FORGOTTEN GENESIS delve
that no book has done bef
changes in DNA that have taken place over millennia and
how Mankind has evolved into what it is today. Some
of the "hot spots" of human history, which have either
remained unknown or have only been considered from
mythological positions, are explained, including: Atlantis,
Troy, Shambhala, and Hyperborea. The diversity and the
accuracy of the explanations presented are clear and con-
clusive, combining pure esoteric knowledge with certain
scientific elements. Particular emphasis is placed upon the
existence and manifestation of inter-dimensional chasms
or portals at the "intersections" between the physical plane
and the etheric plane.

FROM THE AUTHOR:

"Even though the notions presented in this book are delicate, I considered it necessary to take a step forward and
expose some deeper aspects. I also believe that the elements presented in the other volumes of this series have
prepared the ground for the interested reader to gain a fair
understanding of the esoteric and other factors involved
with this fascinating and complex scenario. I will continue with this more elaborate approach which has become a
necessity in the current context of the times. I hope that the
readers of this series of volumes will correctly understand
my approach and the sincere desire to expose to the world
some unknown aspects of the reality we live in."

— *Radu Cinamar*

FORGOTTEN GENESIS

RADU CINAMAR

EDITED BY PETER MOON

SkyBooks

NEW YORK

Forgotten Genesis
Copyright © 2019 by Radu Cinamar
First English language printing, January 2020
International copyright laws apply

Cover art by Creative Circle Inc.
Typography by Creative Circle Inc.
Published by: Sky Books
                Box 769
                Westbury, New York 11590
                email: *skybooks@yahoo.com*
                website: www.timetraveleducationcenter.com
                www.skybooksusa.com
                www.digitalmontauk.com

Library of Congress Cataloging-in-Publication Data

Cinamar, Radu / Moon, Peter
        Forgotten Genesis
        276 pages
        ISBN 978-0-9678162-9-6
1. Body, Mind, Spirit: Occultism 2. Body, Mind, Spirit: General
Library of Congress Control Number: 2019953450

This book is dedicated to
"The Ancestors"

OTHER TITLES FROM
SKY BOOKS

CONTENTS

INTRODUCTION

For those of you who have picked up this book without any prior knowledge of the circumstances surrounding Radu Cinamar and his previous work, I will lay out a background and summary.

During the Cold War, there was a natural alliance between the two communist nations of Romania and the People's Republic of China. Trying to keep up with the West in regards to the most advanced and esoteric methods of reconnaissance and espionage, the Romanians sought out the help of the Chinese as they did not really trust the Russians. As part of a cultural exchange program whereby Chinese students were able to participate in educational programs in Romania, the Chinese government sent the Romanians an expert in parapsychology who would set up a secret department that would deal with all abnormal occurrences. These were referred to as "K events", but in pop culture terms of today, these might now be termed as "X-File" events. Known as Department Zero, this special unit was only known to the head of state and the head of security. Besides housing and caring for paranormal subjects, Department Zero also trained them. The expert in parapsychology who set up this unique department is known to us as Dr. Xien, and he was introduced to us in the first book of this series, *Transylvanian Sunrise.** Although Dr. Xien is an intriguing character, we do not learn too much about him in that book. We do know that he was called in after the birth of another very interesting character who also turns out to be one of the progenitors of the *Transylvania Series*. His name is Cezar Brad, and he is born with an umbilical cord that is so thick, the doctors have to use an ordinary saw to sever it. As this is an anomaly, Cezar comes under the scrutiny and eventual tutelage of Department Zero and forms a close personal relationship with Dr. Xien from a very young age. Cezar is trained in a host of spiritual and psychic disciplines that would rival the best your imagination might offer.

As fate would clearly demonstrate, Dr. Xien was grooming Cezar to serve as a steward and guardian for what is arguably considered the greatest archeological discovery in the history of Mankind: a secret and previously inaccessible chamber beneath the Romanian Sphinx containing futuristic holographic technology that was put together some 50,000 years ago.

---

* The book you are reading now, *Forgotten Genesis*, is the sixth in a series of books by Radu Cinamar which are collectively, along with Peter Moon's *The White Bat*, known as the *Transylvania Series*. The previous works include *Transylvanian Sunrise*, *Transylvanian Moonrise*, *Mystery of Egypt — The First Tunnel*, and *The Secret Parchment — Five Tibetan Initiation Techniques*, and *Inside the Earth — The Second Tunnel*.

FORGOTTEN GENESIS

In what could be termed a virtual Noah's Ark that far exceeds the thinking and experiential capacity of those who lived in biblical times (or even in our own times for that matter), this chamber includes technology whereby one can place their hand on a table and see their own DNA rendered in three-dimensional holograms. Other devices on the table enable one to see the DNA of alien species from other planets with accompanying star renderings so that one can see where they actually originate from. By placing two hands on different parts of the table, one can also "mix" the DNA of two species so as to see how they might look if hybridized. As the tables themselves are six feet high, the creatures who built them were gigantic compared to humans of today.

This remarkable chamber also includes a "projection hall" whereby one can see a holographic rendition of the history of Earth that is particularly tailored to the individuality of whomever might be viewing it. This history, however, abruptly cuts off in about the Fifth Century A.D., perhaps because it requires some sort of software update. One of the more intriguing aspects of the Projection Hall is that it also contains three mysterious tunnels that lead into the bowels of the Earth and similar facilities in Iraq, Mongolia, Tibet and also beneath the Giza Plateau in Egypt.

Although Cezar, through the tutelage of Dr. Xien, was set up by fate to be the overseer of this remarkable archeological discovery, it was not his role to write the story of what was found and its implications. As these events were unfolding, Cezar handpicked Radu Cinamar to write these volumes. Serving as a mentor to Radu, Cezar gave him a rapid fire education in all of the political machinations going on behind this discovery while also introducing him to the world of psychic phenomena and esoteric studies. We learn about this in the first volume, *Transylvanian Sunrise*, but we are not told exactly why Cezar picked Radu. What I can tell you from what I have learned thus far is that Cezar is a remarkably adept individual, and he knew precisely what he was doing. His psychic sensibilities are quite formidable and proved to be accurate in this case. Radu got the job done, and with the release of this book, he now has five volumes in English.

You might think that this discovery was a wonderful opportunity to enlighten Mankind and take advantage of all that this newly discovered technology has to offer for the benefit of humanity at large. Many, if not most, of the Romanians in the government who were privy to the discovery viewed it that way. Circumstances, however, dictated otherwise.

Cezar informed Radu that the actual discovery of this secret and previously unknown chamber took place when the Pentagon discovered it via the use of ground penetrating radar that operated through satellites. It is understandable that the Americans would use all technology at their disposal for reconnaissance purposes as well as to scrutinize all geographical anomalies and

10

resources on the planet. Right or wrong, this is the purpose of the Department of Defense. What was most challenging about this intelligence, however, was that Masonic interests in the Pentagon funneled this information to a leader in Italian Freemasonry, a Signore Massini, who represents a hidden global elite that wanted access to and control of this chamber for themselves. Accordingly, Massini approached Cezar who was then the head of Department Zero and sought his cooperation. Cezar, who did not trust Massini, was forced to cooperate to a certain extent due to political circumstances. Thus, the evil interests of an Italian Freemason forged an unprecedented alliance between Romania and America with the former suddenly being admitted to NATO. The specifics of these political intrigues are detailed in the book *Transylvanian Sunrise* which is primarily the story of Cezar's life and his involvement with the uncovering of these amazing artifacts.

While the enigmatic and mysterious Dr. Xien set the stage for Cezar to uncover this secret chamber through rigorous training and education, he is a distant memory when the discovery is made and seemingly completely uninvolved in any tangible way with the political machinations and evil intrigues which allowed it to even take place. Dr. Xien, however, is an interested party and a definite progenitor of the information revealed in these books, and this comes into clear view in the second book of the series, *Transylvanian Moonrise — A Secret Initiation in the Mysterious Land of the Gods*.

Transylvanian Moonrise begins with an editor's note from the Romanian editor, Sorin Hurmuz, who includes numerous excerpts from the Romanian press that not only corroborate Cezar's story as told by Radu but give insights into why it is credible. Above and beyond these facts, it might interest you to know that a key area near the Romanian Sphinx is blacked out on Google Earth. Besides that, Americans were seen en masse during the time of the excavations that were taking place near the Romanian Sphinx in 2003. I have also spoken to several well-placed people in Romania who believe the general story to have merit. Exactly what has taken place and all of the details are still largely a mystery, but Radu's books offer us the only clues. In addition to that, they are remarkable stories and teaching devices which integrate the mundane aspects of politics with some of the most esoteric concepts of occultism as well as the cutting edge of technology.

Radu's narrative in *Transylvanian Moonrise* begins with a mysterious man named Elinor trying to contact the enigmatic author through his publisher, Sorin Hurmuz, who has generally been instructed to stonewall any people wishing to meet with Radu. In fact, Sorin has never met with Radu and only communicates with him by special courier or with a prearranged phone card. When it is eventually discovered that Elinor is speaking on behalf of a Tibetan lama, both Sorin and Radu change their tune and a meeting is eventually arranged. This meeting is filled with a panoply of metaphysical revelations which present an entirely new paradigm by which to view the events described in *Transylvanian Sunrise*. After an amazing indoctrination into the ancient art of alchemy and the prospects of immortality, Radu meets the lama who reveals himself to be none other than Dr. Xien and explains that he once served in the royal court at Lhasa under the name of Repa Sundhi at the time of the Chinese invasion of Tibet. Escaping that purge, he somehow ended up in the employ of the Chinese government and adopted a different identity as Dr. Xien.

Repa Sundhi has a very specific agenda for this meeting with Radu and it has to do with what is the focal point of the fourth book in the *Transylvania Series: The Secret Parchment — Five Tibetan Initiation Techniques* (more on that later). In *Transylvanian Moonrise*, Radu learns that the lama wants to take him to the Apuseni Mountains of Transylvania. Once there, a mysterious but well-described space-translation takes place that literally transports them (as well as Elinor, who remains in their company) to certain rarefied high peaks of Tibet which are inaccessible to humans by normal transportation means. Radu is escorted into a cave where he meets another progenitor of the *Transylvania Series*. Her name is Machandi and she is a blue goddess and tantric dakini who not only educates and initiates Radu but gives him an ancient manuscript which is to be translated from ancient Tibetan and published, first in the Romanian language. Having finally been translated into English, it is the centerpiece of *The Secret Parchment*.

While *Transylvanian Moonrise* refers to the characters in *Transylvanian Sunrise* and the lama is included in the dramatic events that take place, the two books are astonishingly different and offer complementary views of the overall scenario from completely different perspectives. The third book in the series, *Mystery of Egypt — The First Tunnel*, is no exception. Radu is recruited to join Department Zero on a journey with Cezar into the mysterious "First Tunnel" in the Projection Hall of the Bucegi complex. This leads to a hidden chamber beneath the Giza Plateau in Egypt. What they find there is no less astonishing than what has already been offered in the first two books. The purpose of the mission is to recover neatly organized slate-like tablets that are in fact a type of ancient "DVD" that project holographic "memories" of the history of the world. The tablets do not require a projector and are so numerous that they can only hope to return a portion of them to their home base, after which they will be sent to America for detailed study. Even though they cannot recover everything in one mission, what they do retrieve would take a team of viewers a considerable amount of time to view.

There is also an occult chamber containing a device consisting primarily of huge crystals that facilitates the projection of one's consciousness back into time. It is not a physical time travel device. It should be noted that it requires a certain amount of psychic and esoteric development to be able to

12

withstand the rigors of projecting oneself into time, even if the physical body is not being utilized. We also learn that this device is bioresonant in that it is tuned to the physiological, mental and emotional conditions of the subject as well as their own past experiences. In other words, you would have different experiences than would I and so on.

Another intriguing aspect of the time device is that there is a certain amount of censorship present. When Cezar attempts to project his consciousness into time in order to see who created the device, he encounters blockages. While it is informative and useful in certain respects, it contains mysteries which it does not want penetrated, at least at this particular time. All of this gives rise to interesting speculation.

These censorship issues further fuel the controversy Cezar ignites by relaying his initial experience in the time device whereupon he returns to the time of Jesus in the First Century. Radu also recounts what he saw in his original experiences in the Projection Hall (beneath the Romanian Sphinx) when he witnessed events surrounding the crucifixion of Christ. This account contains UFOs wreaking havoc amidst a virtually insurmountable thunder storm while a fearing populace scrambles to save their own lives. It leaves us with a hornets nest of information, the result of which has been more than a few questioning the veracity of the authors. I should add, however, that most of the reading audience thus far has not blinked at the accounts given. They have enjoyed the book and are not judgmental about the authors. What is perhaps the most relevant aspect of this experience, however, is the fact that the device which facilitates it is bioresonant. Whether the events presented are indeed real in a conventional sense, they are certainly events that the collective consciousness has wrestled with for thousands of years.

What happens in *Mystery of Egypt*, however, is superceded by what occurs in the fourth volume, *The Secret Parchment*. Radu finds himself in the middle of the political and conspiratorial intrigue that is swirling around the effort to control the holographic chamber beneath the Romanian Sphinx. Accordingly, Radu is sent to the United States to attend a remote viewing program in the Pentagon, all in an effort to defuse the rising political tensions. As the conspiratorial intrigues escalate into a full scale political and esoteric war, there is an intervention by superior spiritual forces, one of which includes Radu being recalled to Romania in order to meet with Repa Sundhi to facilitate the translation of the ancient Tibetan manuscript or "secret parchment" which had been given to him by Machandi as described in *Transylvanian Moonrise*. While the parchment presents five invaluable techniques for spiritual advancement (these are not the same as the already known yoga exercises known as the "Five Tibetans"), its very presence in the world has ignited a series of quantum events, extending from a bizarre structure emerging from the snow in Antarctica, serving an antenna function, which is at the crossroads between signals to Jupiter's moon Europa as well as Mount McKinley, and Transylvania. As incredible as the discovery of this extraterrestrial connection is, it only escalates the attempt to undermine the structure of Romania's Department Zero when the Americans learn that the signal to Transylvania reveals a passage way of solid gold tunnels, extending miles into the underground, leading to ancient hieroglyphics, embedded in gold, indicating the locale as the nexus of the Inner Earth where "all the worlds unite." Not too far from the nexus, accessible through more passageways of pure gold, is an incredible room of golden thrones with panels of yet more hieroglyphics and a mysterious portal that appears to be a direct conduit to outer space; and, presumably, an outer space of another universe. These discoveries were made by a certain Professor Constantine who, upon reporting them and taking a team from the government to investigate, was whisked away and never heard from again. Although the investigators were killed, Professor Constantine was able to make a summary report to Cezar Brad; and the file for such was deemed to be the highest state secret of the country of Romania. Even so, Department Zero was unable to find any access to these passageways and, despite considerable effort, no further discoveries were made. Although Machandi's secret parchment is translated and we are treated to its specific wisdom, *The Secret Parchment — Five Tibetan Initiation Techniques* leaves us with a very great mystery that is left dangling.

I also contribute to the book by revealing my own adventures in the area and learning of the ancient legends and how these fit into the scheme of Radu's adventures. It turns out that Professor Constantine was indeed a real character who disappeared, and I am even shown where he once lived. There is also a Valley of the Golden Thrones, and it is in this region that I make one of the most remarkable discoveries that I have ever stumbled upon.

Although it has not been mentioned in any of the previous books, I was led to a cave by a Romanian archeologist in 2014. Known as Cioclovina Cave, it is the site of one of the greatest archeological finds in Romania which indicate a civilization did indeed occupy caverns within the inner earth and in the vicinity mentioned by Radu. Cioclovina Cave represents a sort of grand central cave station with some seven other caves interlinking with it, representing at least seven kilometers of tunnels.

While the aforementioned findings concerning Cioclovina Cave are of great relevance with regard to Radu's claims, there is an even more startling confirmation from Dr. David Anderson, my scientist friend who originally brought me to Romania in 2008. In an interview conducted by myself in 2015, he revealed for the first time that Cioclovina Cave was the site of the largest discharge of space-time motive force ever recorded. Space-time motive force is a term Dr. Anderson coined to signify an energy that is released as a result of time dilation that occurs in the process of frame-dragging. If you are further interested in this aspect and would like a full explanation, you can watch the video series *Time Travel Theory Explained* at my website *www. timetraveleducationcenter.com*. This function is also explained in the appendix of the book *Transylvanian Moonrise*.

What all of this means in layman's terms is that Dr. Anderson's findings indicate that this area was the site of heavy duty time travel experiments. He was completely surprised that I happened to come across this very area by happenstance during my adventures in Romania. Note that this area was never a targeted area of interest for me. I had an off day and was brought there by an archeologist I knew at his instigation. He had no idea of the time experiments or the like. The archeologist, by the way, told me that the stories I relayed to him about Radu's books, which he had not read at that point, correlated with many stories he had heard about the area.

While there are many so-called "side tunnels" or supplementary threads of great interest that involve Dr. Anderson and my other associates in Romania, I am getting off subject. Radu is very well aware of Dr. Anderson and is even interested to meet with him. It is quite possible that all of these different threads might coalesce into a single homogeneous thread some day.

Radu's fifth book, entitled *Inside the Earth — The Second Tunnel* refers to what is referred to as the "Second Tunnel" in a series of three tunnels in the projection room located within the chamber beneath the Romanian Sphinx. The First Tunnel, named in the title of the third book in the series, *Mystery of Egypt — The First Tunnel*, leads to a chamber beneath the Giza Plateau. The Second Tunnel, leads to underground cities and installations. The Third Tunnel leads to Tibet with an offshoot branch to the Carpathians (near Buzau, Romania) and then towards Iraq; and from there to Mongolia and the Gobi Plateau.

Inside the Earth — The Second Tunnel begins with a rather sober evaluation of geophysics and how it relates to the core of the Earth and the myriad misunderstandings that have profilerated on the enigmatic region which is often referred to as the "Inner Earth" and often incorrectly as the "Hollow Earth." Radu's old friend and mentor, Dr. Xien, gives him rather thorough explanations on these various aspects and gives remarkable new insights into the science and origin of black holes that will eventually reach into the halls of academe and revolutionize the way that science thinks about such topics. There is also an exhaustive explanation of the fatal error of the Cavendish Experiment, done in 1799, the "gold standard" for justifying that the Earth's core is a mass iron-nickel alloy surrounded by molten lava. You will learn that later experiments to justify this conclusion is based upon what amount to outrageous assumptions based upon an experiment which has not been subject to rigorous inspection and is, in fact errant. You will also learn that what resides at the core of the Earth is indeed a black hole.

Beyond the science are Radu's remarkable adventures with Cezar where the two visit mysterious regions within the Earth and the multiple civilizations that occupy that region. There are lots of amazing meetings as well as descriptions of technology that facilitate transportation between the mysterious regions "Inside the Earth." Radu also provides us with a glimpse of the fabled city of Shambhala, a paradise at the core of the Inner Earth itself where balance and harmony are the basis of civilization. Whatever your final opinion of Radu's adventures might be, you will be exposed to a paradigm that is novel and will change your view of the world.

One of the most admirable aspects of Radu's book is that, while familiar aspects and characters are common to all of them, each one is unique and focuses a different look. *Forgotten Genesis* is no exception and herein you will read about the forgotten orgins of the history of Mankind.

Peter Moon
Long Island
May 11, 2019

AUTHOR'S NOTE

I wrote this book with a keen interest in giving the readers the real basis and essential points of the history of Mankind. This was an older project, a quest that had begun in 2004, after having been stunned by various images from humanity's "forbidden" past that had been witnessed in the Projection Hall.

There were two main reasons why I did not fulfill this project more quickly. On the one hand, I did not have enough information to present an appreciable view on the destiny of Mankind from its origin to the present time; and, on the other hand, I did not have permission at that time to reveal even a very small part of what I already knew.

Even today, I have been advised not to disclose certain "delicate" events in the history of humanity which could shake the religious foundations of various segments of the population. There are also other sensitive political and geo-strategic events that should be withheld due to the governmental problems or "embarrassment" that may arise.

After I finished writing the text of this book and reviewed it for correction, I realized that what I have to offer could be quite complicated and make for a sticky situation. For a few days, I was in doubt, not knowing what to do. Eventually, I realized that a simplification of the entire matter could later give birth to other questions, so I decided to "risk it" and publish the full version.

I do dare, however, to make an important suggestion to the reader. At the very least, the fourth, fifth, sixth, and seventh chapters of this book must be carefully scrutinized in order to understand the roots of the "Human Project". Rereading segments of their content will prove itself useful in contributing to a better knowledge of what happened in those very distant times.

Even though the concepts presented in this book seem difficult, I thought it was necessary to take a step forward and expose some deeper issues. I also believe that the elements covered in the previous volumes I have written have prepared the ground for presenting a fair understanding to the reader with regard to the esoteric and other meanings herein so that the reading of the present volume and those that follow will have context and coherence.

I will continue with this more elaborate approach as it has become a necessity in the current context of the times. I hope that readers of this series of books will correctly understand my approach and sincere desire to expose to the world some unknown aspects of the reality we live in.

Radu Cinamar
March 1, 2019

FORGOTTEN GENESIS

CHAPTER ONE

THE EARTH IN CROSS SECTION

After my return from Utklaha,* the city of the ancient Mayans in the center of the Earth and located very close to Shambhala's sublime citadel, I had to come back to terms with the rather tough reality of our planet. The difference in perception and the level of vibration was huge. During the first few days, I felt virtually suffocated with everything seeming primitive to me, and this included the habits of people, their ideas, their ambitions, their way of conceiving life as well as the standard of living that we are all familiar with.

Unlike me, Cezar seemed to be in his element whether he was inside, the "interior" of the Earth or on its surface. When we returned to the Base, he asked me almost immediately to give a briefing to Lieutenant Nicoara, our colleague who had replaced him in leadership of Department Zero. In the following hours, Cezar was already distributing tasks, making plans, having telephone conversations within the country as well as abroad and making important decisions. I admire the extraordinary power of focus, self-control and the force and energy that radiates out of his being; and his determination and good intentions and motives are always expressed with wonderful simplicity.

As for myself, I had to go to Bucharest for two days in order to resolve some personal issues. The excitement of the capital and the affairs I was involved in there were not exactly what I needed then, especially since the impressions of my recent trip inside the Earth were very much alive in mind. I returned quite quickly to the Base, however, and the normal flow of activities resumed before I was then pressed to make an immediate departure on an expedition through the Third Tunnel, the tunnel to Iraq, which was scheduled at the beginning February 2015.

PROBLEMS WITH TEAM CHANGE

Shortly before we left, some of the basics of this expedition had already been set forth in discussions with Major Cross.** The team was to be made up of five members for a short-term trip with a precise purpose. For me ,it would be my first trip through the Third Tunnel,*** but as I had already accumulated

---

* One of different cities that Radu visits in *Inside the Earth — The Second Tunnel*, Utklaha is the closest to the fabled region of Shambhala. Although Radu is only able to get a glimpse of the storied city, he is told that it lives up to the fabulous legends that have told about it.
** Introduced in *Inside the Earth — The Second Tunnel*, Major Cross is the American liason to Department Zero and has a positive relationship with Radu and Cezar Brad.
*** The Third Tunnel leads to Tibet with an offshoot branch to the Carpathians (near Buzau, Romania) and then towards Iraq; and from there to Mongolia and the Gobi Plateau.

considerable experience in the expeditions through the other two tunnels, I felt ready for such an attempt.

The task of organizing this expedition was up to me and Lieutenant Nicoara. I was charged with the administrative part of the protocol which included the composition of the team and their general plan of movement, including all activities and links with the American side. Lieutenant Nicoara was assigned to take care of all matters regarding logistics and security as well as the scientific aspects.

As this expedition was going to be virtually lightning quick, the training was relatively simple. In the first stage of organizing the trip, the team was formed of Cezar, Lieutenant Nicoara, myself and, in accordance with what the Americans asked, two officers from the U.S. Navy's Secret Service. As we did not understand the reason for the Navy's involvement, I had asked for an explanation, but we received a confused response which made us reconsider the composition of the team. Accordingly, we asked for members from the internal secret structure of the Pentagon as this had been the case with the other expeditions. The situation, however, was a bit tense, especially due to the arrival of the Venerable One* with whom we had a discussion that was attended by Major Samuel Cross. Nevertheless, that discussion did not influence the collaboration with the American party for the travel that Cezar and I had taken to Yosemite.** It turned out that the Venerable One had other intentions and did not put any pressure on us regarding the composition of the team that was to travel through the Third Tunnel. He only asked for the rights to study a particular artifact. To be specific, he wanted the rights to study the crystal pads which he knew already knew had been discovered in the Third Tunnel by reason of previous reports from those who had traveled through it.

Following our request to change the team, the Americans reconsidered their decision and included two young officers on the list from the Pentagon. Besides this change, there was also a surprise that Cezar and I had learned of upon our return from Argentina. It was initially just a brief verbal briefing from Lieutenant Nicoara, but it was subsequently presented in a full report that had been requested by Cezar.

---

* The term "Venerable One" is a term used to designate an esteemed officer in Freemasonry. In this case it refers to Signor Massini, an Italian who is in the highest echelons of Italian Freemasonry and also is a member of the Bilderbergers. Discussed extensively in *Transylvanian Sunrise*, it is Massini's high level connections in the Pentagon and his acumen and connections with the Romanian government that precipitated the discovery of the Projection Hall beneath the Romanian Sphinx in the Bucegi Mountains.

** In the book *Inside the Earth — The Second Tunnel*, Cezar and Radu visit Yosemite at the request of Major Cross because the Americans are having difficulty accessing and dealing with a portal to the Inner Earth. The expertise of Cezar and Radu are in concert with the Yosemite Indians who provide access to another region of the Inner Earth by non-technological means.

"THE SPECIAL CHAIR"

From the briefing presented by Nicoara, we learned that a team of scientists had been able to develop a technology that allowed for downloading the information from the platinum tablets that had been retrieved from the chamber beneath the Giza Plateau that had been reached via the First Tunnel.* The research to accomplish this had taken years.

The unknown material and the coding system used in the recordings remained a mystery for scholars, but somehow, they eventually managed to access the stored information. Immediately after the discovery of the plates in the Egyptian chamber had taken place, the biggest problem faced was that the data contained therein could not be accessed in any way so that it could be delineated and therefore evaluated. In the first years after their discovery, intense studies were carried out, and although it was very difficult, they were able to download the information from one tablet, but it took about a year to accomplish this. There were, however, thousands of such tablets in the Occult Chamber in Egypt, but Lieutenant Nicoara informed us that an important step had been taken in this direction and to the point where downloading could be done in less than a month. More importantly, technology was provided so that multiple tablets could be downloaded simultaneously. The fact that such extremely important data could be downloaded in digital format has made it possible to inventory and classify it and, of course, under very tight security. In his report, Lieutenant Nicoara specified that the Americans had inquired about this protocol, wanting to know if the decoding and downloading of the information would be done by them or us. Cezar, however, was very clear in this regard.

"If the operation is done in the United States," he said, "that means transporting the tablets there. We cannot afford that. If it were an ordinary treasure, this factor could be overlooked, but certainly not such an invaluable treasure as this which is beholden to the vigilance of all Mankind.** Decoding and classification operations will be done here."

This step forward made me very happy because it allowed me to have easy access to study all of those records. The protocol, however, proved to be a bit more complicated. In the subsequent bilateral talks, the Americans tried for a long shot, advancing the idea of "blackmail" but they gave up quickly because our arguments were obvious. They attempted to make us addicted to this new downloading technology that they had discovered,

---

* The First Tunnel referes to a tunnel that leads from the Projection Hall to beneath the Giza Plateau in Egypt where there is a similar installation to that beneath the Romanian Sphinx. It is the subject of the book *Mystery of Egypt — The First Tunnel*.

** [from the Romanian Editor] Cezar is most likely alluding to the royal Romanian treasure being transported to Russia during the First World War under the pretense of keeping it safe. This treasure, however, seems to have "vaporized" as most of it has never been returned.

but they recognized the huge problems that could arise if the tablets were taken from here. It was much easier to assemble a laboratory in Romania that was dedicated exclusively to this task, and to ensure optimum security, it was decided that the plates would be taken back to the Occult Chamber in Egypt after the decoding and inventory of the information. It should also be mentioned that a very strict protocol has been developed for the security of the information with regards to its storage, accessibility and protection. The accuracy of the data extracted from the tablets was almost 80%, and this was significant. A synthesis of scientific reports on the matter indicate that the loss of information is the result of a strange interaction that emerges at some point between the technology used and the unknown material that supports the holographic information. It has some very special magnetic properties that is congruent with a particular algorithm that has not been fully deciphered up to the present. Although there was some loss of information, the percentage of accuracy was acceptable, especially since we could hope for a complete solution to the problem in time.

In the report, Lieutenant Nicoara repeatedly mentioned the existence of an element that we had to take into account. With digital information provided that had been extracted with American technology, I watched most of those extraordinary recordings, and I noticed that in many of them, as the images began to flow, there was a "seat" which, by all appearances, made it possible to move individual consciousness across great distances, both for the purpose of facilitating "meetings" with other beings or entities as well as for "seeing" places, planets, stars or other cosmic elements that would otherwise be ignored by the common human mind. The association between the chair and the images indicated that the latter were accessed by the former.

We already knew from Cezar that the underground complex in Iraq, accessible through the Third Tunnel, contains a "room" similar but smaller to that of the Occult Chamber in Egypt. After I watched the visuals from platinum tablets, Cezar informed me that there was such a "seat" in the Occult Chamber in Iraq, similar to what I had seen in those images. The fact that the images on some of the platinum tablets in Egypt featured a special "chair" similar to that existing in the complex in Iraq is the element that Lieutenant Nicoara had mentioned in his report, and he did so because it is a common element between the two chambers.

THE WEAK LINK

Even though Cezar had been in the Occult Chamber in Iraq several times, he could not clearly understand the functionality of the "seat" with regard to human beings because it just did not work. All attempts to make it work were doomed to failure, including the attempt to connect it to an external source

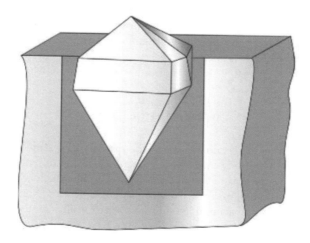

SIMPLE REPRESENTATION OF RECESSED ETHERIC CRYSTAL

of energy. The "chair" was not "booting up" and had not been brought into operating condition ever since the time it was discovered.

This enigma persisted until, after Cezar watched recordings on some of the platinum tablets in the great Egyptian library, it became clear that the functionality of the "seat" depended upon a fairly large crystal being placed to the right of the chair. The crystal emanated light, and its radiation varied in intensity, depending upon the elements of the information that was presented. As far as we could tell, the crystal had the shape of a tetrahedron and was recessed with the tip pointing downwards.

The problem was that there was no such crystal in the Occult Chamber of Iraq. There was, however, a designated place where it was supposed to be to the right of the "seat", but it was empty. This was quite odd because it made no sense to just have a "seat" without the presence of the crystal upon which it functioned, as had been revealed in the recordings on the tablets.

That is why, after the informational report was sent to the Pentagon, some voices from its senior staff requested the presence of an IT expert to be a part of the team that would be traveling through the Third Tunnel. Their argument was that a computer scientist might eventually solve the problem of operating the special "seat". Personally, I would have liked this expert to have been Aiden[*], but I knew he had left the service of the U.S. Army six years

[*] A character in the book *Mystery of Egypt — The First Tunnel*, Aiden is an American who is a tech expert who accompanied Radu and Cezar on the trip to Giza and brings along a holographic laptop computer which is indispensable to the success of their mission. A fascinating and complex character, Aiden feels like he is mentally "wired" to the holographic computer.

earlier. In our advisory meetings at Alpha Base, however, we decided not to supplement the number of team members. Thus, after several deliberations with Pentagon, this option was abandoned as, in my opinion, it would not yield any result. As such IT experts were civilians, potential leakage of information was possible. An exception, however, could be made for Aiden as he was a special case.

AN IMPORTANT HELP

Although there was no answer to the mystery of the missing crystal in Iraq's Occult Chamber, Cezar made a decision during one of the planning sessions for the expedition through the Third Tunnel. He decided to contact Dryn, the wise man of Tomassis, to ask for his opinion and help.* By the end of January, Cezar had accomplished this by the familiar method of contact in the Projection Hall. After returning to the Base, Cezar told me that Dryn had agreed to help us and that he would also ask the Apellos Council for support.** Dryn justified this by the fact that those in Apellos would know more about this because they are hybridized from a race of cosmic beings, and the technology of the secret complex in the Bucegi Mountains was obviously of extraterrestrial origin. It was therefore logical that the people of Apellos would better understand this technology and be able to help us.

Cezar's idea was not received with much enthusiasm at certain levels of the Pentagon. Some of the generals there did not want to create a precedent of "indulging" other civilizations inside the planet. In other words, there was no desire to share the technology in the Projection Hall or the chambers in Egypt and Iraq, even if the population of Apellos was more advanced than ours. This information came to us unofficially from Cezar's good friend, Major Samuel Cross. The fact that we learned this was due to the gracious and direct authorization of Major Cross, an honest man with integrity. Such tensions between the Romanians and the Americans sometimes arise at the decision-making level, but they are usually quickly overcome, with or without diplomacy. As I have said before, the most difficult moments are those in which we have to cope with the intervention of the Venerable One, as when such occurs, the issues are more complicated.

Dryn's response was not delayed, and as a result of his consultation in Apellos, where he is very respected, doors opened in an extraordinary way

---

* In *Inside the Earth — The Second Tunnel*, Radu meets Dryn on his first journey to the Inner Earth. Dryn lives in Tomassis, a city beneath the surface of the Earth that is an actual subterranean region, heated and lighted by natural elements. It is an in-between area with regard to the more inter-dimensional aspects of Inner Earth culture and Dryn is a liaison for Radu and Cezar.

** Apellos is another city Radu and Cezar visit. More advanced than Tomassis, they travel from there to Apellos which is not in the physical plane. It has very advanced technology which is discussed and even illustraed in *Inside the Earth — The Second Tunnel*.

to share an objective and trustworthy knowledge of the past of Mankind, the main points of which I will present in this book. Dryn told us that those in Apellos have agreed to help us, and moreover, in turn, they have proposed that there will heretofore forever be a link between them and the surface world. My own wonder over these matters reached a climax when Cezar informed me that, at the request of the Apellos Council, that liaison would be me. They did not give much detail about this decision, but they said I had made a good impression during my meeting with them in Apellos. With a happy smile, Cezar also told me that it would require a person with relatively good esoteric training in order to properly understand the revelations they wanted to share.

As they have presented the situation, their decision is part of a very large plan to facilitate a transcendence of human society that will emerge on the surface of the Earth by spreading information that will serve as an important link that will enable at least a part of Mankind to experience a transformation in their level of consciousness. Dryn said that, at our planet's level, this plan is coordinated by the Wise Men of Shambhala.*

Although I was very keen to get to Shambhala, I was aware that this suggested that I would have to have a certain level of consciousness and understanding that would allow my presence there. The visit I had taken to Utklaha, in the center of the Earth, had clearly shown this to me, but it has also laid in my heart the nostalgia of that dream realm to which I have no access save for to look at that fabled city from afar. Now, with this wonderful opportunity offered by the Apellos Council, I was thinking that maybe the moment of my penetration into Shambhala was not that far off.

APELLOS REACTIVATED

Things evolved quickly. Dryn brokered the connection with Apellos and gave us a set of precise coordinates that indicated a meeting place. Quick research showed us that the place was on a deserted hillside near a small town in Transylvania, at the foot of the Apuseni Mountains. An exact date and hour were set to get there, and I went unaccompanied. It looked like what I saw in the visuals, but it was perfectly recognizable. In fact, the place indicated was virtually impossible to miss: the small hillside was bare, covered with only a thin layer of snow, and over its wide expanse, the same landscape was uniform, almost devoid of trees, shrubs or forest. The city was in the distance, about five kilometers away. As there is no access road at ground level between the other hills and the surrounding mounds, you cannot get there by walking.

---

* In *Inside the Earth — The Second Tunnel*, the Wise Men of Shambhala refers to a council of elevated beings who monitor the region of Shambhala and allow accees to those who demonstrate an elevated state of consciousness.

It was obvious that this place had been ideally chosen to block any attempts to be pursued. I do not, however, think that those in Apellos did so because they suspected we would have been followed; but rather, it was probably a minimal and even necessary protection measure, given that, from time to time, certain national or foreign forces and factions have shown that their occult interests and ambitions have been onerous and lacking in transparency. The tendency to control, seize, conquer and even to suppress has caused much suffering over time, and the situation is no better today, even if things seem to be paved with good intentions.

When I arrived at the meeting place, there was a man waiting for me. I thought then that the situation seemed to be a replay of the meeting in Argentina where Cezar and I also waited in a deserted place and were met by a strange shaman. Now, the man at least seemed more "normal". Middle-aged, he looked like an ordinary man, clothed in sporty winter gear and very relaxed. Besides, I felt relieved that, unlike the shaman in Argentina, he talked, but in German, speaking with a slight Bavarian accent. He showed me the direction in which we should go and I was amazed to see that we were actually heading for the city where I had just come from. I expressed my perplexity about this, and the man explained to me, as I suspected, that the meeting place was only a minimal protection measure.

"I was instructed to drive you to where you will get your supplies," he said.

I raised my eyebrows.

"Detecting us could be very easy, even if there are only two of us," I said, in order to prevent any misunderstanding that might later come up.

The man smiled finely and spoke.

"From the moment we met, any device that you have on you no longer works. You have 'disappeared' to the outside world for some time."

As I looked at him questioningly, he paused briefly, then cryptically added, "The Apellos technology."

I realized that this was the case, but the man did not show me any device. Instead, he remained quite steady and focused. Curious, I pulled my phone out of my pocket and the special GPS from the Base. Indeed — both devices were "dead". I did not say anything, but the level of that technology was admirable.

We travelled the rest of the road in a few minutes, engaging only in pleasant and general conversation, but I noticed that the man had not introduced himself. We were already close to the outskirts of the small town, an area suited especially for warehouses. I was quite amazed because I was expecting to be going to a much more isolated and mysterious place, perhaps again to Apellos; but in fact, the man led me to the front of a well-maintained and well-kept hangar in a courtyard guarded by a modern fence. We both walked to the entrance and, to my surprise, I simply entered the door into that hangar and saw that it was just like a regular warehouse of a retailer.

I have to say that I was expecting something unusual and mysterious about that meeting, but it turned out to be quite ordinary and even trivial. If it were not for the protective stealth technology demonstrated by that man of German origin, I would have said that everything was the product of a bad joke or perhaps that he had brought me there to shop. In reality, as I was going to understand very quickly, things were completely different.

The hangar was just one of the bases of civilization of Apellos that they had told me about when I had visited their city. Indeed, looking around, I noticed that the place was full of commodities and especially food. Everywhere I looked, I saw balloons, sacks, big boxes, containers, and forklifts. In a word, the usual activity and items one would expect in a warehouse of goods.

AMAZING TECHNOLOGY — AN INTER-DIMENSIONAL HELMUT

The man who had led me into the hanger closed the door behind me, remaining outside. Inside the lighted hangar, I saw five people coming to me and immediately recognized that they had characteristics of the people found in Apellos. Although they looked like us, their faces featured a distinct pale-

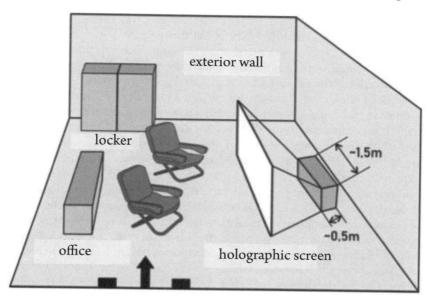

**THE ROOM IN THE HANGAR WITH
THE HOLOGRAPHIC PROJECTION SCREEN**

ness with higher foreheads, and their gait was harmonious in a manner that could even be considered noble. Their brown hair is slick as if anointed with oil. Coming to my right, they greeted me, speaking this time in Romanian. Dressed in simple but elegant brownish-red overalls, the skin of their faces was white, making a strong contrast with their dark hair, and their eyes were more elongated than ours, slightly almond-shaped. One of the five seemed to be their leader, and I exchanged a few pleasantries with him. He spoke Romanian well although his pronunciations were strange to my ears. His freely relaxed and spontaneous nature generated a feeling of great comfort that was also supported by kindness in his communication.

Three of the men went to another area of the hangar while I was left with their leader and another person who followed us, respectfully staying behind. These two showed me a more secluded area in the hangar where I saw a circle on the ground with a diameter of nearly three meters that was bounded by lights whose source I could not see but which I likened to LEDs. The light emitted was a very fine white color that was continuous but barely perceptible. The surface of the circle was covered with small squares and lines, also discreetly luminous, but in a whitish-blue color. Based upon the earlier explanation given to me during my previous visit to Apellos, I recognized that this was a "lift" with specific teleportation technology.

A few meters further, we saw a space separated from the rest by three tall walls, the fourth being the wall of the warehouse. It was a rather large room with a surface that I estimated to be about thirty square feet that featured a thick carpet of a rubber-like material on the floor. Beneath the carpet, the floor was somewhat porous and dark blue. Surprised by the cleanliness and perfect order of the interior, I saw only a desk, two armchairs, and a folder. In front of one of the sidewalls, we noticed a metallic silver surface on the ground in the shape of a rectangle with a large side of about a meter and a half. It was explained to me that this is a device that facilitates the projection of Akashic records that Apellos uses to investigate certain present time situations in relation to their own security. While we were listening to these explanations, the metal rectangle began to take shape, but I did not see anybody giving any special command for that. When it reached about a meter in height, it stopped. A rectangular metal box, it was perfectly smooth and appeared to be a brilliant silver. After a few seconds, some of the light blue lines close to the surface appeared to the side of us, some of them changing to red. Suddenly, a holographic projection appeared in front of the metal box and about a meter away from it. Also rectangular, but rounded at the corners with a depth of about half a meter, this was a genuine holographic screen with large dimensions. Although I could see through it, there were holographic waves of blue-light undulating slowly, somehow appearing inside the "edifice" of the screen, the surface of which retained its smooth quality.

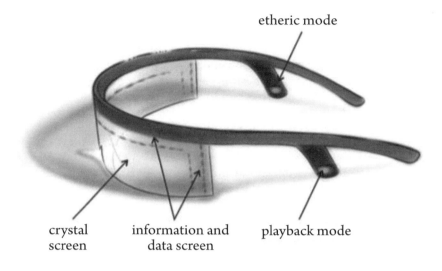

etheric mode

crystal
screen

information and
data screen

playback mode

INTER-DIMENSIONAL HELMUT

Gradually, images of the nearest city appeared with sequential snapshots of streets, buildings, people, and interiors, all clearly put before me in a manner I could readily understand. I immediately realized that I was being shown how this holographic screen worked.

The leader of the group from Apellos that had first greeted me then showed me a small device that was like a very thin and small helmet into which he inserted something similar to a card. He told me that in order to better understand some of the elements that were to be presented to me, I needed to be somehow "coupled" to the rectangular device on the ground, and for that, I had to put on this miniature helmet.

As its main element, the helmut had a ring resembling a narrow luminous band at the level of the forehead that surrounded the entire head. At the front, the ring had a very fine transparent crystal screen. If it were not for two small branches of the helmet extending down to my ears, I would have said this was a modern pair of glasses. It was a very technologically advanced "smart" device. The man told me that the device would couple to my personal vibrational frequency in a subtle way so as to serve as a kind of additional accessory to my consciousness that is aligned with the specifics of my mental processes. In other words, I understood this to be a customized personal accessory.

The Apellos man told me that the device would automatically record anything I would see as soon as it was put on my head. For playback, he told

29

me it was only necessary to touch the left side of the headset with the hand and then focus on the moment, the image, the being, or the object I wanted to evoke. Yet, from what I was told, the pièce de résistance of the helmut was its ability to visualize in the etheric plane. Switching views between the physical and etheric planes was done automatically or "on demand" by gently touching the right side of the headset with your fingers. The Apellos man then urged me to experience this special function of the helmut.

At first, I did not see anything unusual in the external world. After a few seconds, however, I began to perceive otherwise as more colorful and clearer three-dimensional details came into view. At the top of the "lens", figures and other specific signs appeared, but in a holographic format at a certain distance ahead. The visual information was unfolding pretty fast, just as I had witnessed with the rectangular metal box in the room.

I then turned my gaze to the holographic screen and saw pictures of a rather crowded market. It was as if I were watching a documentary, but the interesting part was that I could not only see the simple projected images on the screen, but it was as if I were actually there amidst those events and images, perceiving everything through my senses. Somehow, with the help of the helmet, I was able to perceive the images from the large holographic screen but with the emotional aspects added in as well. I was not really a stranger to this sort of thing due to Cezar's explanations as well as the time displacement I had experienced with the device in the Occult Chamber in Egypt. Slightly touching the right side of the helmet, I saw the images become somewhat "milky" with a slight glow around objects and people, thus indicating that I had gone into "etheric mode".

With regard to the helmut I was using, I did not understand how all of this could happen, but I suspected it was an integral part of the advanced technology of Apellos. I was seeing everything on the holographic screen, but I also had a deeper sense and understanding of the images. There was obviously a link between that helmet and the holographic screen, but I did not understand it.

In a certain way, I was a part of that "documentary" and was taking part in the environmental images I was watching as if I were actually there. At the same time, however, I knew too well and could feel that I was in the hangar together with the beings of Apellos. I did not have the feeling that I had "gone somewhere" or that I was losing contact with the physical reality I was in; but still, I felt as if I were both in that room in the warehouse as well the "inside" of the images I was viewing on the holographic screen.

THE EARTH IN CROSS SECTION:
PASSIVE ZONES AND SUBTLE CONNECTIONS

Just as I was seriously wondering about seeing those images of a crowded city, I felt like I was being "lifted" to a certain height, as if I was levitating over it. The ascension was so fast and so high that I could quickly see the planet as a whole, and when the Earth turned around on its axis long enough, I could see a cross-section of it on the left.

I was stunned because it seemed that those in Apellos wanted me to come to terms with viewing the Earth in a cross section, just as it had been brought up for discussion during my meetings with Dr. Xien. I explained this to myself as if this was the result of the helmet technology having access, at least in part, to my neural activity. I was glad, however, that I could see "live" what I had just imagined mentally. It would have been very exciting to know what technology they used to facilitate that, but this was not the time to ask such a question.

Initially, I thought what I was going to be viewing would be a graphic rendering, but I realized immediately that everything I saw was very real. In a way that I cannot explain too well, I was clearly seeing our planet in a half-section, and I was even able to modify that vision in terms of distance. It occurred to me that those in Apellos wanted to show me a map indicating where to get to Apellos from the surface.

We saw many caves, grottoes, and tunnels, including the large tunnels through which the population of Apellos travel inside the planet via shuttles. Wherever I looked in that section, the visuals were perfect. That is, wherever I looked within that section of the Earth, I saw everything clearly, including details.

We also saw the tunnels through which the Apellos send material such as "goods and merchandise" by their specific teleportation technology. I have counted four such transport tunnels in the area corresponding to Romania, but I think there are actually more. No one spoke or explained to me those things, but I did understand what I was seeing and what the images meant. I was already firmly convinced that the technology implied a highly evolved software; but besides that, I think it included something else that had a direct interaction with the etheric plane.

The section that I was viewing then amplified and "approached" me, so to speak, and clearly separated Transylvania and the northwestern parts of Romania. On the side of the section from Oradea, I saw an opaque silver sphere at one point, serving to hide what was there. When I asked what this was, the man who had accompanied me with the leader and had remained respectfully behind us told me that such opaque spheres were areas where I was not allowed to see for the time being. He specified that there are five such major areas beneath the Earth's crust which are located under the territory of Romania.

These areas contain entrances to the "inside" of the Earth which must remain hidden. One is in Dobrogea, another is in the area of Buzau, two are in Transylvania, and the fifth is in the northeastern part of the country. These are areas on the surface where one can access the tunnel networks within the Earth that connect with subterranean cities and their populations. They are inter-dimensional chasms, i.e. entry points through which you can move from the physical plane to the etheric plane and penetrate into certain precise locations underground. There may be more such input zones, but they have shown me only five of them, even though they were obscured.

Rising higher and higher, as I noticed the outer shell of the planet in sectional format, I became more and more astonished at the sight of the network of subtle etheric links within the Earth as well as their extensions into the material plane which included inhabited regions such as grottoes, cities, tunnels and big cavities.

In that extraordinary cross-section of the Earth, I saw brighter dots, some of them shining in a such a way that they were emanating power. Asking what those lights were, it was explained to me that there are powerful magnetic distortions that serve as portals, making it possible to move from the physical plane to the etheric plane, even from the "inside" of the Earth. They are basically links between the surface and the interior of the planet.

"As such etheric connections are not limited to the Earth, they are inter-dimensional," the Apellos man explained to me. "These portals not only connect the exterior to the interior of the Earth but also serve as a conduit between the Earth and other planets. Those who have sufficiently developed technology use these links with much wisdom.

I confess that, at that moment, I did not really understand how this took place because I was shown only what was connected to Earth. The colossal etheric links appeared to me to be like silver arches whose exact localizations remained obscure. Watching them, I realized that they were etheric in nature by reason of the direct understanding that was transmitted to my brain as well as the fact that they were brighter, being encompassed in a distinct shining halo. For example, I could make out the difference between the natural caves or voids in the Earth's crust that were in the physical plane and those on the etheric level that were radiating out in that particular way.

Just as subtle energy meridians support the circulation of energy in the human body and "nourish" the being on different levels, so does the Earth have its own "meridians" and "subtle channels" that are very active and at the same time "nutritious". I understood at that point that the populations living in the Earth are "nourished" to a great extent by these subtle tellurian energies, and that is why it is easy for them to come into contact with the etheric plane. They do not use our planet but rather can be said to live within it in a kind of harmonious and efficient symbiosis. This is fundamentally different to the paradigm of understanding and thinking of people on the surface of the planet which endures systematic destruction by reason of pollution, waste or irrational exploitation.

"COVERED" SINGULARITIES

Some of the points where subtle meridians "intersect" the surface were very bright, drawing attention to their importance. Beginning to understand how the helmet worked, which I realized was a very technologically advanced converter of human psychological experiences, I wondered if those points were populated or deserted. This amazing technological device somehow made the connection between the human mind and certain information stored in subtle dimensions of Creation; otherwise, I could not explain the "dialogue" that was possible within certain limits. After I asked the question, the image immediately and intensely zoomed in to some of those bright dots on the surface of the planet. I was somewhat surprised to see that some of them revealed houses, castles or old buildings while others were placed in forests, on the coast of the mountains, or even on the flat surfaces of plateaus.

I was particularly interested in those buildings that had been built exactly upon the points of intersection along the etheric meridians. I turned my head back to the Apellos man who was assisting me and asked him what those constructions represented in the areas indicated. I already knew that the Apellos man was interested in correctly understanding what was being revealed to me and had the telepathic ability to follow my journey with regard to the visuals I was seeing via the helmet.

"You might call them 'houses of cabal' but these buildings actually cover essential points of passage between the physical plane and the etheric plane. They are like portals," he explained.

"Okay, but then who lives in them?" I asked with puzzlement.

"Some of us are the Apellos, but there are also other advanced civilizations inside the planet with whom we work in the sense of using portals to move from one plane to another. We cannot afford to let go of these essential passages in the etheric plane and within the Earth, at least for the time being, because they would disturb the population, and your rulers would want to use them for military purposes."

"Some of them are very old I see," I commented.

"Yes. The castles are hundreds of years old, but there were other settlements before them in the same place, even thousands of years older. It is, however, sensitive areas of convergence in the cities that are the most important because they are exposed and must be well guarded. There are property titles for all of this, of course; but this is sometimes not enough. Over time, there have been various incidents and some even in these times. With the development of your technology, your monitoring capabilities have become finer. The secret services of developed countries have become suspicious and have begun to gather information on these points, but they still do not understand what is really going on there. The are some critical situations when breaches occur, and we have to intervene and cancel the etheric charge of the place, alter its structure and move the 'convergence point' of the etheric meridians into another more secure area."

"So why do you not do the same with all of these sensitive areas and locate them in very safe places?" I asked candidly.

"Nature must be left to play its own game. There is a reason for everything and a meaning that is often hidden. If we were to take some tendons from their natural position in a human leg, do you think the person could walk just as well? It is the same here, too. In cases of force majeure, we appeal to such extreme methods, but even so, the move takes place at a certain time and in a succession of well-calculated steps to help induce a circumstance that aligns with nature.

"Have you had such a situation?"

"Yes. One of them was a few years ago," replied the man from Apellos.

He focused his eyes for a few moments and then touched a small device attached to his temple that I had not noticed up to that point as it was almost covered by the black hair on his head.

Within my helmet, different images immediately began to appear from what I had seen before. I was shown a pretty old house in a German city. Then, the picture suddenly changed, depicting another home, this time in the U.S., which I was able to identify by the specific way the streets were named and arranged. The image suddenly changed again, and I could see the Earth from extreme heights that highlighted the clear outline of Europe and North America. Between two points on the two continents — which highlighted the two locations I had been shown — a rainbow-like conduit appeared, blurred and accompanied by many symbols.

We therefore had a space distortion, a discontinuity in the fabric of the space-time continuum which was known of for a long time and guarded by this unique method of building old properties exactly over such portals. It was basically the same method used by the Yosemite Indians with the cabin that had been built in 1776 over the portal leading to the "inside" of the Earth. The Apellos man told me that some of these cases were already being hunted down by the intelligence services of different countries. As I know from experience that information about such things is offered in exchange at a certain echelon, I resolved myself to check this out upon my return to the Base. I was curious to know what had actually happened in this regard and how such situations were resolved. Having access to good intelligence information from two countries, I was hoping to find records about this.

SUBTLE FIELDS AND REALITIES

The man from Apellos then brought back the series of images with the Earth onto the holographic screen. The best comparison I can make about what I was experiencing is that I was watching and even sensually and emotionally "participating" in a very well-documented documentary. I was amazed by the very large number of areas populated under the terrestrial surface and the many variations of "relief" regions inside our planet. These areas looked exactly like the nerve networks in our body, full of life and branching out to the body's extensions. I never imagined that the activity inside the Earth could be so complex. Being now at a great height and having a wider perspective of the planet's section through her crust to the mantle, I could see many of the aforementioned spheres of silver in other parts of the globe, all of which were designed to obscure the knowledge of what was there. Some of those silver spheres were smaller, others larger, but some were really huge. Showing my curiosity, I asked what was there.

In the case of the large silver spheres, I was told that they represent more than just important passages from the surface of the Earth to the "interior" of it. Some of them also overshadow extraterrestrial bases that have been placed in those regions. For example, I have seen such spheres inside the crust which correspond to areas on the bottom of the Atlantic and Pacific oceans at their different depths. From those bases, I have also seen subtle etheric networks connected to various other structures or settlements within the Earth. I then asked myself if the bases were built into existing cavities or if it had been necessary to cut rock to form the cavities. The information I received is that there was no need to cut rock to get the space needed for the construction because the Earth's crust is full of voids and many already extant underground cavities, each with its own specific characteristics.

I began to see the cross-section of the planet I was viewing more and more clearly, observing that the structure of the Earth is not chaotic, but in a precise way, aligned upon magnetic field lines generated by the black hole in its center which, in their turn, are extremely complex, somehow resembling the striated muscles of the hands and feet. I saw a complex overlap of these lines extending deep into the planet. In holographic imagery, these were rendered as brilliant arcs with varying colors of different intensities in the etheric plane.

My mind then grasped that the planet's crust is formed by magnetic field lines and that vortices appear in different places where it is empty. I then understood matter could not be formed in these areas because of an

35

accumulation of intense magnetic, electric and gravitational fields and that those spaces are the cavities, caves and great voids found inside the Earth. I also saw that the field lines have different characteristics and, depending upon how they combine in different areas of the planet, they push the matter upward, forming the mountains; and in others, they pull down, forming the great valleys.

The hypothesis of scientists concerning the way the mountains were formed — by the collision or interaction of the tectonic plates that are stuck to one another — is not wrong, but it is incomplete. For example, I have clearly seen how the crust does not float on the magma such as contemporary science tells us. It is true that there are large areas of magma inside the planet, but there are also areas where the Earth's crust is self-contained and arches (based upon magnetic field lines manifesting as arcs), just as I have described as seen in the section of the planet that was presented to me.

Magma is therefore a kind of "by-product" and the mountains do not necessarily form by reason of different tectonic plates floating on its surface colliding and pushing against each other. On the other hand, they are born due to cumulative factors related to magnetism, electricity, pressure, temperature, and also certain moon movements which cause fluctuating stresses on the Earth's crust and influence the characteristics of the field lines that manifest in those areas. I could see that there were a bunch of complex fields, the nature of which were not identified. Any fluctuation of the field lines causes a rearrangement in the crust. The rocks there are no longer solid but are rather soft, like clay.

I also witnessed that the field lines generated by the central hole of the planet are not static but dynamic. They move continuously, and where their structure changes, solid matter is tensioned. At some points, there are gaps and tensions, and these rearrangements and shifts cause earthquakes. Volcanic activity has a similar explanation as, depending upon how the field lines are directed, the magma bag can retract or push; in which case, a volcano erupts.

I then understood how difficult it is for contemporary scientists to understand these realities which start from something ethereal and invisible and end up manifesting on the physical plane on a large scale, resulting in volcanic eruptions, tremors or mountainous formations. It is extremely difficult to present something that belongs to the subtle domain of such a manifestation within the parameters of modern physics because the laws and phenomena of the subtle worlds are much more complex than the physical one. Neither Newton's classical physics nor even the general relativity of Einstein can be applied to an etheric or astral reality. Even though the understanding of such phenomena is valid and is recognized by the academic world, it is still limited by the conceptions and prejudices that most scientists still retain.

CONSCIOUSNESS OF THE PLANET EARTH

Then, as I continued to watch the cross-section of the planet before me, I saw where the magma ended, but the visual below me was already darker and more obscured. After a few seconds, I began to see this part of the interior structure of the planet more clearly. It was based upon the gravitational distortions caused by the central hole, but the "texture" or "fabric" was different.

It was then shown to me that the passage between the physical plane and the etheric plane is about 2,300 to 2,500 kilometers, and beyond this "depth", starting from about 2,800 kilometers, is the etheric dimension. I found this astonishing because I had already learned from Dr. Xien that the transition to the etheric plane was made from between 1,800-2,000 kilometers. When I raised this issue, the Apellos man explained to me that what Dr. Xien said is not wrong but that differences arise due to the dynamic forces manifested by central singularity which may vary from time to time depending upon what the consciousness of the planetary spirit wants to accomplish. On the other hand, we have already explained in the preceding volume of this series that the "division" of the dimensions of existence — the physical plane, the etheric

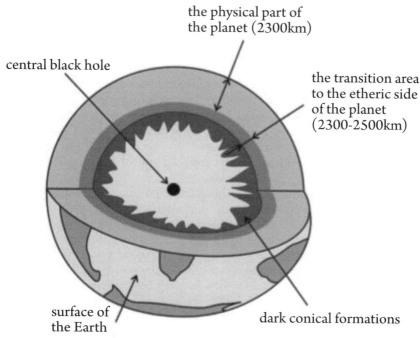

the physical part of the planet (2300km)

central black hole

the transition area to the etheric side of the planet (2300-2500km)

surface of the Earth

dark conical formations

EARTH IN CROSS SECTION — DISTANCES AND CHARACTERISTICS

plane, the astral plane and the causal plane — does not imply a "slicing" of the dimensional planes; that is, a stratification that would appear as a "sandwich", as some readers might incorrectly understand.* Rather, the planes of creation are differentiated by their specific vibrational frequency, each falling within a certain margin, but they coexist along with the physical plane. This reality is just like that of radio waves that coexist in the same space. They do not "mix" but can be accessed as soon as the radio switches to their specific frequency. Of course, there may also be "interferences" in some cases that are generated by energy anomalies.

In the case of our planet, the vibrational frequency of matter increases from a certain "depth" and begins to resonate with the vibrational frequency of the etheric plane, an aspect which is dictated by the proximity to the central singularity or black hole. So does the change in vibrational frequency occur as one moves from one subtle dimension to another, all of the way up to that of the causal plane that surrounds the central singularity right in the very "center". It should be understood, however, that the subtle planes do not exist by themselves but rather are there by reason of the presence of the black hole and its enigmatic nature in the Earth's center.

Inside the cross-section of the Earth that I was seeing, there were some roughly tapered cone-like formations that were pointing towards the black hole in the center. This surprised me because, when I actually entered the planet, I saw sea, earth, and vegetation, but as I looked through the special helmet, there seemed to be a dark void marked by those conical formations.

As soon as these questions occurred to me, the image changed a bit and rotated at a small angle, and I then found myself looking right over the center of the planet, just above the black hole. I immediately realized that what you see varies from area to area, all depending upon the vibrational frequencies of the area where you are looking from. I had been "placed" just above the center of the black hole whereupon I noticed a kind of glimmer, a wondrous splendor that I had never before seen.

I understood that it was very important for me to observe the beautiful reality of that poetic grandeur which is almost impossible to describe. At the very moment when it is viewed, it imparts a trance-like state in one, a nostalgic thrill and even a mystical hue. That vision is almost hypnotic, impossible to replicate accurately and undoubtedly not to be seen on our surface world. As it has been presented to me, this manifestation represents THE celestial entity, inclusive of the celestial spirit that gave birth our planet. Its mystical glow triggers a state of absolute fascination, but even as I admired that reality, I remained fully aware of what was happening to me and the place where I was on the surface world.

---

* These aspects are very well explained in volume 5, *Inside the Earth — Second Tunnel*, 2017, pages 58-60.

The first impression I felt after that state of fascination and amazement was the wonderful sense of gentleness that came from this ancestral spirit. And, contrary to general belief and what is written in the mythology of humanity, the spirit of the planet or the subtle entity that represents it is male, not feminine. I understood this instantly when that overwhelming glimpse also transmitted to me the state of strength and dignity that are of the masculine nature.

When men and the esoteric tradition refer to Gaia as "the spirit of the planet", they are actually alluding to its bioenergetic component, the life that exists and manifests itself on its surface as well as the interior of the Earth. This is why Gaia is soon conceived as the soul of the planet, a term which implies its life and dynamism. On the other hand, the spirit of the planet is the very consciousness that created all this and which represents the planet itself, being of a male nature. This observation is important in the context of understanding the laws of manifestation where everything is based upon polarity. So, the male spirit of a planet that creates the lines of force upon which it is formed corresponds to a feminine nature which is the soul of the planet that sustains and develops life.

Virtually overwhelmed by the depth of the impression I was experiencing, I was allowed to quietly and without disruption digest a transcendental vision. I appreciated the respect and understanding of the two men from Apellos. At the same time, my observation of those images, which turned quickly into contemplation, was neither passive nor only in a singular sense. Almost immediately, I felt that the very profound "contact" I was making was actually being reciprocated because I then perceived a mood similar to the one in which you are allowed to enter a home where you are well received.

CORRESPONDENCE OF SUBTLE PLANES INSIDE THE EARTH

I gradually emerged from the trance state and returned to the careful observation of the cross-section of the planet.

I understood that, even if from our point of view — metrically speaking and corresponding to the physical plane — the etheric plane within the Earth begins about 2,500 kilometers below the solid surface of the planet, the cavity inside is larger because the metrics of space there are in another dimension that is different from that of the physical plane.

The information I received telepathically was that the inner diameter of our planet, with regard to its subtle dimension, is roughly equivalent to the diameter of Venus which is very close to the diameter of the physical Earth.

The Apellos man explained to me that there is a lot of confusion among scientists because they say that entering the "cavity in the center of the Earth" is not supported by a complementary series of factors, laws, and measurements which would corroborate this idea. The laws, factors and measurements that are used in this instance, however, belong to the physical plane whereas, within the planet beyond a certain depth, we pass into the subtle etheric dimension and then into even more subtle dimensions where the type of measurements to the surface of the Earth can no longer be applied.

One of the concerns is that those who have been inside the Earth and talk represent the area as being very large which leads to an interpretation that the crust of the Earth would have to be very thin. While I was seeing this, I was shown that scientists' criticism in this direction would indeed be valid if the metric at the surface of the planet, i.e. the metric of the physical plane, were used. Other energies and other realities, however, manifest themselves inside the Earth which are specific to the etheric plane and have another metric, another space and another manifestation of time. We cannot therefore simply take a reality that we have become accustomed to — for example, the one on the surface where we live — and just apply it anywhere, regardless of the conditions.

Entry into the etheric plane therefore requires our ability to adapt to the reality there and to the metric that applies. In connection with this, the calendar of the Mayans was shown to me. While their year was 260 days, a number pretty close to one year on the planet Venus, their calendar is not related to it; rather, it is actually based upon the duration of a year within the Earth whose inner cavity has an "etheric diameter" close to the physical diameter of Venus.* Since I had already been in Utklaha and met the family that descended from the ancient and very special civilization of the Mayans, I was not surprised that they were calculating their own calendar and correlating it with the one inside the Earth, just as today's big companies, banks and hotels account for time zones in different regions of the planet.

The cavity inside the Earth has two important seasons. It was shown to me that even though there is not a real physical hole at the surface of our planet's poles, the way that the Earth moves and the fact that the sun's rays reach the north or south of the planet have an important influence because light and heat bring in energy and cause some changes in the eco-system inside the planet. Even though the brightness of the central Sun within our planet — which in fact represents the effect of the black hole in its center — is almost constant, the influence of the Sun in outer space causes some changes within our planet, bringing more rain or extending droughts, especially in the Northern and Southern regions. The central areas inside the Earth, however, have a certain temperature stability.

One of the extraordinary aspects that greatly impressed me was when it was shown to me that, at certain times, the physical and etheric planes are "aligned" in a manner that the beings within can see the nighttime stars,

---

* A year on Venus takes almost 225 days.

provided they are in certain areas. It is through this precise correlation of planes that it is possible.

The details of the section in the center of the planet now became clearer to me. I have especially noted a lot of lush rich vegetation and very high mountains which correspond vertically to the Pacific Ocean in particular. The central sun has a luminous light, and I could observe this by directly looking at it courtesy of the special headphone technology. The intensity of its light is about 55-60% compared with the light reaching the surface of the planet that comes from the Sun in cosmic space. It has also been transmitted to me that the inner sun's diameter is several hundred kilometers. Telepathically, I understand it to be about 700-800 kilometers.

From place to place, I was shown by a zoom effect various details, especially in terms of fauna, both on the soil and in the waters. I smiled, observing pterodactyls in flight and other dinosaurs, thinking that perhaps those who wrote or made films about the interior of the Earth did not do so unknowingly or perhaps just took some information that was long ago forgotten. In fact, such information is very real. Dinosaurs, for example, are exactly as we know them from museums or paleontology books, but I have nevertheless appreciated that they are somewhat smaller than the dinosaurs that roamed the surface of the planet in times long ago.

I have not seen, however, destruction or interventions in the harmony of Nature's play such as that which has been generated by the hand of man on the surface world. For example, there are no hydropower plants or other such industrial exploitation or pollution. Instead, there is a perfect communion between the human beings and the exceptional nature that exists there. It was also shown to me that there is absolutely no feature of our planet, either externally and internally, that is unintentional. Rather, the very aspects of manifestation are a direct and very clear decision of the male consciousness that gave birth to it. Both the specific position of the Earth in space and the amount of light or heat it receives from the Sun, as well as the other characteristics that it has such as density, mass, volume, etc., all are the manifestation of the will of His spirit which is determined from the center of the black hole.

For example, while watching those images, I telepathically received the knowledge that, from the very beginning of the formation of the planet, the subtle entity representing it decided that its surface would have a certain kind of life so that certain souls can come here to have the necessary physical experience. From time to time, the entity or consciousness of what is basically the Earth modifies the planet's integration parameters to enable the DNA to change according to the change that is desired. All of this, as it was transmitted to me through a profound telepathic understanding, is in perfect correlation with the whole universe where we are with the cosmic cycles and energies that surround us.

41

Next, the transition from the etheric plane to the astral plane was shown to me with reference to the visual cross-section of the Earth. The transition is about the diameter of Mars.*

Of course, these analogies are given in order to present a clearer mental picture of the inner dimensions, but we must not forget that a different metric applies in each of these cases. For example, in the case of the diameter of the planet Venus, this analogy was correlated with the magnitude of the inner earth's dimensional capacity in the etheric plane. On the other hand, the analogy with the diameter of Mars is made to give an idea of the magnitude of the size of the astral area in the "inner" Earth. In other words, if we use the metric of the physical plane that we live in, the etheric dimension inside the Earth would have the approximate magnitude of Venus, and the astral dimension would be about the size of Mars.

I found it very interesting that, by reason of observing the cross-section of the Earth, the causal plane within the interior of our planet corresponds approximately to the size of the Moon, if we relate it to our metric from the physical plane. It has also been suggested that the size of the Moon is not at all accidental. Although I now know the real elements about the Moon, its origin, what it represents, and the reasons for its presence in the sky beside our planet, I did not have this knowledge at that particular time. The details of these issues will be presented in the next volume. What was explained to me, however, was that the spirit of our planet wanted to have a "mirror reflection" of itself and from the moment it appeared in the sky, that Moon was that "mirror" and especially so due to its strong feminine nature.

Thus, the information that comes to Earth is somehow controlled through the surface of the Moon. It is an extraordinary experience at a Macrocosmic and Celestial level that all these elements — both from the outside of the planet and from within it — are combined in the Earth. This experience has made me intuitively understand that the implications for our planet are in fact much deeper and more complex than just the mere formation of a celestial body or the appearance of life on its surface.

After this last presentation, the images were interrupted, and the two Apellos men, both of whom had carefully attended my "trip", told me that it was their mandate to transmit what information that was relevant. I was, however, slightly puzzled, given the reason I had come there; that is, to receive some information about the missing crystal from the Occult Chamber in Iraq. Just when I was preparing to talk about it and bring up how my experience in observing the cross-section of the Earth could possibly solve this issue, the leader from Apellos told me that this could be accomplished by reason of the special helmet that I had been viewing with.

---

* Earth's diameter is about 12,700 km, and the diameter of Mars is about 6,800 km, almost half of our planet.

"This is our gift to you," he said. "It will help you solve the mystery surrounding the 'chair' in Iraq and its crystal. Just grasp the nature of that crystal."

Upon hearing this, I felt a deeply emotional and extreme gratitude as I could not imagine that such a piece of advanced technology would be left with us for our use. That was a great gesture which made me cherish even more the friendship between us.

Before saying goodbye and leaving the man from Apellos, he told me that there would be two more visits that I would make there, and this was according to the information he had received from the higher echelon, the wise men from Apellos. He revealed that these visits were meant to provide me with important information about the unknown past of Mankind so that it could be brought to public knowledge in a coherent and clear way. He also showed me exactly the days and times when those meetings would take place and commented that I would have a pleasant surprise at the first one.

FORGOTTEN GENESIS

CHAPTER TWO

THE FLAT EARTH DELUSION

I spent the next two days sorting out documents and files but mostly solving the communication and organizational aspects of the forthcoming expedition. Additionally, I investigated the database and other informational notes from the past to find references in connection with the portals of the "houses of cabal" mentioned by the Apellos man. The few holographic images that I had seen of these had impressed me. I wanted to know how things happened, both from the experiential perspective at the level of the Secret Service as well as to see the type of reaction of those involved in such special cases. I focused in particular on the German and American information because I suspected that it was not a mere accident that I had been given that example with the viewing device. There would surely be some information on this, and all I had to do was either look carefully or ask our overseas colleagues where it might be. Although I worked almost continuously, taking only short breaks for rest, I realized that it would not be possible to meet again with anyone from Apellos until I left through the third tunnel. I felt somewhat dissatisfied in this regard because I was very impatient to investigate the past of Mankind, even if some events and situations had been shown to me years ago in the holographic images of the Projection Hall.

According to my calculations, however, and if I managed my time efficiently by delegating some tasks to Lieutenant Nicoara, I had the opportunity to obtain extraordinary information corresponding to the invitation from Apellos. I did not quite understand the reason why the two meetings scheduled were not to take place until the expedition; and while this obviously put pressure on things, I suspected it was based upon a certain necessity, probably dictated by a "window of time" related to that activity.

A STRONG THEORY

Drawing on references to the "houses of cabal" that hide inter-dimensional gates, I came across an informative note I had not seen before that was floating amongst a few dozen others on my desk. Generally speaking, I prefer to work in electronic form or to wait for notes or files in digital format, but given the particular interest I had on the subject of dimensional portals, I decided to check everything I had on my desk, including an update of current events.

I do not know why and how, but the information I had found had been overlooked. After checking notes and information summaries, I found one titled "Flat Earth - References." I had heard of such a "movement" that made some waves amongst people for many years, but I never imagined it would

45

ever be worthy of becoming a subject for our department. The delusion of such an idea is obvious, especially for those who have good sense and personal experiences regarding our planet from the perspective of outer space.

A little confused as to whether or not I should read the few page summary on the Flat Earth Theory, I sought out Lieutenant Nicoara and asked him about it. He told me that the information came from the operational department of another SRI section* and had the status of a secondary circular. The Lieutenant specified that the only reason why this information came to our department was due to the abnormal "phenomenon" it had triggered in the world, but less so in our country where the number of "followers" was at a relatively low and reasonable rate.

The Flat Earth Theory seems to be the "gold rush" of our day, an aberration which, in my opinion, the only merit of which is that it can leave you speechless and even in a state of "shock" if we take into account the progress of contemporary science and the technology that Mankind currently has. I could understand that a lack of knowledge, amplified by bigotry and other obscure interests hundreds of years ago, could take hold of the minds of a relative few but for it to grow to the level of an international movement in the 21st Century was beyond rational belief. From a celestial perspective, I wondered if human stupidity could go beyond this level, but I was not very convinced of that prospect.

As it is, however, one of the tasks of the Secret Service to take into account even the most quirky phenomena, at least to the extent that such concerns the masses and their opinions. I did read the summary which very clearly exposed the main points of the problem, but it did not offer any conclusions.

"THE FLAT EARTH" — A SERIOUS DEGENERATION

That same evening, taking advantage of the fact that Cezar was free, I shared the Flat Earth issue with him, presenting it more as a social case rather than as a direction of study. Cezar laughed loudly, talking a little bit about the subject before the conversation then took a surprising turn towards some very interesting issues. He told me that, three to four years ago, this subject was introduced to him and discussed with other colleagues in the intelligence services as there were signs that this idea was trending towards becoming a common opinion. Out of respect to the reader, I would not normally include such a discussion in my book series. It requires only a little intelligence and minimal scientific training to understand that the arguments for such a theory amount to ignorance and fanaticism. Beyond that, however, there are some psychological implications that have been revealed by Cezar that seem to have some importance with regard to general knowledge and social experience.

---

* The initials SRI are an abbreviation for the Romanian Intelligence Service.

The first point in the discussion with Cezar about the Flat Earth Theory concerned the great number of its followers.

"The mechanism by which the number of followers of this bizarre theory increases is related to the segregation of human beings," Cezar said. "It is as if the population is divided into two distinct categories, but this separation is actually based upon the level of consciousness of each human being, and that is directly related to their vibrational frequency."

"But," I replied, "I cannot figure out what caused this outbreak by which more and more adhere to these 'arguments' without meaning. It's more like a silly virus."

"Such a major change in the thinking paradigm does not come, as might typically be understood, as being on the same wavelength with what is known in the world today. That is to say, such new ideas are not related to the knowledge of our times. This is an effective method to use because the idea of a flat Earth is strongly supported by occult factors, by those who are interested in seeing that things remain stagnant and do not progress. That is the best way to control: break people out of reality, make them dream of nonsense, support their fantasies, and encourage them to project. So it is that popular masses are controlled by imposing upon them that which someone else wants. The followers of the idea of the flat Earth, believing in it firmly, will seek to meet, gather and even separate themselves from others for they will regard others as fools who are deceived by lies. In other words, they will be convinced that they are the ones who "discovered" the truth.

Although this was sad to hear, the situation was, unfortunately, quite real. I spoke.

"Although I have the report under my eyes, I find it hard to believe it has arrived here. I have the feeling that this is an ugly dream, as if a part of the population of the world has willingly regressed several hundred years. That's the feeling I have. It is incredible that the minds of today's people can still be influenced to such an extent by delusions that not only defy decent intellect but also scientific reasoning, carrying everything right to fanaticism. Look at the results!"

I showed Cezar estimated figures and graphs.

"I know. We've talked to other colleagues about that," he said.

"Your astonishment is justified precisely by the great difference in conceptualization and frequency of vibration that is already beginning to be felt amongst people. It is a reality that is accentuated by each passing day and cannot be ignored. It is part of the segregation I was telling you about. In principle, people are interacting with those who are evolving as well as those who prefer to remain in the purely materialistic, coarse, or involuntary mind-set. Those in the first category refine themselves, realize the changes that occur on Earth, and experience certain emotional states and specific sensations.

That is why it is incredible that some think in a medieval mind-set, such as the followers of the Flat Earth Theory."

Cezar saw the wonder on my face and rushed to confirm what he said once more.

"Yes. I do not exaggerate. It is a return to the Middle Ages because these people cannot evolve; and instead, return to an older state of consciousness that is closer to their true level of consciousness."

"Why cannot they evolve?" I asked, amazed.

I knew the answer, of course, but it was always a pleasure to capture Cezar's explanations. In addition, there could always be a new element that would enrich my knowledge.

"Because they have no affinity with the current state of things and with the higher vibrational frequency of the Earth, a feature that is increasing more and more."

"For the followers of the Flat Earth Theory, their comfort lies in the fanaticism with which these primitive ideas are sustained as free spirit and thinking are blocked. So was it also during the Inquisition: a set of stupid and false conceptions were raised to the rank of law, and any violation of them was enforced."

As I thought about all this, I was hoping I was wrong.

"Are we back in the Middle Ages? History raises waves of conceptions that sweep across extremes. Those in antiquity already knew that the Earth is round, but the situation deteriorated in the Middle Ages.* Then there was the modern scientific revival, but is this just so we can now backslide into medieval retrogression?"

Cezar answered calmly:

"We do not; but for that segment of the population that has regressed: yes. There are several elements that contribute to this. There is the indignation with which the followers of the Flat Earth Theory cling to their idea, their refusal to think logically or rationally based upon real arguments and evidence, and there is also the denial of evidence — justifying their position fraudulently — and, in general, a kind of proselytism that masks fanaticism.

PSYCHOLOGY OF THE "FLAT EARTH"

We have noticed then that whenever fanaticism has prevailed, society faced a lack of discernment and a limitation of individual freedom. Cezar offered me an example to better explain how it is possible to reach this predicament in the context of a civilization that is relatively developed.

---

* The author is undoubtedly refering to the knowledge shared by Pythagoras and Aristotle, both of whom asserted that the Earth is round, as well as the demonstration made by Eratonese in ancient Alexandria.

48

"The phenomenon is the same as in quantum physics. If there is enough energy, an electron can make a leap into a 'higher' orbit. If there is not enough energy, then it can remain on a slightly higher level and be relatively stable; but at some point, the surplus energy is emitted as a photon and the electron returns to where it started, in the orbit it was originally found. In quantum physics, this is the fundamental orbit of the electron. In other words, the electrons with these characteristics turn back to the level at which they have a safe trajectory."

I was on topic and chimed in.

"I know that, throughout the history of humanity, the idea with the Flat Earth has long existed in a few religions. Modern astronomy has since developed extensively. The planets Uranus, Neptune, and Pluto have only been known for about two hundred years. In this sense, the Flat Earth Theory is not really very old and its memory is still fresh. Maybe that's why some of humanity returns to what it knew before."

"This is also another factor," Cezar admitted. "In any case, human society is changing from 'having' to 'feeling.' That is, the sense of possession, egotism, competition, and violence tends to be gradually replaced by pure and positive emotions and feelings of which love, altruism and compassion are fundamental."

I was somewhat skeptical.

"This is hard to believe as almost all of us see the proliferation of these negative manifestations."

"At first sight, it probably seems so. Remember, however, that most of the population on Earth is uneducated and 'resorted' to this illusion of competition, money, business, and lack of spirituality. The great number of human beings who indulge in this dream tips the balance against those who are looking for a pure life with a definite meaning who are guided only by spiritual values. Here is the segregation we are talking about."

Cezar, in fact, wanted to say that every man is invited to take part in the great spiritual transformation of Mankind and our planet, to ask with aspiration and dignity that his life be a germ of light, spirituality, and hope for a bright future to which we can have access. This is a superb ideal but followed by too few to date.

SPACE AND TIME IN THE PHYSICAL AND SUBTLE PLANES

Consider, for example, the concept of the "Flat Earth". I was thinking that, by reason of scientific and technological progress thus far, such an idea — both from a conceptual point of view and from an existential reality — should have been considered, at most, a joke. It seems, however that, due to its multiple nuances, the problem was not that simple. Cezar gave me a much deeper perspective on this issue.

"The adherents of this theory confuse a certain kind of subtle perception with physical reality," he explained. "There are indeed accounts of Oriental mythology concerning the 'Flat Earth' being supported on the back of four elephants, turtles, or even diamonds. But, you have this vision with time and space having the same 'value'. The physical world, that is, our world, is characterized by three spatial dimensions and, apparently, a separate one of time. We can talk about this as: 3-D (space) + 1 (time). It is a 'three-dimensional' world if we are only talking about spatial dimensions. This situation is so because we are moving through space using time, but you already know that, in reality, and according to the laws of relativity, space and time 'work' together. If you perceive them as inseparable, then the spatial curvature does not matter to you, such as the curvature of the Earth as a sphere. This is what Oriental sages perceived when, traditionally, the Earth was represented as 'flat'. Stretched like a plate or as round as a sphere, it was the same for them except that the 'flat' option was probably easier to represent."

I thought this was hard to understand for those who did not have the necessary subtle experience. Such a reality cannot be properly integrated into the physical plane because it is superior to it. The way the problem was posed was also new to me. Anticipating a little, Cezar's subsequent explanations would be confirmed by what I was going to see on the holographic screen during the next two encounters with the man from Apellos. Cezar continued explaining to me.

"Suppose, for example, that you have a lucid dream or consciously decided to go from the Earth to the Moon without traversing the space that is normally between them in the physical plane, just as if you were walking from one garden to another. And so on would you go, from the Earth to the Sun, the Sun to Saturn and so on, between different heavenly bodies, but still within a certain limit, usually within our galaxy. Practically speaking, you do not have any 'empty space' between these heavenly bodies. If you then return from the astral plane to the etheric plane, you notice the difference because you cannot do the same and even less so in the physical plane."

"What do you mean by 'there is no empty space between these heavenly bodies'?" I asked. "How then are they?"

"Laws take other forms in the higher planes. You cannot claim to understand the phenomena that exist there by simply applying the physical laws that govern the material plane. The differences are too great. In the astral, the vibrational frequency of a thing, a being, or a phenomenon is very important. It's not like here where something miserable can stand next to something clean or when a liar can deceive a lot of honest people. In that realm, you can only be in the 'space' and company that match with your own personal vibrational frequency. You cannot deceive as is so common in the physical plane; and this is to say that you cannot be where you do not deserve."

"And if I still want to go higher than my vibrational frequency, what happens?"

"You have access to the lower frequencies below you but not to those that are beyond your reach. Even assuming that you try this, the space you see is a blur, even becoming opaque. This gives the feeling that things are linked or 'tied together' in some way with no space to separate them."

"Well then, what is the connection with space and time? Are they are unified or not?"

"The connection is that if you look from the higher to the lower levels, there is no space between the bodies because space and time are united, but when you return to the physical plane and take things from the perspective of the current system of thinking, that is 3-D and time, then even the calculations of mathematics show that the most effective form for matter to be structured is spherical because there is no other method that is suitable. This is to say that no other model would provide an explanation with regard to the nature of the physical universe. Therefore, a rectangular disk or rectangular plate does not suitably fit the image of the Earth in this plane as they are neither recognizable or adaptable with regard to macrocosmic laws. Those who try to credit the idea of the "Flat Earth" lack the capacity of subtle observation and then struggle to inject there idea into the physical plane at all costs, resorting to all sorts of 'explanations' and 'observations' that can bend the weak and ignorant who then become confused and full of doubts."

I then brought up the point that when matter is in a vacuum, even water tends to take a spherical form when there is not any external intervention.

"Yes," said Cezar. "This is precisely the case with the large-scale telluric bodies in the cosmic void. There is, however, a minimum limit before they can become spherical. For example, planetoids need to be about 500 kilometers in diameter before gravity and other types of forces are strong enough to structure the spherical material."

Cezar also told me that the followers of this bizarre Flat Earth movement adopted this variant because they cannot "jump" from the physical plane (3-D) to the etheric plan (4-D), all of which implies a unitary vision of space and time. When you cannot do this, you "condense" into three dimensions and even lower than that.

He explained this to me in the following way. The physical plane is characterized by three spatial dimensions which are rendered graphically, generally speaking, through the three-dimensional axle system: x, y, z. But, when we add time as a variable to this axle system, the three axes are no longer found in the classical three-dimensional system x, y, z.

---

* Einstein's *Special Theory of Relativity* applies right here in the physical plane: it replaces the separation between space and time within the space-time continuum in 4-D (Minkowski space).

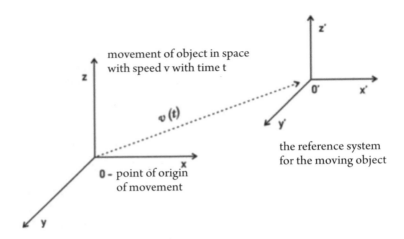

O-X,Y,Z SYSTEM OF REFERENCE

To make this explanation easier, I'll show the motion only on the 0x axis, because it's easier to track.

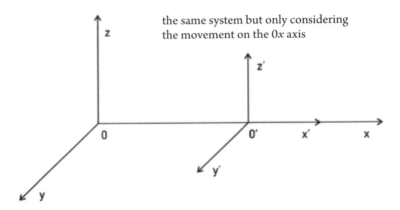

"When we talk about the space-time continuum, you really have the feeling that things are somewhat flat, being a 'continuum,'" Cezar went on to explain. "This is not about volume. It is like a wide strip of paper, and the astrophysical representations also show this continuum as being, in fact, bi-dimensional, as a 'net'."

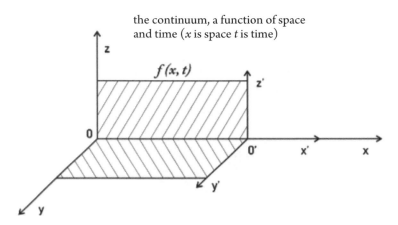

the continuum, a function of space
and time (x is space t is time)

$f(x, t)$

**REPRESENTATION OF THE SPACE-TIME CONTINUUM
(IN THE PARTICULAR CASE OF THE OX AXIS)**

"This, however, is only for our ease of understanding because things do not actually exist in this way; rather, it is just a notation or a convention of physics. The point is that if you cannot embrace this concept and cannot 'digest' it intuitively in your mind, then you go back to what you know you have; that is, something that is easier to understand and belongs to the past."

the distortion of the continuum
under the action of a large mass

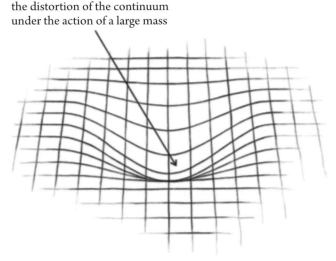

**TWO-DIMENSIONAL REPRESENTATION OF
THE SPACE-TIME CONTINUUM AS A "NET"**

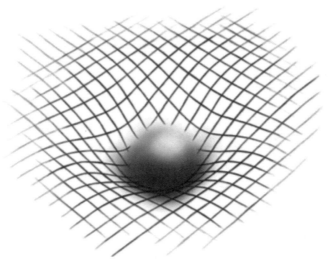

**THE DISTORTION OF THE CONTINUUM CAUSED
BY A LARGE BODY (SUCH AS A PLANET, ETC.)**

"Very well," I said, "then they will return to 3-D, that is, to the physical plane."

"Not at all," replied Cezar. "For us, 3-D clearly represents three spatial dimensions. We move from 3-D to 4-D considering that 'time' exists in a unitary way with 'space,' i.e. 3-D + 1-D. On the other hand, the followers of the Flat Earth Theory say that they do the same, but if we analyze their idea with the Flat Earth as a 'sheet', 3-D is not actually three spatial dimensions, but only two, to which they add time, i.e. 2-D + 1-D. Their impression is that there are three dimensions, but in fact, they only refer to two spatial dimensions because the third, that is height, is negligible in relation to the other two dimensions. It is a significant regression."

"That's why you said we cannot apply situations from the superior planes to this world. However, even if the idea of a 'Flat Earth' is more of a 2-D reality or something located between 2-D and 3-D, those who express it and believe it with so much conviction live in 3-D physical reality. That cannot be denied."

"No doubt, but here you tend to state things in black and white. In reality, there are, as everywhere, transitional areas. In the case of those who move to the 4-D space-time continuum, that is, those who can be said to ascend in some way, the process is not yet definitive and we can associate it mentally with a kind of 3.5-D. This, of course, is a simplistic explanation at this time, but at least it has the merit of being intuitive, and yet it provides an incipient basis for understanding what the difference between 3-D and 4-D really means.

The 'intermediary' numbers I have given you that are not natural — that is, between 2-D and 3-D or between 3-D and 4-D — only suggest a condition, a level of consciousness that some people can reach at some point. On the other hand, in the case of those who subscribe to the Flat Earth Theory, we can talk about a kind of 2.5-D; but for them, the transition is inferior and, this fact itself is somewhat dramatic because the decline for some is quite great, especially from a moral and psychological point of view as can easily be seen from a brief analysis of the global situation. So, they come back to where they feel safe, at a level that allows their individual consciousness to manifest, and this level is very rough."

POPULATION SEGREGATION

Listening to Cezar, I almost slipped into philosophical reflection because I could not accept the reality of the times we live in. For example, how can such divergent attitudes, such as atrocious evil and sublime good, coexist side by side on the same plane? I raised this issue in my discussion with Cezar.

"It's possible in the physical plane. In recent years, however, we are in a period of transition to the etheric superior plane, 4-D, and even though such actions and attitudes may still exist here in the physical world, it is appropriate for the situation at hand because such actions and attitudes are appearing faster and firmer. Currently, many people are capable of reprehensible, coarse and illogical actions as a result of the decrease in personal vibrational frequency. It is like a sort of compression of individual consciousness because it resists the rise of energy, the amplification of the general vibrational frequency of our planet. That is why the followers of this bizarre theory in the physical plane, who say that the Earth is actually flat, want subconsciously to separate themselves from high frequencies, precisely in order to preserve the frequency of vibration that suits them and with which they are accustomed. This results in a segregation of the population.* It is a 'contraction' of consciousness,

---

*In Volume 3, *The Mystery of Egypt - The First Tunnel*, 2007, p. 248, there is a passage in which Cezar makes a similar comment about the law of affinity and the segregation of values in society.

"(...) part of the immediate future destiny of Mankind is determined by the lack of unity of people and their incredible opacity in the perception of what is good, positive, authentic and valuable. Many times, this attitude degenerates into a foolish stupidity," he explained to me at that time. "Those who are misleading, dogmatic and aberrant in their opinions, rejecting many issues of common sense or lacking a profoundly spiritual side that could turn many things into goodness, are not even open to dialogue. In a sense, they imagine they are the only ones that can do anything. In fact, they cannot do anything from a practical point of view, but they still claim to be the only holders of truth."

To the contrary, I asked Cezar, "Okay; but then why do not all the forces unite to change the balance of evil for the better?"

"Do not forget that under no circumstances can evil unite with good. That has always been the case. The one who is evil will flee from what is good, and for this reason the union you suggest cannot be achieved. You can only realize the union of (*continued on next page*)

a separation; and that is why it is a decadence: because they have so far evolved into orbits of existence which are unstable and cannot be maintained at that level.

I reflected a little before sharing my own observations.

"Indeed. People are grouped by affinities. We also see good, altruistic and active organizations in a superior way but also many that are bad and even destructive. People are 'distributed' according to the tendencies that each of them manifests. What amazes me very much is how they all manage to be together in the same space. It is clear that the physical plane manifests from this perspective, but at the same time, it represents a great 'risk' for evolution.

"But, it can also be a great chance for it if you do the right thing and you understand your experiences correctly," Cezar said. "It is true, however, with the groupings that observe and resonate at the same type of vibration: people gather together according to affinities because this is a universal law. For example, consider those who have reached 4-D or close to it because there are such people who have a fairly broad and fair understanding of the world. They attract those who have the same aspirations around them, and they are gradually elevating themselves, listening to and even practicing certain spiritual techniques that are shown to them until they themselves reach the 4-D level. The others who have 'come down' have reached the level of fanaticism which is very well known as the 'medieval area' with its specific representations: religious conceptions of the world and its existence. They consider us to 'lost' because 'we do not see the truth'. But, this 'truth' is their truth, a medieval relic embedded in the inability to understand things correctly. It is also a common sense problem."

"It's the kind of reaction that happens with those who cannot even listen to explanations because the difference in vibrational frequency is considerable," I said. "Whatever you say, anything you show or prove is rejected de facto and a priori. Yes; it's amazing where human stupidity can go."

"Not just stupidity," Cezar said, "but ignorance, too, for they often complement each other. For example, in the case of those who adhere to such ideas and mentalities that correspond to the Middle Ages, you can notice that they do not know the basic principles of quantum physics, all of which leads to an understanding of how energy is transmitted at such a level. Instead, they sometimes invoke those principles and bring them into question from a safe and authoritative position, but the vibrational frequency of their consciousness does not allow them to understand the quantum realities. Further, they imagine electrons as particles of matter, continuing to manifest

(continued from previous page) good and good because people who are mutually oriented 'speak the same language'. Unity can only be achieved between those people who have affinities that are close on a mental, emotional and spiritual level. You cannot, for example, have a very bad friend if you are good because that friendship cannot stand. Where there are no affinities, it is impossible to unite with unity, brotherhood or sympathy."

their skepticism about quantum fields and their objective reality. In other words, they want to 'solve' the quantum world through the knowledge and notions of the physical plane, but that's like trying to put a huge French key through the eye of a needle. Their lack of knowledge of what energy means forces them to mechanically revert to the principles of classical Newtonian mechanics, about four hundred years old."

I spoke thoughtfully.

"That could be dangerous in the future. If more and more people are looking for this 'safe' thinking, that could lead to some sort of social schism; not necessarily conflict between countries, but rather social segregation, just as you said."

"Yes, it could. Let us hope, however, that it will not be so," Cezar replied with a sad smile on his face.

FANATICISM AND IGNORANCE

We were both silent for a while, and then I spoke.

"From the report, I noticed their lack of reason and knowledge but especially their fanaticism. It seems that any discussion is doomed to failure precisely because of the fanaticism that manifests and is routinely encountered in those with poor intellectual training and suffering from a lack of general culture. They are able to find explanations for any evidence or answer that contradicts their theory, but they are often hilarious or simply fanciful. In fact, nothing can be said to them because they consider from the beginning that all the ideas and arguments relating to Earth, other than those supported by them, are erroneous. For them, the fact that the Earth is flat seems to be an axiom that cannot be countered or discussed."

Cezar was caught up in the subject, and he responded clearly to me.

"Some time ago, we were talking to someone in our echelon about this subject, but we were more interested in the psychological factor of the problem. The Major told me that the followers of the Flat Earth Theory go so far as to assert that they know nothing of sciences such as astronomy, physics or biology, yet they tell the whole world with the utmost certainty that the idea of a spherical Earth is completely false and that all Mankind must believe their word. This is like saying, 'I do not know Chinese, but I certainly tell you it does not exist.' Meanwhile, however, a billion and a half people speak Chinese. They use all sorts of 'experiments' and 'demonstrations' which can divert their audience, for those less well prepared or even angry, from the values of common sense. And, when faced with indisputable evidence, they say they it is actually fake. You cannot reach an understanding with such people because they are an expression of fanaticism. In a way, it is dramatic to see such thinking behavior. They do not know, do not document, do not read, nor seek to understand. The only thing they do is postulate from the very beginning that everything is one great scam."

"Whose scam?" I asked.

"They say it is all of the decision-makers and important institutions of the world who 'conspire' to make people think that the Earth is round," Cezar said ironically. "According to the Flat Earth Theory, scientists, NASA, ESA, and other research institutions all seem to have talked to each other in order to present to the world false evidence that the Earth is round. It is not clear why NASA would do this, but the followers of the Flat Earth Theory know better and say for sure that this is the case.

"Now, considering the problem more seriously, much of this fanaticism comes from the interdisciplinary manner in which science develops. Many of the results of modern science have emerged from the continuous 'movement' or active way in which it has evolved, even though it has many bugs, especially from a conceptual point of view. To give you a better idea, consider the idea of a wheel with spokes rotating very quickly and to the point where you do not see its spokes. At some point, there is an alteration of the image that gives you the impression that the spokes are just three or four. Moreover, there is also an aspect when you feel that the wheel is spinning in reverse, as if it were going backward. It is a dynamic aspect, and while it is obvious that it is not real, it appears as if it is real. Therefore, it is an illusion; but for the followers of the Flat Earth Theory and their mentality, this becomes a big problem. They do not take into account of the fact that such illusion is a result of the eye not being able to properly discern the movement due to the high speed of rotation, but they say that this movement cannot be seen because it actually does not exist."

Somehow, I was overwhelmed by what I heard, but I nevertheless spoke.

"If this unfortunate idea of a flat Earth continues to be followed, I would expect that their way of thinking, which is essentially aberrant and fanatical, would be extended to many other phenomena, both in the physical and abnormal realms. As far as I understand, they go on the general theory of global conspiracy wherein everything is a conspiracy that is meant to make us think in a certain way, but they are the only ones who know the truth and tell it."

"Such phenomena is regrettable and even worrisome, but it is likely to grow in the coming years," Cezar said. "Indeed. It is true that deviants can believe in and advocate those who adhere to this false conception.

"If you were to take some of them to the International Space Station or a cosmic shuttle in orbit around the planet, they will say exactly what they say about the tens of thousands of photographs that were made in cosmic space: that this was an 'arrangement' made to make them appear stupid, that everything is actually a fake and that nothing of what they see in connection with our planet being spherical is true; or that it is just an optical illusion caused by camera lenses or photographers."

"Still, how is it possible for the rest of the population to 'swallow' such nonsense?" I asked, annoyed, indirectly citing the cellular perception and sensitivity as well as the individual discernment that every human being in the present society should have.

"This is possible due to lack of education and individual training. People simply do not know, do not study, and lack general culture. Also lacking guidance and common sense in the interpretation of such things, they are at the hands of anyone who tells them that something is so or different. Here too, the education system contributes a lot, tending to become somewhat unidirectional with only certain things being taught with regard to their own personal skill-set. Nearly all other sciences or life-enhancing aspects that could give a much wider and pertinent view of life are neglected. Because of this, the majority of the human population on the planet is helpless and, in a way, it makes them 'prey' to strange influences. What should be the discernment factor of those who have no knowledge of or have never heard of the physical laws of matter, energy, the cosmos, or the multitude of phenomena that are happening in the world? They live only within the very narrow range of small needs and daily satisfactions."

"This represents a great decline for our society," I said sadly.

"It is true, but we must see this decline also from the perspective of the transformations that come. Part of humanity is evolving. That is indisputable. There are beings who have refinement in thought, who are intelligent and have good sense, and who aspire to superior consciousness so as to pass through the specific vibrational frequency from 3-D to 4-D. Those who are unable to achieve this will automatically descend to a lower level, i.e. to 2-D, because maintaining 3-D is difficult due to powerful disturbing forces."

DRAMATIC INVOLUTION FROM 3-D TO 2-D

At this point in the discussion, I wanted to clarify one more aspect because I was not sure that I understood the problem that I had raised a little earlier. Cezar clearly explained that this 'dimensional' representation, i.e., 2-D, 3-D, 4-D and so on, is one of the methods used to designate the perception or degree of consciousness of the surrounding reality.

"In other words," I said, "to understand within the perspective of the 3-D system, time is considered as a separate variable."

"Exactly. On the other hand, in the 4-D system, time is an integral part of the coordinate system that represents this reality. Understanding time as being 'fused' with space — as is the case in 4-D — requires a higher degree of consciousness."

"So what is time in 4-D?" I asked, a little confused.

"In 4-D, space and time will form a stand-alone reality. Then, we no longer have $x + t$, $y + t$, and $z + t$, representing a three-axis system, plus the movement in time; but we have a permanent collaboration between x and t, y and t, and z and t. They seem to constantly correlate, as if to say: xt, yt, zt, as if to be united permanently. Do you understand?"

"And, one should not confuse $x + t$, $y + t$ and $z + t$ with addition nor xt, yt and zt with multiplication because we are using different units of measure," I said thoughtfully.

"Obviously. They are just a way of rendering features in the absence of better notations. But, if you want, we can better consider $0xyz + t$ in the case of 3-D and $0zyzt$ in the case of 4-D."

Cezar then looked through the room for a few moments, searching for something with which to give me a good example. He saw a small metal ball on his desk and said, "Here is a ball. Do you admit to it being part of three-dimensional space?"

"It can be represented by a three-axis system," I nodded.

"Now, look at how we add time as the fourth dimension when we move the ball from one point to another. I move the ball from here to here and you see this as a linear motion, like a thread."

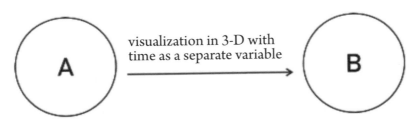

visualization in 3-D with time as a separate variable

MOVING A SPHERE IN TIME (T) FROM POINT A TO POINT B

"All right. I get it. And how would this move in 4-D?"

"Then, instead of seeing a moving sphere, you actually see a 'bar'. This is actually the four-dimensional plane; that is, a unification between space and time. For those who have diverged away from and out of 3-D, like the followers of the Flat Earth Theory, time is not even taken into account because it is interpreted as a mere 'quantity' that measures an event. For them, time is just a measurable quantity which is not perceived as a very subtle energy in relation to the superior aspects of Creation."

"If so, then those who adhere to this Flat Earth Theory are returning to the mechanical theories of classical physics, that is to say, Newtonian physics," I commented, drawing the natural conclusion.

visualization in 4-D in which time creates
new forms that are visible as a whole

*THE MOTION OF THE SPHERE OVER TIME IN THE FOURTH
DIMENSION (4-D) CREATES A KIND OF TUBE, LIKE A "CANE"*

"Newton revolutionized physics, explaining gravitational attraction
and many other phenomena, but the followers of the Flat Earth Theory do
not even accept the existence of gravity so they actually descend more and
more, over time, to the 'flat' concepts of the Middle Ages."

What I heard was almost unbelievable but unfortunately true, and the
report I had read was testimony to that.

"It is interesting, however, that this drama of humanity — because it is
still is a drama that will continue this way for decades — has its need, and you
will see this after you've progressed quite a bit," Cezar continued. "Otherwise, the segregation of human beings would not occur. The Earth would be
virtually sick because nothing would be done to get it out of the numbness
of a perpetual mire in which different categories of people are combined at
relatively close frequencies. Those who want to know and learn would have
no conditions or sufficient momentum to evolve due to all kinds of pressures
that come from others. It would be like collective suffocation."

What he was saying was overlapping with the concept of raising the
vibrational frequency of the planet. The Earth is preparing to activate its
superior dimensions, first of which is the rise to the subtle field characteristics
of the etheric dimension of 4-D. In the meantime, "Old Earth" in the third
dimension still remains with its limitations and vicissitudes.

This segregation of vibrational frequencies also inexorably attracts human
beings because some of them will aspire to spiritual evolution while others,
most of them, will prefer to stay with what they already know; that is, to live
on Earth in the 3-D physical plane.

This process in already in progress and will be amplified more and more
towards 2020-2025 when some galactic energy 'pulses' will take place that
will have profound effects on human consciousness.

This, however, being primarily a matter of choice, which in turn is
based upon individual inward tendencies, will not be easy for many human

beings to deal with in order to choose another life that is bright and pure. Instead, they will prefer to remain in their own sphere of reference and low resonance sensations because this comfort zone is better suited to their inner structure.

Cezar then strongly punctuated his point.

"With this severe segregation, there will be a massive gap between frequencies so that those who want to harden will harden even more; and the others who are moving forward will find the opportunity to easily distance themselves because the difference in consciousness between the two factions will increase significantly."

"Yes. It makes sense," I said.

"Those who will ascend in 4-D will be well prepared at some point and will be quite stable to descend later and try to help those in 3-D or below. This will all depend upon the choices and decisions of those there."

"From what you say, I see two clear tendencies: the hardening and even the deepening of this hardening of a large part of the population, of which the followers of the Flat Earth Theory are a good example; and the freedom of other people to evolve and break away more easily from the rest of involuted humanity."

Cezar nodded his head, approving. Then, after a few moments, he spoke again.

"Let's hope there will be enough of those in the second category."

I did not insist on this last reply because it was already very late. Generally speaking, I now had a clear idea of what this "Flat Earth phenomenon" represents with regard to correctly understanding the situations we are likely to face in the years to come.

I went to my room to rest because two American team members would be arriving the very next day, and this would involve some preparations that had to be made before the expedition. Several briefings were needed as well as preparing accommodations for two American officers to visit the Projection Hall.

It turned out, however, that they had already done their homework; so the talks were very productive, expeditious and efficient. As an exchange of information, they brought several evidentiary documents and the discussions derived from these were very interesting; so, with the approval of Cezar, I have decided to present in this book, in summary format, some pieces of interest from the content of those discussions.

CHAPTER THREE

Important Corrections

The two officers sent by the Pentagon were young, professionally trained and agreeable. Not all of those with whom we have been dealing with in the past with regard to expeditions have possessed such qualities. In fact, in such situations there have sometimes even been animosities and hidden intentions or thoughts on their behalf, but this depends upon the people involved. The Pentagon's secret orders are never absent; for in a way, it's like going fishing. "If one gets caught, then it's good; if not, we are still trying." It is important, however, to what degree they are influenced and dominated by those who sent them as the nature of human beings is different.

These American officers proved to be a pleasant presence, and the conversations with them went very well. There were two rounds of talks, the first focusing on technical elements, and the second being related to information and documentation that the Pentagon officials wanted from us.

It was a procedure that worked on the basis of sincerity and fairness, a sort of "barter" that was mutually beneficial for each of the parties involved, both the Romanian and the Americans. While we have had access to the very advanced technology of the secret complex in Bucegi, they have offered us other types of immediate advantages in return for being allowed study the artifacts and the other elements that are there. Politics were also involved but only as an outward form of things. This exchange, however, does have its limitations, being structured by General Obadea on ethical and moral principles which are still in force today.

The basic rule was that the nature of the information they were to request would be neutral, not to be used for onerous purposes or to exploit or harm other nations. Things have worked well since 2010; that is, since the protocol was implemented. This has resulted in a mutual trust which has led to a very good and close cooperation in this direction. This does not mean that everything was "milk and honey" but we believe that the present state of things is an example of how to work in a balanced and honest manner, even though the "object" of common interest — the secret complex in the Bucegi Mountains — is extremely important and delicate for all Mankind.

ANTEDILUVIAN HISTORY

During the briefings and discussions that took place before expeditions or other types of cooperation, it was usually Lieutenant Nicoara and myself who participated on the Romanian side, but Cezar attended this time because

63

it involved the exchange of information at the highest level of security. The general explanations given here are to show the context in which the discussions turned to the direction of Mankind's history, all as a result of details requested by the American side. It is not necessary to insist upon mentioning them, but they have led to an excellent presentation of historical realities which Cezar has summarized.

At that time, I did not know about these aspects as I had not had time to ask about them. That is why I was much more interested in listening to and understanding the true nature of some important events in the past of Mankind, the ordinary historical description of which has either been truncated or modified by the prism of understanding of the people from that time. In reality, as I was going to find out, the historical events to which I will refer have to be addressed in another form and with other connotations than those that have been handed down to us from history, transmitted from the darkness of those times.

A significant part of that discussion, more than half of it, I do not yet have permission to report on. From what remains, I have summarized some elements that I consider important, especially since they correlate with what I myself would soon find out, learning much of the unknown history of Mankind in summary form.

The discussion I am referring to took place in the second round of talks with the two American officers. It was a free, open and formal discussion. In short, the question arose concerning artifacts discovered by the U.S. military in Afghanistan and also in another area in the Far East. The two officers presented a written report and several photographs depicting a rather strange object. We were told of its amazing characteristics which were described to us in some detail. The Americans wanted some past information about the place where the artifact was found and an in-depth view of the topography of the soil, a request which could only be fulfilled by accessing either the dome in the Projection Hall* or the "Time Machine" in the Occult Chamber in Egypt.**

They also wanted information about the past populations who had lived in those places. As I am not allowed to give details of all this, I will confine myself to saying that the discussion veered off quite a bit with regard to the distant past of Mankind which Cezar presented and explained in a novel way. In two of the issues raised, Cezar could not answer on the spot as a special inquiry was required, but he answered the other questions that had been asked, at least for the most part. At one point, in direct connection with some investigations they themselves had made, the two American officers raised the

---

* The book *Transylvanian Sunrise*, Chapter 5, discusses a device in the Projection Hall beneath the Romanian Sphinx by which one can view historical events.
** See Volume 3, *The Mystery of Egypt - The First Tunnel*, Chapter 4, which discusses a "time machine" that will enable the viewer to travel in time with their mind but not the body.

issue of the Flood in the Middle East region. They wanted to clarify rescue efforts that had taken place for the people who lived there at that time. As Cezar had studied that time period, he responded immediately.

"If we consider the *Bible* and how the Flood is presented in the text, it follows that all the Earth was covered with water. We need to consider, however, how the inhabitants of that time understood what the Earth to be like. To them, there were no other continents. The area in which they lived and what was around them was the entire world."

One of the Americans, the younger one, then spoke to make a point.

"The biblical flood does not seem to be the only one in the history of humanity. There are other traditions and populations that speak of a devastating flood but in different parts of the world, including our continent."

"That's how it is. Various populations have experienced such a phenomenon in different periods of history and in different areas around the globe. But to say that the entire surface of the planet was covered by water at the time of the biblical flood is a mistake. Things did not happen like this. Over time, there were vast territories and even entire continents that fell under water, burying civilizations. There is, for example: Mu, much of Lemuria, and especially Atlantis."

In the holographic images of the Projection Hall, I had seen many things about the Flood. This, however, had occurred many years prior, and they were very few in number, presented in the format of a very brief summary amongst many other events in the history of the Earth. For example, I had seen large areas covered by water, starting from old Cappadocia (central Turkey on today's maps) and extending down to Syria and Israel with a flood of water destroying everything in its path, like a tsunami. I could no longer distinguish the shore of the Mediterranean from the land. The layer of water that flooded the soil, however, was not very deep. The landscape seemed desolate: an endless stretch of water with a few rare trees above the water or an isolated temple that had resisted the diluvian forces. This was largely due to the fact that there were no tall buildings as most of the buildings then were small and precarious, made of clay and stones.

I did not, however, see the source of the Flood nor other implications related to it, but I did not doubt such existed.

SPECIFICS ABOUT THE BIBLICAL FLOOD

Seeing that the discussion had quieted on this subject, the time seemed right to clarify a few unknowns in this regard, so I came up with a question.

"How is the Flood described in the *Bible*?" I asked.

"The Flood in the *Bible* is the same as the Sumerian description of the evolution of the society over the past thousand years," Cezar replied.

"When the cataclysm took place, it was desired to preserve the fauna and flora in the area which was covered in water. Noah's Ark was not so great and not all animal species were taken in it. The boat was indeed built, and Noah and his family even took on board a few pairs of animals but relatively few in relation to what was written. His ark played the role of a necessary "double" or backup on the ground. The real preservation and subsequent resurgence of fauna came from space."

Seeing the stunned faces of the two American officers, Cezar continued.

"At that level, the problem was put in another way. There was a fairly large 'library' full of containers containing DNA samples of living creatures from Asia and Africa. Those who wrote the *Bible* could not explain this scientifically so they stated that Noah took pairs of all animal species on his ship. In fact, the taking of DNA samples was done by beings from another stellar system who were considered to be 'gods' on Earth."

"They had a virtual biological data bank," I said, "but what was the point with the Noah episode?"

"It was the evolution of humanity, of its own destiny," Cezar replied. "Help was given, but people had to build their own future. Their contribution was necessary as it was part of their destiny. Even if everything was well established and preserved in the DNA samples of living creatures, the process of 'rebirth' of the fauna was to be initiated by humans as a 'backup' on Earth. The recovery of animal species lasted several decades after the Flood. Humanity, of course, was helped by an extraterrestrial civilization, but that took a long time."

The two American officers did not seem too convinced. One of them then asked a question.

"But why did they do that? The fauna and flora were rebuilding themselves after the Flood. It would have taken longer, but it would have recovered."

"In a cataclysm of such proportions, you have no way to recover," Cezar replied. "Everything is destroyed. The flora would still have a chance but not the fauna."

"It all seems quite nebulous," the younger major insisted.

"Indeed. That period was very tense," Cezar admitted. "It's about 5,000 years since then. There were many divergent interests even between the 'gods'. What has happened, however, was due to the necessity of evolution on Earth. Greater diversity of wildlife was needed as evolution was impetuous. The more diversity there is, the quicker it is that souls can incarnate and evolve."

"And what guarantee is there for that?" the other major asked.

"None," said Cezar, "but the chances for evolution are great with this rhythm. Unless there is diversity, a great effort from one species would be needed to evolve sufficiently in order for it to ascend to become the higher species. But diversity, through the many experiences that it promotes, allows for 'learning' in an accelerated way; that is, an accelerated evolution. The easiest path by which beings can rapidly evolve is by small evolutionary steps that are 'accelerated'. This avoids sudden changes that strain the structure and can make certain events unpredictable."

"Okay, but does that mean that there was a need for a flood to be triggered?" I asked with wonder.

"Things are always correlated in the Universe. What you think serves a purpose at a certain time is also a solution for other needs. Something may seem to be bad or terrible at a certain time and space, but when you look at it from a broader perspective, it proves to be necessary, even leading to a higher level of evolution. The cataclysm that involved the Flood — especially when it encompasses a wider area such as the biblical flood, i.e. much of the Middle East and Southeast Europe — has undoubtedly meant a massive purge of the area of inappropriate practices and tendencies with regard to the correct development of the human being, but it also represents the possibility of a rebirth with regard to the sense of a significant leap on the scale of evolution.

TWO MAIN CHALLENGES IN THE EVOLUTION OF HUMANITY

The room was silent. We each thought of how it is possible that a flood, which undoubtedly means much suffering and massive loss of human life, is still a trampoline for human evolution. Cezar was also silent, letting us soak in the idea. Finally, I put my heart in my mouth and said that maybe some extra explanation was still necessary.

"The point is, when we talk about an evolutionary leap, we have to consider a change in the structure of DNA," I stated.

Cezar answered with goodwill.

"This cannot only happen through genetic engineering but also as a result of environmental changes. What do you think that the great migrations of peoples meant when they took place? Even the most stable seeds eventually migrate. It is an impulse of life that determines evolution. An environmental change for a population always means more than just the immediate needs that are reflected in everyday life. It also means a profound change in DNA."

"The location, the topography, the geographical area ... all this affects DNA?" the other American officer asked in amazement. "That would partly answer some of our questions."

"Undoubtedly. Food, climate and the area influence DNA over time, it being modulated according to the basic information structure within it. Everything then changes, even the spoken language, at least to the extent of an accent if not a complete transformation of its structure. Migrations by communities, groups, or even entire populations, in time, have resulted in combining races and diversifying human DNA. It's like 'grafting' a plant to affect a slow transformation of DNA."

"But, there were more evolved populations on Earth among the people," the officer commented. "Besides the 'gods' with their technology, there have been human communities or even civilizations that have developed amazingly. We have artifacts and evidence in this regard that we have discovered."

Cezar approved of what he said with a nod of his head.

"In the history of humanity, we can talk, more or less, about two great categories of human beings who have developed differently: one of them has reached a high degree of evolution; the other has been somewhat left in nature so that its progress was much more strenuous. This is how we can explain why some areas of the Earth developed and evolved to a great extent while others were inhabited by people living in caves and organized in tribes. We see this even today at the level of monarchical or certain genetic lines or even in the cultural tradition of some peoples. For example, the caste system of the Hindus represents a rough classification of what once dominated life on this planet. Then there is an issue of purity and not mixing the DNA between 'pure' and 'impure' races. It is, to put it this way, a sort of struggle to preserve the superiority of those who come 'from above'; that is, those who have a special structure of DNA in their genetic tree. The problem is complex, but in summary, we can say that the current human civilization is a reflection of the second category of human beings, the ones that have evolved strenuously.

MIGRATION THROUGH INTER-DIMENSIONAL PORTALS

I did not know anything about these issues, but I was hoping to find out more about the two upcoming meetings with Apellos. I decided to ask a question.

"Why has this happened?"

"It was not just a single cause; but more recently, in the last few thousand years, it took the form of a 'blockade' from certain alien civilizations who wanted to exploit this category of human beings for their own use. In other words, they were not interested in the evolution of humanity. This gave rise to many divergences between 'gods' as I have already alluded to, for some wanted to facilitate the extraordinary capacity of the human being to evolve."

"And others wanted to exploit them?" I asked, amazed. "Why did an advanced alien civilization want to use backward beings?"

"Nevertheless, they did. This planet is alien to them, has resources, and some of these had to be exploited. Additionally, some of the 'gods' were to be serviced and especially so that they could control everything. They wanted to keep humanity very close to an animal level; that is, not allow it to evolve in order to use it. Later, they advanced their plans in order to take over total control of the planet, using as an intermediary an 'elite' class human beings that had somehow been hybridized with the DNA of those extraterrestrial beings."

Cezar's indirect references were obvious to all of us.

"It seems though that their plans did not go as they wanted," I said. "I understand that the migration of people has just resulted in a slow but safe change in DNA. Otherwise, control would have been total."

"Yes; because such negative 'gods' have a limited mandate. They cannot do exactly what they want. There is a sort of a 'galactic control' imposed by some very advanced civilizations to which they are subjected. Even so, because they are very patient, the negatively oriented 'gods' have done much harm, especially through the people they have appointed."

The younger officer intervened, wishing to bring the discussion back to the information the two were particularly interested in.

"About the artifact we discovered — the data we have is leading us to the Huns, but something does not fit because they seem to have come from elsewhere."

"That's right," Cezar replied. "The Huns were a migratory people, but they not only came from the Mongolian steppes, as it is supposed, but from three distinct directions. They have emerged from the Arctic, along the Nordic countries, in the Siberian region; and from the steppes in the east, in Mongolia. The Huns, however, did not actually come from these physical regions but 'entered' into their respective areas through the secret passages which still allowed for a connection between the physical and the etheric planes. From there, they began spreading to Europe, giving the impression that they were coming from the Mongolian steppes."

I saw the two American officers look at themselves, a sign that the information corroborated with what they had discovered and knew. Cezar continued unhindered.

"They came from some areas of the etheric plane close to Shambhala. This explains why the Huns suddenly occupied a vast region; not because they conquered it but because they arrived from other areas, seeming to have conquered new land. True, there were also struggles; but their empire, as it was, was rather due to the speed with which they had occupied the area. They also, of course, contributed a lot of their warrior qualities. There were not many, but the other peoples felt the specific energy of righteousness that the Huns manifested, and some of them united with them against the Roman Empire."

"Yes; they fought with the Roman troops, so there were more than a few," said one of the officers.

Cezar nodded his head, then explained.

"Here we have to clarify who the Huns actually are. The name 'hun' comes from 'inn' which means 'leader'. They were a tribe of 'rulers' or special beings with obvious qualities, both physical and intellectual. Indeed; these were few, but the rest — that is, the great mass of the tribe — were made up of ordinary and rather primitive people, most of the time being part of the already conquered tribes which bloated the army ranks of the Huns on their way to Europe. Only the rulers were Huns because they were part of a special race of human beings. This also explains that they originally came from the etheric plane through inter-dimensional chasms."

The two majors shifted a little bit in their chairs, and the youngest finally dared to ask a question.

"Could we know precisely where the etheric plane crossed the physical plane?"

"The eternal problem," I thought to myself. On the other hand, I understood them, for their demand was somewhat legitimate. They were in possession of a very valuable artifact found in those areas, and they wanted to know more, to find out and explore.

Cezar smiled discretely, making an elegant denial.

"Even if I precisely knew those locations, I would still not disclose their position. You know how things are in such cases. They are the territories of other states, and we have no jurisdiction there and do not want any suspicion."

"We could act punctually and efficiently without destabilizing anything," the other major insisted.

I knew Cezar well, and I knew that from this point on there was no way to convince him otherwise. After a while, we all got up to go to rest, the time being quite late. There were five days left until the expedition, but the program was still full. The two American officers had to go through some predetermined training steps in connection with the secret complex in the Bucegi Mountains. I was the one who had to deal with their training, practically and theoretically, and Cezar had to go to Bucharest for some important discussions. To get the opportunity for the two meetings with those from Apellos, I had to delegate my duties to Lieutenant Nicoara, and he accepted with extreme goodwill.

INTERPOLATION OF PHYSICAL AND ETERNAL REALITY: AN AMAZING CASE OF GERMAN AND AMERICAN SECRET SERVICES

I woke up early in the morning and decided to reserve that day for rest and relaxation in order to prepare for the next day's expedition to meet with those from Apellos. Although I focused on preparing myself mentally for the expedition, there was no peace of mind because I could not forget what the man from Apellos had told me about those so-called "houses of cabal". I went to the office and started researching, hoping to find some information in our database about a possible secret operation between the U.S. and Germany that had taken place in recent years. I was not successful, so I had to resort to using some of the relationships I had in the BND.* We already knew that the German Secret Service was never too generous with the exchange of information, but we rely on the collaboration that sometimes exists between agents to obtain data of mutual interest.

Relationships spoke, and the same day we received a secure copy of the preliminary report for that secret operation. I immediately realized that it was just a two-page summary of a full report on the event, and details were lacking. The operation had taken place in 2005 and was immediately classified into the highest category of security. I wanted to read the whole report, but my source in the BND told me that they had no access to that level. I thanked them and decided to try my chance with the Americans because, according to the summary report and what I had seen on the holographic screen, both countries had been involved in that activity.

Finding Cezar in the training room, I briefly addressed the situation. He had tangentially heard of a U.S. Army secret division which only dealt with the study of space-time distortions in the U.S. and Antarctic. He knew about this from some talks with Major Samuel Cross who, in turn, had come across such information several years ago.

"The division was led by a Colonel Finnegan," said Cezar. "Cross met with him several times, but he did not give me any further details. I do not know if that colonel is the head of the division anymore, but I'll check on it."

Towards the evening, Cezar sought me out and gave me some good news. He told me that he spoke to Major Cross and that he had confirmed that Finnegan was still the head of that secret section. Over time, it had become very important. Cross knew about the 2005 incident with the Germans, so it was easy for him to ask about it, especially by reason of the fact that he had the necessary security clearance. Since there was already a collaboration agreement between the Romanian and the American side, based upon mutual exchanges of sensitive information related to unusual phenomena, the Colonel finally agreed to disclose the details of the operation, even if his division had not been mentioned in the 2007 agreement. He had a great friendship with Major Cross, however, and he knew about the Bucegi complex. Surprisingly, however, Finnegan did not ask for anything in exchange. Surprised, I noticed that even the Secret Services can have a human face.

I received a dossier with several dozen pages the same evening which I immediately read with great interest. There was a corroborated analysis of the BND report with that of the FBI. Indeed; I can say that it was a most unusual operation, having disturbed both sides enough to the point where it warranted the establishment of a special division under Finnegan's leadership.

---

* BND is an abbreviation for Bundesnachrichtendienst, the German Secret Service which was created and run by Reinhard Gehlen, the Nazi who also set up the CIA.

The situation was such that both the Germans and the Americans were somehow on the same wavelength without knowing it. Somehow, there were parallel events in both Bavaria and the city of Detroit. In Germany, special troops were alerted but only after what began as mere routine curiosity turned into genuine perplexity and suspicion.

In a German city, there was a very old house, built almost 300 years ago. Having been rebuilt and renovated several times, it somehow kept its late medieval appearance. The problem was that it was in a demolition area where a large park was planned. The surrounding buildings, all very old, had already begun to be demolished, but that house was well defended by property law. Besides, it also had a historical protection status. Discussions, proposals and even legal proceedings had gone on for many years, but no one had ever seen the owner. Lawyers said that he was always abroad, being an important businessman who did not want to sell or give up that old building. In the legal papers, it appeared that he had inherited the property, with all of the other papers referring to the "descendant". It seemed to be a problem with no solution. At one point, the city officials asked the police to do some discreet research because, despite the efforts of state officials, they were unable to contact the owner of the house to conduct direct talks and negotiations. Any such dealings, at the order of the owner, were to be done only through the law firm.

After a time, however, things became very strange. Taking advantage of the cameras already fitted for the future park, discreet observation of that house began. The reports indicated that it was not inhabited during the first four months of 2005. Then, at the end of April, the first person, possibly the owner, went inside and came out only four days later. In the summary note I had received from my BND colleague, the police report stated that the man who entered had no luggage but only wore a raincoat over his clothes. There were obviously no goods in the house because it had remained uninhabited for several months. Even so, the man did not go out until four days afterward.

The police became suspicious and informed the BND, believing that the situation contained a certain risk of terrorism or other dangerous actions. The observation of the house continued, this time with a superior technique and Secret Service personnel dedicated specifically to that operation. The house was again deserted. In just two months, another person, a tall brown-haired man with a small backpack, was seen entering it.

The team carefully monitored the house for the next seven days without seeing lights, movement or other people entering or going out. Intrigued by the unusual situation, the head of the team made the decision to penetrate the inside. Additional outside help was called upon for observation, the German team being ten in number.

On the other side of the ocean, the situation was slightly different. While the Germans merely observed a building, the FBI actually chased a suspect. He was a tall brown-haired man with unnaturally white skin who did not appear in any civil or visa records of the United States, but he had been involved in a particular accident. He had been sporadically observed from 2003 to 2005 in various cities on the East Coast of America, but each time, he was lost. The case was solved in 2005 when an alert was given that the person had suddenly appeared in Detroit whereupon he was arrested.

The FBI team, however, wanted to closely follow the subject to see if he had any associates. Additional trigger forces had been mobilized so that the character could no longer "disappear" as had happened before. The man was traced to a house in a neighborhood near the outskirts of the city where he entered alone. A special FBI intervention team of seven members then arrived and were strategically placed around the building.

What developed from that point precipitated even more confusion. Reading the American report, I had the global vision of what had happened there, but none of the parties involved, neither the Germans nor the Americans, knew each other. When six members of the German team entered the old Bavarian town house, they found no one there. The rooms were large enough, measuring about three meters tall, and were modestly furnished.

Four of the German agents walked into the middle of the house through a hallway that led them into a room that was larger than the others that was placed perpendicularly to the direction from which they had entered. On the opposite wall, they saw an ordinary door located exactly at its center. The only strange aspect was that on the side of that door facing them, there were ingrained stones on the wall that were just like those from a river at the base of the house. The German agents were tense as they heard more voices on the other side of the door, addressing them in English in a commanding tone.

The U.S. report mentions the "hot part" of the operation as follows.

> "The German team violently broke the wooden door between the two rooms, being prepared for automatic weapons. Our team, more specifically three of the four agents who entered the house (sergeants # 1, # 2, # 3), also had their weapons on the door because we had heard voices giving orders in the German language. They had four agents and we three. At first, we screamed at each other to drop the guns, but in all of that tension and agitation, we could not understand anything. Then, we suddenly stopped because we were all stunned."

The German and American operatives were staring at each other after finding each other in a large but completely empty room. What follows is a fragment from the summary of the German report according to what the team commander said.

"I looked in the room from behind one of the windows. It was evening and was raining hard enough Our clothes and equipment were wet. I turned my head towards to view through the window inside the empty room where the American agents were, and I saw it was noon time there with the sun shining in the blue sky. None of us could articulate a word. I knew that the images were being transmitted in real time, but everyone was silent during those moments. The surprise was colossal."

In the report, it was mentioned that when agents were at the broken door; that is, when interacting with inter-dimensional space, the image was distorted, but it was still possible to distinguish what was going on there. After the portal area was entered, images returned to normal.

Obviously, that house contained an actual distortion; that is, a spatial portal, and the door between the two chambers was actually a discontinuity between two worlds. When they broke the door, the German agents broke into the "other side", meeting with the American team who had already entered the room but through the opposite door. For the Americans, that door was in Detroit; for the Germans, the portal door, which they broke, was in a city in central Bavaria.

Even though the German report was only two pages, it was still surprising. I particularly liked the attitude of the German team leader as he seemed to have shown a great deal of self-control, and he quickly focused in on the new situation. He responded very well to what he had encountered when he walked through the broken door into the empty room: "I felt a tingling when I walked through the portal."

He also showed himself to be a keen observer with a presence of mind, making some observations about the weapons after having passed through the portal: "The guns electrified and sparked when they were touched by hand."

Of the four German agents who entered the room, only one — the commander of the team — showed any curiosity about that phenomenon of discontinuity in reality and not losing one's bearings. Two of the American agents showed a presence of spirit and interest in the situation, and one of them — mentioned in the report — even sent a report to command through the microphone attached to his combat gear, stating: "You should see this."

In the days that followed, the other agents took part in a few psychological therapy sessions to alleviate the emotional and mental shock that they had due to a lack of understanding of what was happening there. In some people, the structure of the mind is so rigid that it cannot withstand sudden changes of reality without giving rise to unpleasant side effects.

In the U.S. incident file, almost half of the volume concerned the analysis of the operation as well as conclusions and proposals. Research began immediately, and in the archives, it was revealed that, in fact, that house in Detroit was built more than 200 years ago over a place where there was known to be a portal or spatial distortion described as: "which takes you away to who knows where because no one will come back from there to tell you."

There was no reference as to who had built the house over the space distortion. Indeed; people were "jettisoned" somewhere to a hill in Bavaria, suffering complete disorientation and even losing their minds. For those who managed to get over that shock, it was probably very difficult to ever return to America, and so the legend was created.

A good initiative from the Americans was that, after the incident in 2005, they set up a secret division to research into such phenomena, the head of which to date is Colonel Finnegan. Apparently, he drove this department with an iron hand and managed to impress his superiors in the Pentagon by virtue of results — some remarkable, as Major Cross revealed to us — that he obtained. He was the one who presented, for example, a classification of spatial distortions based upon all the years of work and activity of the division that had taken place since its establishment.

By summarizing Finnegan's material, it can be said that spatial distortions can be divided into three main categories:

1. Fixed Portals — These are very rare and not very well known (this category includes, for example, the distortion in Germany).

2. Multidirectional Portals — Passing through such spatial distortions can be reached in different places, depending on the individual characteristics, the time chosen for the passage, and the weather or other elements.

3. Dynamic Portals — Also called "Earth wormholes", these are continually moving space-time distortions in the sense that they appear and disappear very quickly, changing their position, size and even subtle energetic characteristics.

Major Cross told us that Finnegan's division gained an even greater reputation a year ago when he managed to implement a special program — after a long collaboration with several IT geniuses — that allows him to, in a certain way, "foresee" the place and moment when the third category of portals will open.

Finnegan's study is based upon a whole series of mysterious events that have taken place over the years, from the late Middle Ages to the present.

One of the instances, indicated by the uncertain reference of an obscure antiquity in Paris, shows the case of the great physicist Isaac Newton and how he apparently experienced passing through a spatial distortion on the edge of a forest. Newton was projected about 30 kilometers further from that location. Although he returned there, the portal had disappeared, and so it was designated as a "wormhole".

The division led by Finnegan provides a map of the portals discovered and classified according to the above division. Many of them are found in Iceland, Northern Ireland, Canada, in the passage to Alaska, and also on a significant part of the Alaskan surface. This also included locations on the ice as well as the Kamchatka Peninsula.

I finished reading the file later that night, but I was pleased to have documented it and to understand how "houses of cabal" work. Such notions were not new to me because I had already experienced many such "passages" up to that point. Besides, they were commonplace within the secret complex of Bucegi and its tunnels. But, the impact of such a situation on human beings who are not accustomed to this kind of situation is often intimidating.

Reading the two reports, we have found that there are two main categories of people: those who are open to such experiences and have a level of consciousness that allows them to adapt quickly to them; and those that do not support the "vibrational jump" or change in thinking paradigm. For them, the "threshold" is too high. I then remembered the phenomenon of population segregation which Cezar had put in the spotlight shortly before, a factor which will dramatically increase in the years to come. This was an additional reason to better understand that the radical transformation of Mankind can only come from elevating the level of individual consciousness.

CHAPTER FOUR

HUMANITY'S ORIGIN ON EARTH: FROM THE COSMIC TO THE QUANTUM LEVEL

I was glad I that I had managed to arrange everything in order that I could attend the two meetings with those from Apellos. Lieutenant Nicoara dealt with the training of the two American officers, and this gave me the time to prepare for the next day and also to solve other pressing tasks within the Base. Everything went really well. The officers from the Pentagon proved to be cooperative, and they assimilated perfectly.

Arriving punctually for the meeting, things went quickly as far as I was concerned. Although I was told we were early, everything worked out as it should. We were in the hanger that the Apellos used for surface activities.

MENTOR

The Apellos man received me very kindly and with friendliness, leading me to the holographic viewing room. Already in front of us were two comfortable armchairs that had been arranged for our visit. I was given the special helmet in order to access as much information as possible.

"Someone in our world wants to give you some important things," he said with a smile.

I looked at him with wonder and an inquiring gaze as the Apellos man directed my attention to the holographic screen that was projected in front of me. It was big and blue. Appearing immediately with it was the image of a very beautiful woman who looked at me carefully, almost serenely. She was about 5'7" tall and brunette with her hair cut straight in the back, descending a little bit down to her shoulders. She wore a one-piece suit of glossy skin-like white material upon which discreetly beautiful designs were emblazoned. Her eyes were almond-shaped and long, and her eyes seemed to veil a hidden flame. The white skin, characteristic of the Apellos, contrasted strongly with her black hair and dark eyes. Her body, harmonious and supple, gave the impression that she was very well trained, and she exuded a special magnetism. It was virtually the first time I had seen a woman from the Apellos civilization, and the effect it produced upon me was one of sincere admiration, with a fascination for the special charisma that she manifested in a natural way and for the energy that radiated out of her.

Addressing me in the Romanian language, which she had mastered very well, she had the same easy but "sweet" accent that I had also noticed in the man who had guided me in the surface hangar. I heard the sound of her voice coming from the direction of the rectangular device that came out of the floor, but I could not figure out how it worked. I did not see speakers or anything else in the room.

The woman said her name is Méntia and that she is one of the scientists of the Apellos civilization. Her field of activity corresponded to the term "medicine" in our world, although her explanations of this notion is much more enriched and nuanced than you would typically hear in our society. Better said, Méntia deals with the health of the people of Apellos, being a kind of "minister" in this respect. They regard health as being inseparable from spirituality. You cannot have one without the other because they are inseparable.

"Being healthy is a necessity for man," she said. "You cannot be healthy in the body without having a healthy soul. Body sickness means a sickness of the soul and vice versa. Your medicine has developed only in a horizontal direction which is of little use. It does not provide or offer effective and genuinely powerful treatments for healing."

Even though I knew very well that what she was saying to me was true, I did not really understand the purpose of our meeting. As if reading my thoughts, she replied immediately.

"What I want to tell you about is the physical condition of people and their spiritual condition, both of which are degrading more and more. From our point of view, it is worrisome because our analysis and observations even show a degradation of 'base' DNA in many people on the surface of the planet, and this is very dangerous. This is primarily due to neglect of health. In turn, health is linked to a much deeper understanding of human nature and body composition. The physical part must be correlated with the subtle part of the being. This means that what is material, that is, the body, must be correlated with what is spiritual, that is, with subtle energy and consciousness. Your people not only separate the body from energy and consciousness, but many of them completely ignore the spiritual side. This is a sure recipe for decay, suffering and involution. My hope is that you will be able to share this with as many people as possible."

Méntia spoke with a lot of passion, force and feeling, drawing my attention to the fact that the human health situation in the world has become alarming. The solution, she said, is not in national and international health associations and bodies, all of which are merely administrative machinations of political, personal or group interests. These organizations do not improve the situation. At best, they perpetuate it on the same level. I noticed anger in her which I interpreted as a sincere concern and expression of compassion for human beings.

"There's not much to do in this direction," I said. "It's a terrible octopus at this level: of drugs, hospitals, and medicine in general. The change must come from a profound level."

"Of course. One has to first of all change the vision and mentality," she replied quickly. "This will lead to new discoveries of great value which integrate the human body into the universal holographic structure."

"The problem with this," I said bitterly, "Is that I do not want that." Having talked with Cezar on this subject a couple of years ago, I knew the subject quite well. We even had access to some sensitive files in this area. Unfortunately, we always butt up against a colossus in this area which seems to crush everything and not let any flowers grow. My metaphors were immediately understood by Méntia who was not at all foreign to the subject.

"We know of this serious situation on the surface world. To you, a number of harmful factors cause disastrous combinations. Governments are avid for money, power and political influence. In order to obtain them, they allow the use of very harmful products in food and treatments. Many of the laws are insidious, and the knot of financial interests is immense. We, however, firmly say that change comes from the population; not from riots, but from a change of mentality. People must understand that they must produce a transformation in their conceptions and then be firm in maintaining those superior ideas that in some way imply the ascension of being."

She paused for a few moments before speaking with great determination. "Transmit this further because any seed has its fruit later."

I smiled to myself, noticing that Méntia was taking over the style of expressing herself through occasional metaphors. Ultimately, however, she was perfectly right because a superior world is primarily a world of perfectly healthy people, full of radiant energy and vitality. It would be difficult to imagine a sick and afflicted society which is also advanced from the point of view of technology and spirituality. Human health and evolution are two aspects that correlate and go hand in hand, such as chains that are inseparable. A sick or distressed man, trapped by all sorts of physical or psychological problems, cannot concentrate, nor is he efficient; but most important of all, he is not happy. What evolution can come from such a state?

I knew this all too well and even expressed this to her, but Méntia told me that those in Apellos had found solutions and are willing to help us if there is openness and desire in this respect. She told me that, at a given moment, the relations between Apellos and the population of Romania would have to become public; but until then, they are willing to help indirectly.

"People must understand that health depends on certain factors that can neither be ignored nor excluded. First of all, this is about their evolution at all levels; and that means refining and then transforming their DNA, but in a beneficial sense and on many vibrational frequencies."

"And how will they figure this out?" I asked curiously.

"There are three main factors. First, senses will become more sensitive and more developed; and people will use their brains more and more efficiently. Some of them will gain paranormal powers because their DNA structure will be refined enough on certain frequencies. It will have affinities with some material or subtle realities in the universe, and this will lead to the ability to influence matter or certain subtle energy fields at will. This is combined with the second essential factor that must be taken into account, and this is the psychological and mental balance of the being. The third factor is the physical body. A person will actually 'feel' the problems that exist at the two higher levels and how one's will translates them into the physical plane through various diseases. As you can see, we cannot separate one of these areas from the other two."

"Is that what you do in Apellos?"

"Spirituality, psychology and medicine make up a collective body inside of us. They are not treated separately, such as is the case in your world. But, we believe that it is time for an invigoration of these ideas, none of which were at all strange to the ancient inhabitants of your country. The Dacians applied this style of 'holistic medicine' and the Greeks adopted certain notions from them, enough to propel them to a higher stage of evolution."

I wondered that if this was the case with the Greeks of antiquity, then what was the level of the ancient Dacians in this regard? I realized in a flash the truth of what Méntia said as I already knew that the inhabitants of Tomassis,* direct descendants of the ancient Dacians, applied this style of "holistic medicine". I now had a better explanation as to why I have noticed harmony, well-being, balance and, generally speaking, the perfect health that these people always radiated.

In practical terms, Méntia told me that the spiritual transformation of the human being, which refers to raising the vibrational frequency of consciousness, is directly related to the health of the body and that one cannot achieve one without the other. The Apellos woman surprised me again with her telepathic perception and answered my thoughts immediately.

"Indeed. A perfectly healthy body has every chance of evolving, for one is then able to go through the stages necessary for their spiritual evolution. Your ancestors knew and accepted this, applying the principles I am telling you. This information is 'imprinted' in your DNA, and all you have to do is re-activate it. There are many other populations on the planet that have the same characteristics, especially in those territories that have maintained their ancient roots."

I raised an issue that seemed a logical question to ask concerning a trend that is quite extensive nowadays.

"If the health and spirituality of the being go hand in hand, what is the situation with atheists or agnostics? They are also healthy and can live long

* Tomassis is an underground city that Radu visited and is below the surface city of Tomis in southeastern Romania. See Volume 5 of the *Transylvania Series*, entitled *Inside the Earth — The Second Tunnel*.

enough without suffering despite the fact that they are not evolving spiritually. They have their own system of interpreting the world and life, none of which seems to affect their body."

Méntia immediately responded with a charming smile on her beautiful face.

"An atheist only 'lives' within the context of playing their role in what amounts to a simple mechanical participation in a much more complex process, driven by many forces and energies. He participates in life in a somewhat gentle way, but he still thinks he is complete.

"This does not mean true health or harmony, however, because 'life' is lacking. An atheist is like a dry tree which, although it continues to exist for many years in the forest after it has died, nevertheless has a dry trunk without the slightest trace of the essence that gives it life. He 'lives' in a way, however, because he is still standing on two legs."

"Then what is the difference between a person and a spiritual being?"

"A spiritual and physical being 'lives' as opposed to just existing," replied Méntia. "Do you perceive the difference? She is more or less aware of what she really embodies while an atheist remains stuck in an individual, self-contained and seemingly self-sufficient system of thought. In fact, they consume themselves without even realizing it. This is because they are not connected to the true source of their existence, thought and feeling. Such an attitude ultimately exhausts individual energy, drains the cells of vitality and inhibits the true joy of living."

As it occurred to me that a superior attitude does not emerge out of nowhere, I had a question.

"Are there perhaps some internal changes necessary for the being to have access to a superior condition of thought and existence?"

"These are happening at the DNA level," Méntia said. "What your civilization is living in now is a very special time period of limitation. Such stages and evolutionary leaps in the history of Mankind have taken place and are essential pillars in the understanding and development of human civilization. In the past, Mankind was supported to achieve those significant leaps in vibrational frequencies at the DNA level; but this time, human beings have to demonstrate that they really want it. This requires an increased awareness of what you truly are and are embodying on Earth."

I was very interested in the opportunity to know more about those essential moments in the evolution of Mankind, and I asked Méntia to talk about it. She replied that this was the main reason why I had been invited there and that I would immediately begin to view the main elements of the origin and nature human beings on the holographic screen.

Then, after assuring me that we will meet again in the near future, Méntia acknowledged me and the Apellos man with a short bow of her head. She then disappeared from the holographic screen, leaving me in a very pleasant and comfortable state. I was impressed by her pleasant presence, the tone of her voice, and the fire that radiated from both her gaze and her very being. I did not expect the "intermezzo" that she provided, but it proved very welcome, preparing me for the very special viewings that were to follow.

After closing the image on the holographic screen, the Apellos man told me that there would be many hours of viewing and talking, and that is why he suggested to me to concentrate as best as I could. A little excited, I prepared my inter-dimensional helmet and sat down in the comfortable armchair, anxious to find out the mysteries of our civilization's history that had not been revealed to me so far.

A SPECIAL STAR CONFIGURATION

I was happy with the fact that I already had some experience with the holographic system of presentation and interpretation of the images I was seeing as well as the way to interact with the screen through my helmet. It had been explained to me that the processing of Akashic (defined in footnote at bottom of page 96) images could be done very easily, but in order to receive them, I had to mentally connect myself as efficiently and quickly as possible to the flow of images that appeared on the screen. In this way, I could have full personal control over the emission of the visual flow, all of which would be modulated by my psychological and mental characteristics.

I sat comfortably in my chair and put on my helmet. The Apellos man sat down on my right and looked inquiringly at me to see if I was ready to start. I nodded, and then, without any visible command, the first holograms began to appear in front of me, naturally and with extraordinary clarity. I then started to watch the most astounding, complete and correlated epic of Mankind and its evolution from its first moments to the present day.

I will attempt to faithfully reflect what I saw during the two days of visuals, but the volume of information is too great, and the explanatory ramifications are too many. I will therefore first give a general overview of the subject and then a summary thereof. In this, I will include other associated information in order to allow for the best assimilation of the elements present. While watching, I learned this method over time and realized it was the best suited to imprint the information in my memory, at least to a certain extent. Additionally, because the wealth of information was so immense, I often stopped to write down some points or sketch out what seemed important to me.

The first session lasted nine hours and the second eight hours. Both have marked a profound transformation in my being through the incredible accuracy of the presentation and the integration of the stunning images I was able to see. It was a virtual course in "The True History of Mankind", conveying a knowledge that destroys any myth and prejudice through the realism and clear truth presented.

Even knowing some of those aspects which I am now able to present, I was enthralled by the perfection of the way in which I was shown everything. Correctly, I considered this to be a "Royal History of Truth" that was, at best, only known partially, usually distorted and manipulated.

As a necessary part of my training, the man from Apellos revealed to me that the evolution and development of human beings was, among other things, due to a number of influences from several stars, planetary configurations and solar systems. Every star, planet, satellite, or other heavenly body, such as comets, more or less acts to develop biological systems, a phenomenon that is constantly happening.

Even though I was still not fully aware of the circumstances, the evolution of primates on Earth has been deeply influenced by both natural influences and so-called artificial influences. On the holographic screen, I first saw a starry sky, but on an azure background with the stars looking like circles with a bright glow.

It was not the black of cosmic space, but I saw a fairly bright sky of blue that was very pleasant. Some of those stars were somewhat highlighted, having a shape like a rectangularly-shaped file with rounded upper and lower edges, just like the icon you would see for a file when working on a personal computer. There were always three circles with certain marks at the top left of each file. I noticed that the first symbol, the one on the left, was on each of the stars, being similar to the letter *E*.

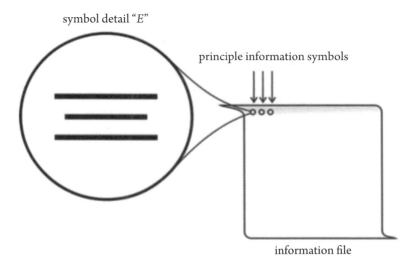

symbol detail "E"

principle information symbols

information file

THE STELLAR SYMBOL "E"

To the right of those files, there were two "dynamic" vertical lines, full of symbols, changing and having different intensities of luminosity.

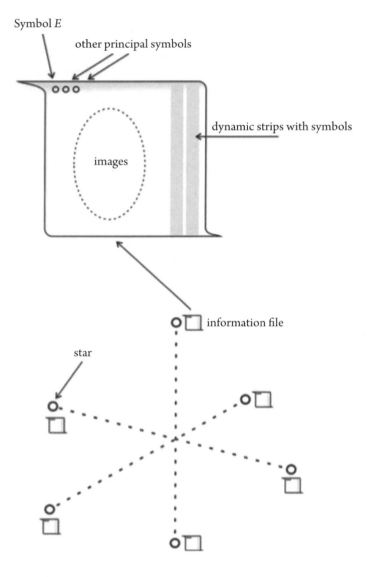

SYMBOLS AND REPRESENTATIONS OF INFORMATION FILES ATTACHED TO EACH STAR IN THE COSMIC ALIGNMENT OF STARS

Our solar system then emerged with its planets at the intersection of several "relationships" or links between stars which can be likened to "stellar rays" of force.

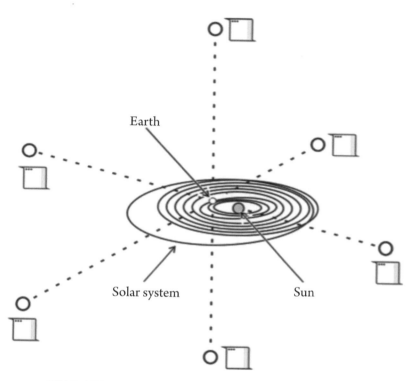

STAR ARRANGEMENT CONCENTRATING IN THE MIDDLE WHERE THE EARTH IS LOCATED WITH A WEAK BUT CONSTANT GRAVITATIONAL INFLUENCE

The image grew even larger and the planets of the Solar System were highlighted. I noticed that it was somehow "rotated" with respect to how the Solar System is conventionally understood, and it did not have the same tilt of the axis as the present one. For example, I saw that the area that today corresponds to Egypt was close to the Equator.

The image then approached the planet and the fundamental symbol *E* was designated in three places which "signaled" three different areas: one in today's Egypt, more precisely in the Sinai Peninsula; another in Arabia; and the third somewhere on the surface currently known as Poland. The symbols shined with different intensities: the one in Sinai was the strongest, then the one in Arabia, and the one in Poland was the most blurred and less visible.

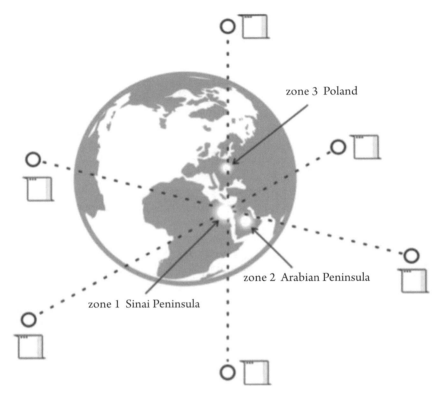

zone 3 Poland

zone 2 Arabian Peninsula

zone 1 Sinai Peninsula

EARTH WITH TILTED AXIS
THE THREE MAIN AREAS OF SYMBOL "E"

I concluded that this probably indicated a certain time line of events, but it could also be an indication of the importance of those areas in a particular context.

THE FIRST IMPORTANT MODIFICATION OF DNA

The picture became more detailed, focusing around hills in a valley in the designated area at the bottom of the Sinai Peninsula. Unlike the desert that exists today, the region was covered with rich vegetation.

The images of the valley then showed a large primate, an evolved bipedal monkey. I noticed that the facial and skull features were different from those of a regular monkey. That primitive bipedal creature was part of a not too large group of individuals who set themselves apart. As far as I could tell, he seemed to be the leader of the group because he was directing the other creatures to certain places where they were looking for food.

Everything that appeared to me in the images was accompanied by a specific sign that appeared to the right of a being, an object, or an area. Though I did not know the significance of those signs, it was often suggestive in the sense that it indicated the direction in which I needed to pay particular attention. For example, a sign near the hologram image of the leader of that group would be indicated with a red pulsation. Later, I would understand that when a signal had such characteristics, the creature or work indicated was very important in the context of the situation being presented. In other cases, the mark could be static and otherwise colored.

Wanting to see a close up, the zoom increased to the specific biology of that primate, first "entering" into its tissue, then into the cells, and ultimately into its DNA structure. During this process of penetration, I felt that I was being comfortably guided by the man from Apellos. The images on the screen were accompanied by the "stellar rays" intersecting so as to indicate the influences of the stars in the first images that were part of that specific star alignment.

They were like threads of white yarn that suggested a certain kind of cosmic action. In fact, those "rays" had been part of the images until then, but I did not understand their meaning previously, and that's why I did not give them too much weight. I noticed, however, that as the image penetrated more deeply at the microscopic level of the anatomical structure of that primate, the "rays" became more and more powerful until, at some point, when they came to a certain layer of the spiraling DNA structure, the stellar rays concentrated in one place in the DNA of the primate.

That point corresponded to a certain moment of time and to a certain place in space in which a certain cosmic influence was implemented into that primate, and I saw this as a specific symbol that appeared at the beginning of each file. I understood then that this represented a very fine but fundamental influence for subsequent changes that were to follow.

Even though it is difficult for some to accept that stars can have such an influence on the development of human beings, I have realized, as a result of following the evolution of humanity on the holographic screen, that the stars and configurations they form permanently act in this manner.

In some situations, it is possible for it to take hundreds of thousands of years for a specific stellar arrangement to decisively influence the DNA of some species in order to create a special structure. Those structures or stellar configurations may remain active for thousands or even tens of thousands of years, during which time modifications to the DNA of those species become complete.

It was shown to me on the holographic screen that such a period of time was essential to the facilitation of an important transformation of DNA of a "great grandfather" on Earth that was from long ago. I saw how the influence

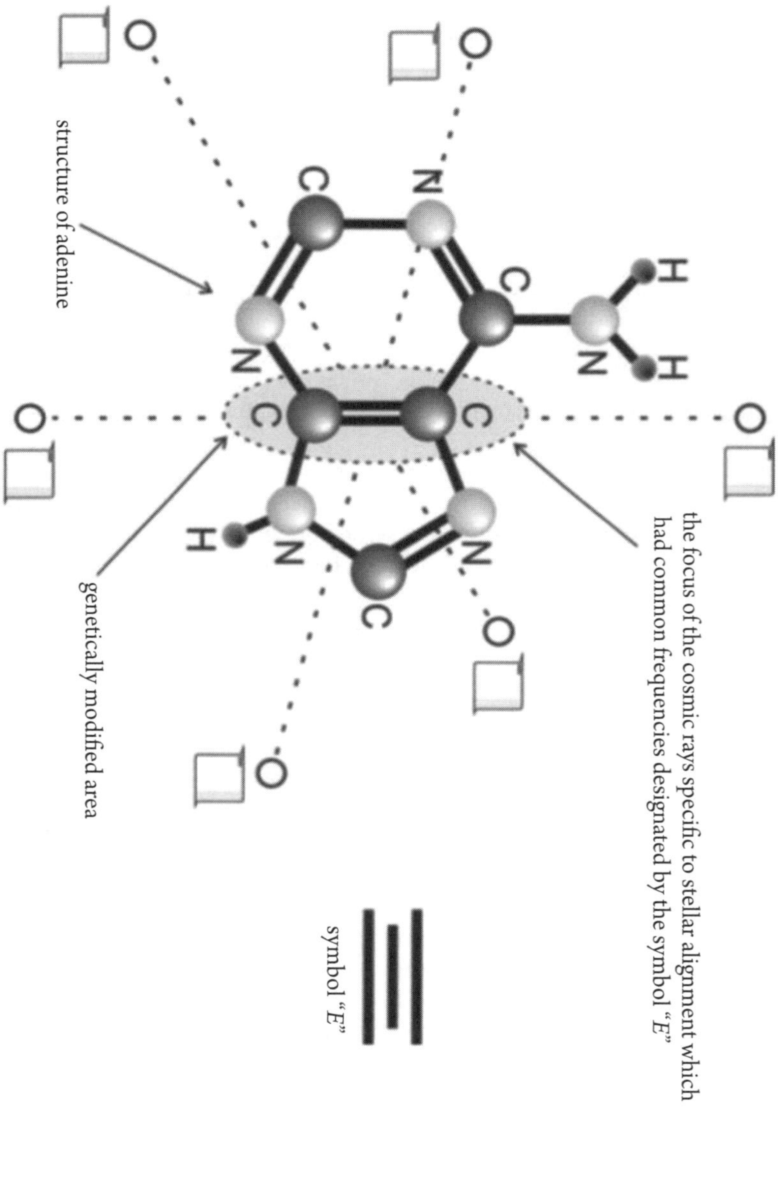

INFLUENCE OF STELLAR ALIGNMENT UPON THE BOND BETWEEN TWO CARBON ATOMS

structure of adenine

genetically modified area

the focus of the cosmic rays specific to stellar alignment which had common frequencies designated by the symbol "E"

symbol "E"

EDITOR'S NOTE: Adenine is a compound which is one of the four constituent bases of nucleic acids. A purine derivative, it is paired with thymine in double-stranded DNA.

of the stars acted at a precise point in the DNA structure of that primate, highlighting what seemed to be an atom with its bonds. I easily recognized the carbon atom and saw that the stellar "rays" had "changed" one of its bonds as well as the rest of the DNA structure.

Within the DNA macromolecule, carbon "uses" its four valence electrons to form covalent bonds. The DNA macromolecule supports the bonds between the oxygen atom and the nitrogen atom, but the geometry of the electronic orbital arrangement in the carbon atom can modify the future type of bonds that form between the oxygen and nitrogen atoms and the four basic components of Human DNA.* Until then, the links created by the carbon atom have certain patterns of manifestation, but through the new cosmic "implementation", there is a "branching" of these patterns; that is, an increase in the probability that the carbon atom will create more types of bonds.

Therefore, multiplying the quantum possibilities that create covalent bonds has caused changes in polarity in DNA. Thus, the likelihood of other new links being created has greatly increased.

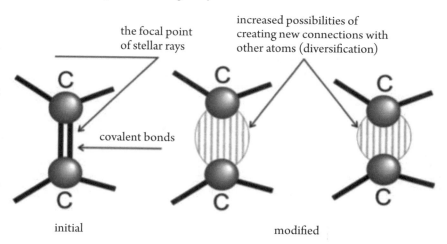

DIVERSIFICATION OF POSSIBLE BONDS TO THE CARBON ATOM IN THE DNA MACROMOLECULE

We have clearly seen how the stellar rays have come and "multiplied" the possibility for the electrons to move in several trajectories, virtually increasing the electron cloud of the carbon. Electrons have become more free in that area, creating new connections and opening the way for a new development of that primate's DNA.

---

* The four different types of organic molecules or bases in the DNA structure are Adenine (A), Cytosine (C) Guanine (G) and Thymine (T).

THE SYMBOLS E-I AND E-U

I was glad that I had deciphered the meaning of the major star symbol, but as soon as I had that thought, a new symbol appeared. Bright and very close to the star (E), this was also a fundamental symbol with the line in the middle having a "protuberance". The emergence of this new symbol was accompanied by a sonorous representation which was clearly similar to the vocal speech of "E-I". Then, another star symbol appeared on the screen, and in that case, I heard the representation of the sound of "E-U". The E-I symbol appeared as a slightly sharper sound while the E-U symbol sounded like a gentler, quieter, and more permissive sound.

E-I   E-U

The nuances of the E symbols E-I and E-U,
representing distinct families of frequencies

In fact, these symbols, which I present here as *E-I* and *E-U*, are graphically close to the *E*-shape as we know it, but in reality, they form and represent symbols designating certain cosmic frequencies in the form of stellar arrangements and positions which reveal a certain influence from a group of stars in the galaxy. Later, however, I found out that this feature also exists with regard to planetary positions or other important celestial bodies.

I have in particular noted the fundamental symbol with the three horizontal lines which I have associated with the letter *E*. In fact, it is more like the Greek letter *Xi* (Ξ), the middle line slightly shorter than the other two. It is no coincidence that we also find this in some very old spiritual traditions such as Shivism in India where three lines are drawn on the forehead (white or red) by the followers of this system. This is, however, not just a local custom but is also universalized at the galactic level.

I found it very interesting how I was shown the great importance of those essential cosmic symbols. On the screen, I saw the moment of inception that involved a corresponding area in a large sector in our galaxy. There was a kind of galactic "alignment" of many stars with our planet in the middle. Somehow, I realized that in those times a local galactic phenomenon occurred which for some time created the visual sensation that the Earth was in the midst of those stellar movements. In other words, the reference point of celestial mechanics for that time and in that area of the galaxy was Earth.

Of course, these graphical representations are "paper-based" correlations, but just as in astronomy and astrology, there are very important and significant cosmic synchronicities which cannot be ignored due to the subtle energy impact that is created for a certain amount of time.

OCCULT SIGNIFICANCE IN THE STELLAR SYMBOL E-I

Then, as if practically speaking to me, the scheme of a very special stellar alignment was shown on the screen. It was made up of six stars, linked two by two (see illustration below), which I had up to then thought were only certain gravitational influences on the Earth. In the meantime, I realized that that stellar configuration also represented the correlation between certain stellar characteristics. It was a significant system, consisting of 6 + 1 cosmic objects; that is, six stars and our planet in the middle of that special celestial configuration. The significance of that "moment" of better times, which lasted about 10,000 years, consisted of the fact that the Earth was then a genuine force. It was a cosmic conjuncture that takes place at great intervals of time which — as I understood telepathically — was wisely observed, understood and exploited by very advanced extraterrestrial civilizations.

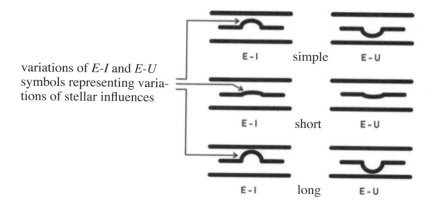

variations of *E-I* and *E-U* symbols representing variations of stellar influences

At that cosmic moment, which was a specific star configuration, it was shown that the conditions for a thriving civilization were born on Earth, starting from the DNA of the great primates that existed at that time on the surface of the planet.

Such a very favorable context also offered advanced alien civilizations the possibility of calculating the need for natural or artificial events that could speed up the development of those primates. Many such highly advanced alien civilizations have fully assumed their "parental" role in the "formation" and development of life on Earth. In a certain way, we can say that they have become the spiritual fathers of Earth and Mankind.

Returning to the holographic images presented to me on the screen, I was shown that the two symbolic representations (*E-U* and *E-I*) could have different nuances, transmuted in several ways, such as a longer or shorter *E-U* or a higher or lower tonality, and so on.

I was, however, intrigued by the semicircle of the *E-I* or *E-U* star symbol because I did not understand its meaning. Knowing that the technology available to me was providing me with an amazing way to access information, I focused my attention and interest on this because my experience there was also a learning process and a personal adjustment to the parameters of a technology that is much more advanced than what is on our planet's surface.

As soon as I focused on the significance of the semicircle in the structure of the *E-I* and *E-U* symbols, I saw on the holographic screen how the semicircle "unfolded" from the graphics of the two symbols and became isolated. To the right of each semicircle, several types of alignments appeared: stars, vortexes (whose meaning I later understood as a yin or yang structure) and even atoms, which we saw as having a great nucleus, a glitter surrounded by a kind of "cloud" or "fog" of electrons, also in the form of a whirl. Then, I was shown that some electrons are characterized by a certain atom-binding energy which seems to be separate from the physical plane. In other words, these electrons are actually coupled into the subtle etheric plane, which is superior to the physical plane, even if they belong to different chemical elements. For example, an electron of a carbon atom could be coupled with an electron in an oxygen atom. This coupling of the subtle etheric dimension was symbolized precisely by the semicircle in graphical representation of *E-I* or sometimes that of *E-U*.

Their coupling means that they come from the same family of etheric subtle vibrational frequencies. In my cortex, the information was telepathically synthesized as a profound understanding which was received as an inexpressible expression: "the same tachyon family".

I knew what tachyons are, as defined by scientists, but they also recognize that they are "hypothetical" particles because they do not depend upon time nor do they manifest in or belong to the physical world. Now, however, I understood that things are not like that at all. I was shown how two such electrons, in their journey through a cloud of other electrons, at one point "found" and "coupled" with each other by virtue of their associated resonance.

I then realized that two such electrons, even if they are not in the same atom, are still "subtly" bound etherically. The reality of this really impressed me and immediately led me to think of one of the strangest phenomena in

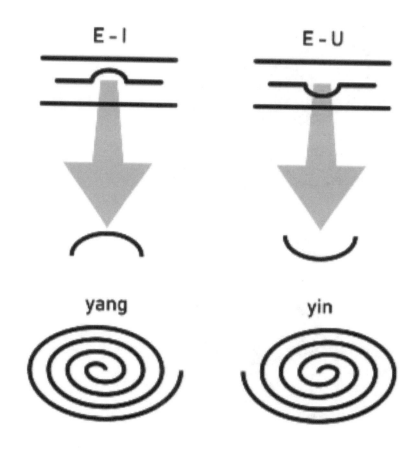

different types of atoms

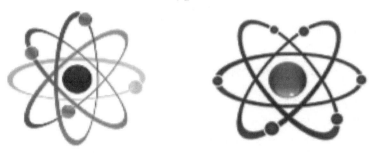

CORRELATION OF THE E-I AND E-U SYMBOLS WITH STELLAR AND SPINNING CHARACTERISTICS AT THE ATOMIC LEVEL

creating new molecules through covalent bonds

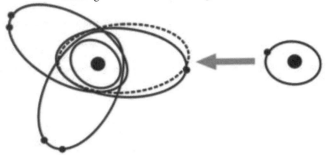

covalent bonds are made only between certain atoms to which electrons are already coupled in the etheric plane

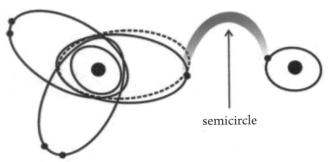

semicircle

ATOMS IN THE PHYSICAL PLANE AND THEIR "COUPLING" INTO THE SUPERIOR ETHERIC PLANE, SYMBOLIZED BY THE SEMICIRCLE

quantum physics, called entanglement,[*] but I will speak of that in another volume because it is the basis of understanding the most fascinating aspects of the cosmos.

MODIFICATION OF ANOTHER DNA "WAVE"

Next, as if the intelligence behind the screen or my special helmet knew that I understood the aspects presented, images appeared on the screen showing

---

[*] The phenomenon of entanglement is a phenomenon specific to quantum mechanics in which microcosmic particles that are separated from each other at great distances can perform instantaneous and mysterious exchanges of information. This leads to the mutual modification of their quantum states. In recent years, however, some studies have shown that the phenomenon of entanglement (translated as "quantum inseparability") appears to manifest itself not only in non-human objects but also in living organisms such as bacteria. [Romanian editors's note]

the bonding of the carbon atom with other atoms, creating virtually another DNA chain in the primates on the Earth due to the stellar influences I have previously mentioned.

Although the shape of the new DNA was also double helical, having the same atomic and molecular composition, I still viewed it as more complex than the DNA of primates. This is because the oxygen or nitrogen atoms that bind to create the DNA were of a subtle quality.

Almost immediately, the screen displayed both the physical DNA macromolecule as well as the subtle bonds that exist between the atoms in the DNA. I saw a bright cloud over the image of atoms that represented the etheric charge of the physical part of the DNA.

Subtly, the macromolecule looked like a twisted sponge, and in some places, I could see some luminous clusters. It was not just a twisted ladder but looked rather like a "tube"; and in some of areas, there were bright dots, representing the nuclei of certain DNA atoms, namely, those in which changes had been made. Being curious, I turned my attention to one of the points that seemed to me to be very beautiful, and the image immediately became very pronounced. Then, more files began to appear, containing a lot of information in the form of signs and symbols that I did not understand. I realized, however, what a depth of information there was in those files that were presenting the reality of these matters at very deep levels.

"In this way, you can find out everything you want about the history of each atom or electron herein or about any other particle or component; and this includes how it appeared, how it developed, what transformations it passed through, and so on. You can go deeper and deeper for further information," explained the man from Apellos.

I referred back to the modified DNA form which was well-known to me. Looking closely, I could see within it the shape of the twin propeller, twisted, apparently the same as before the star-like outburst. As a whole, however, the new macromolecule of DNA appeared to be more dynamic and somehow more vivid.

I noticed that its dynamics came mainly from certain "clusters" of subtle etheric energy, like small bright clouds surrounding the outer DNA and conveying that sensation of dynamism. They moved, interacting from time to time with the electrons in the upper layers and producing various physical lighting effects in the DNA.

Those etheric "clusters" represented complex symbols, but at the beginning of each symbol, *E-I* was found, the influence of which created the possibility that the DNA bonds would be more dynamic, smoother and more sensitive. In this way, I understood that the increase in "quantum sensitivity" at the level of DNA macromolecules has allowed the environment of the planet to further model the genes of the primates and to significantly accelerate their evolution.

INTERNET STYLE "MENTAL TECHNOLOGY" — RESUMPTION OF VISUALIZATION

As I said to myself that all of those links between the physical plane and the etheric plane, which started to become rather complicated, could be correlated with an observable or measurable phenomenon, I immediately noticed that the image on the holographic screen began to blur.

The Apellos man then told me that this was due to my mental intervention with the device with which I was interacting. The principle that had to be respected was for me to understand correctly what was coming to me and to present coherent questions. To have a good representation of facts and events, the man advised me to look at everything without involvement because personal inferences affected the correct rendering of the akashic* recordings.

"Okay, but why does that happen?" I asked, puzzled.

"At this stage of technology, the interaction between man and device is done at the quantum level," he explained. "Everything you think 'interacts' with the device's systems. If there is no consistency between your attention and the subject chosen for viewing, then the images are interrupted. Your thoughts and emotions only help to launch the 'theme' in the beginning, and you can adjust some images on the go, focusing on what you are looking at according to your particular interest. It would be like going in a particular direction of the subject, but if your mind 'slides' into all sorts of digressions, then you interrupt the connection created between your synapses and the cumulative electromagnetic waves emitted by the device; and in such a cases, it will no longer 'respond' to you."

Stunned by the description of the technology, I refrained myself from making any comment, knowing that this was the reality of quantum phenomena in the experiments of contemporary physics. After I ceased the process of deduction and felt ready to stop my own thoughts, I resumed watching the lively experience of what I was seeing in the pictures.

I noticed that my understanding of what I was seeing was of great importance because my cognitive processes then led to the development of explanations rendered in images on the holographic screen.

If my understanding was unclear or even totally absent, then the imaging and information process stopped. My experience with this high-tech device showed me that, generally speaking, it did not emphasize anything if I did not "ask" or were not aware of that particular aspect.

In resuming my interaction with the device, I reconstructed my ideas and initial interest as to the origins of humanity and realized that the interruption

---

* The author refers here to "universal records" which contain any fact, thought or phenomenon that has ever occurred in the universe. The background of these records is akasha, which in Sanskrit means "space", "heaven" or "ether". Elements about this notion were presented in Volume 2 of the *Transylvania Series* entitled *Transylvanian Moonrise*.

actually brought me a further knowledge of what was happening with regard to galactic history at that particular time. Through the mysterious telepathic interaction between me and the helmet, I realized that there had been a cosmic mission which consisted of creating a new species of humanoid beings on our planet; and further, those advanced alien civilizations had to "change" the ancient genetic links that existed in the DNA molecule of primates on the surface of the Earth in order to accelerate evolution, as well as to give it a certain and much improved orientation of the process.

Such interventions, however, are done in full agreement with universal and natural cosmic laws because everything is integrated on multiple levels and in synchronization with the dimensions of the universe, not just at the physical level. For example, I asked how that "change" was made to initiate the process of creating a new and superior human being that is closer to nature. I had already seen how "priming the DNA" was prepared by "dynamizing" and awakening it from "numbness" or dormancy by reason of the energetic influence of the specific stellar configuration represented by the symbol *E-I.*

Now, I wanted to know what was actually meant with regard to the process of forming the humanoid being as a new distinct race; that is to say, Man itself, and what were the details of that process. I will explain this below, but I came to understand that such a fundamental change in the intimate structure of a being, with regard to its very "code" of life, cannot be done in a gross manner with "scalpel and scissors" as some people might imagine.

GALACTIC LEVELS AND BENEFICIAL INTERVENTION

What provoked this necessary "splitting" to begin the process of modulating the characteristics of a "basic being" in order to obtain a much more highly evolved being? This is not done only by reason of interventions with genetic manipulation. Even though this has been done to a large proportion of beings, the random aspect of their development remains because individuals are different by their very nature.

You cannot determine or dictate only through a "surgical" intervention, even if it is sophisticated and technologically advanced. There is no substitute for the way in which Nature will take that change and develop it in those beings. In other words, you cannot simply "fabricate" humanoid beings through endless genetic interventions in the hope that they will become "autonomous" and have a good and stable structure of the DNA macromolecule in order to ensure the success of a new species of intelligent beings.

In addition to such interventions, which are undoubtedly necessary at certain times, the natural course of life must be allowed to proceed according to its cyclical rules as the evolutionary process is not just about certain operations at the physical level but also involves more subtle dimensions such as subtle bodies and the souls of beings. We are not talking about a simple cloning or robotic determination for the new being but rather the integrity at all levels of existence, all of which has to be taken into consideration.

For this, the best method for evolution of the Earth's primates was considered to be the subtle help offered by certain advanced alien beings to facilitate the bodies of those primates that were already at a certain level of development. As I have seen, there has been a very interesting entanglement for some time between some advanced alien beings and developed primates.

This would have been impossible, however, if there had been no initial intervention of primate DNA on Earth involving the "modification" of certain elements within the DNA macromolecule so as to generate a new molecular chain of superior DNA.

As we have shown, this was accomplished by focusing the specific E-I energy at a certain point in the DNA of a primate at a specific time and space in order to make the necessary changes in the way that the bonds in the carbon atom are created. Hence, the possibility of carbon atoms bonding with other atoms and the "building" of a new superior DNA strand was possible under the permanent influence of energy specific to the respective stellar configuration. Further, the deeper "modification" involved the combination of the DNA of primates on Earth with the genes of alien beings, all taking place in various stages, who assumed the role of parents of Mankind. In this way, the process of forming a new humanoid species was initiated.[*]

TEMPORAL DATA TECHNIQUE

When I returned to the history of DNA modification and the development of E in E-I and E-U, I wanted to know the time when that extraordinary phenomenon took place. I noticed then that the spaces between the vertical symbols in the files were not regular, but there were different distances between the signs. At that moment, I had the telepathic understanding of the fact that those distances were representative of temporal values. They were in different colors and widths; some thinner, some thicker.

Then, between the two columns of signs, some sort of "bridge" links appeared which I understood to be "notations" that were correlated with frequencies. I focused on them, and then one of the "notations" grew, and I

---

[*] The extraterrestrial origin of human DNA is already certified by many researchers, but it is not yet officially recognized by contemporary science. Some experts in the study of the human genome in Kazakhstan have asserted, after 13 years of intense research, that human DNA was conceived and engineered in its evolution by an advanced alien civilization that "planted" a very complex program with two versions: one containing an extensively structured code and one containing a simple basic code. At the end of the study, scientists concluded: "Sooner or later (...) we will have to accept that all life on Earth bears the signature of the genetic code of our extraterrestrial cousins and that, in fact, evolution (on our planet) is not what we believe it is. " [from the Romanian editor]

could even hear a sonorous representation. Through the intuitive induction of the inter-dimensional helmet, I then understood that that frequency was correlated with the time I wanted to find out. After this understanding manifested instantly in my mind, it appeared to me that the period of frequency was correlated to the number 4.

I then turned my attention to the other "notations" (i.e. frequencies) and I had the understanding of the time when the first DNA change occurred in a primate on Earth. In other words, when the first implementation of the new information came about, the moment when it all started for the human race was by the action of the "rays" that created the first significant change in a link of a carbon atom in that primate's DNA macromolecule. With the general understanding I had acquired and by continuing the process of understanding how to interpret frequencies, the moment I was looking for was revealed to me in the image as about 432,000 years ago.

I then saw other overlapping symbols that indicated that period of time even more thoroughly, but I could no longer decrypt them. It was difficult to focus my attention, probably because the refinement of the information was too great. I did realize, however, that those symbols showed me exactly the time, the hour, and an even more precisely detailed time than that. The device always determines what a viewer can see, depending upon their level of consciousness.

For example, I can say that the first digit after the number 2 was 7, even if it oscillated somewhat, but something was unclear there. It was as if I could not "perceive" that frequency very well. In other words, the number of years trended toward 433,000 because it was really 432,7(_ _). After the 7, however, everything tended to fade because the information was too fine for my perception, and I was beginning to hear a complex set of sounds that I could not decipher very well.

THE GRAND COSMIC SHOW

I was shocked by the accuracy of the items that the device presented. Almost immediately, the images and symbols on the screen began to rewind. I was then shown another moment in time which I identified to be around the year 421,3(__) B.C., about ten thousand years later, the length of the stellar alignment that influenced the carbon bonds in the DNA of the primates. This was a new phase of development of human DNA because I afterwards saw another primate with more evolved features.

The images did not last too long at this juncture, but they moved to a third phase which I understood to be around 372,5(_ _) years, although I had some doubts as to the figure 5 being accurate as my consciousness sometimes confuses this with the figure 6. This error, however, was relatively small.

An image of a huge alien ship appeared on the screen. It was spherical and amazingly large, like a planetoid. I could make this comparison because it was close to Earth. There were then some quick "flashes" from different areas of that colossal structure before the image stabilized and focused on the central control area of the ship.

We saw a large room where humanoid beings were present, taller than our present average. The image stopped and focused on the man who seemed to be the master of the ship who was in front of a large holographic screen. At that moment, I was shown how the ship's master decided to emit an electromagnetic signal which was blended with the gravitational influence of a star. I noticed that if I imagined a line from that ship passing through the center of the Earth, the star was in the diametrically opposed area.

On the holographic screen in the giant ship's control room, we saw a linear assortment of lines and symbols that resembled stars that we can now see on astrological maps but with an astonishing accuracy of details. I then felt the helping presence of the Apellos man because my mind tended to get stuck due to the complexity of the knowledge I was dealing with.

I received telepathic information that the ship's commander actually looked at the screen towards the possibility of creating a change in the DNA of primates on Earth, supporting in turn the modification of the carbon atoms in the DNA helix chain as was previously mentioned. I noticed, however, that when the subject of the origin of man on Earth was re-launched, the information was then much more detailed than when it was originally presented to me for the first time.

I have interpreted this through the prism of the mental and emotional modes that should be used when working with the holographic screen and the inter-dimensional helmet but also through a certain understanding of what I already knew. At the same time, I thought that such technology is inconceivable to modern science, but I immediately realized that the image was starting to blur due to the fluctuation of my concentration. The Apellos man then intervened again, correcting the image so that I would not have to "rewind" it all back to the beginning. Speaking to me telepathically, he said the following:

"Indeed. There is a huge difference between conceiving something and the technological level of realization. Working in this way with the stellar influences that your scientists do not even suspect might exist, it is impressive even for us. In any case, this moment of time you are seeing on the screen is fundamental. It represents the beginning of your race as superior human beings."

"But you are not part of the same race?" I asked, slightly taken aback.

"Yes, but there has been a further hybridization with us, and we have developed in Apellos in isolation, evolving without any undesirable interventions, but it was more complicated for you."

The man then made a sign, inviting me to follow the historical thread of these exceptional revelations.

The stage of life on Earth at the time that giant ship appeared in our planet's neighborhood seems to have been very important. The images at that time showed me the traces of a space conflict in our solar system. I could not, however, see the nature of that conflict in the cosmos, who determined it or what was the reason for it, probably because it did not come within the scope of the theme upon which I was focusing.

The images showed me only a few sequences during the war with terrible battles in outer space, but I was very interested in how the superior human being came into being on Earth, and this was the reason why those images of conflict appeared in a rather fast and flashing sequence, pointing out only the most important aspects of a secondary story, as was that spatial conflict, but which still had a certain connection with the subject that interested me.

TENEKAU AND MANKIND'S ORIGINS

I was shown some pictures of the period that followed the terrible war in space. I did not understand the reason at first, but it was revealed to me later. The huge ship suffered great damage during the repeated and harsh attacks of the enemy fleet, requiring repairs. I saw that it had been decided to extract ore from Earth because I noticed how many other small ships descended from the giant spherical ship to Earth before returning and bringing various materials to the orbiting vessel. I received the telepathic understanding of the fact that they were carrying some deposits of which the gold ones were the most important because this metal was part of the mother ship. It was practically a confirmation of what is written on the Sumerian tablets discovered and translated in the last century.*

The convergence zone where the ships descended to and then climbed back into space from was the Arabian Peninsula, as I realized from the geography of the area.**

FIRST CONTACT

The image focused on one of the mid-size alien ships that landed in a place with little vegetation that was relatively rocky. The picture then changed when the creatures in the ship loaded more parallelepipedal containers. I saw how manipulation of those parallelepipeds was done by levitation and with just hand gesture, without anything being touched. Such an object, which was quite massive, was pulled out of the carrier, and then, through levitation, it was oriented vertically, staying in the air about a meter high from the ground. "Light tubes", which were buried in the ground, then emerged from it. I could see through them how a kind of "liquid" was extracted from the ground and then stored in the container. Involuntarily, I thought that was the easiest and most advanced and efficient form of "mining" I had ever seen, but the picture began giving signs of instability, so I focused again on what was presented, wanting to see the point of it all.

Among the rocks and vegetation in that area, I was able to see in the picture a group of native beings, a kind of primate that were more evolved,

---

* Indirect reference is to Zecharia Sitchin's books on the contents of the Sumerian tablets describing the process of the evolution of the human race on Earth. [Romanian editor]

** This is different from the descriptions on the tablets which indicate that the exploitation of gold and other metals began in South Africa. The materials extracted in the Arabian Peninsula, however, could be other than the gold which was extracted in Africa, probably by other vessels. [Romanian editor] similar to homo erectus. They looked curiously but fearfully at the ship and the alien beings around it, still keeping a comfortable distance.

At one point, one of the extraterrestrial beings, who seemed to be the commander of the transport ship, saw those primates and the way they showed their curiosity. He then came closer, stopping for a few moments and observing them carefully in a slightly mild state. At first, I did not understand why those images were shown to me so I formulated the question in my mind. At that moment, I began to feel the empathy of that extraterrestrial being as he carefully watched the primitive beings in front of him, creatures that still retained certain features of the great primates. I felt the germ of an idea becoming more and more outlined in that man's mind as he assessed certain possibilities related to those primates.

At the same time, I had the understanding that the alien creatures that lived as crew could not stay for a long time in our atmosphere on the Earth's surface due to some physical characteristics of the Earth's atmosphere which were incompatible with their constitution. As soon as I understood this, the image on the screen changed, and I saw the inside of the ship on the ground, a round and quite large room in which there were five masculine beings, including the ship's commander, who actually talked about this aspect.

By amplifying the telepathic transmission, I understood that the members of the crew had made the decision to start using some of the primates who were more curious and more evolved to carry out the mining work. They wanted to do this by using a mental transmission technology on the primates and then using their bodies for the surface affairs on the planet.

FIRST STEPS IN THE TRANSFORMATION OF DNA

My understanding quickly arrived at new values. For example, it was clear to me that the crew's decision on that transport ship had a double meaning: on the one hand, primates were helped to evolve very quickly due to the mental influence of alien beings and their technology; and on the other hand, the crew also benefited from the aid of physical labor from those great primates as the bodies of those aliens could not withstand the soil very well.

I then asked which alien civilizations those beings belonged to, and I immediately received the response in my cortex that it was one of the civilizations derived from the Sirians which originated from a system in the constellation of Orion's Belt. The images then suddenly changed and I saw a multi-planet system around a relatively small star located in the vicinity of the main stars of the Belt.

The process of modifying primate DNA in that area of the Earth — which would then trigger the entire chain of transformation to reach the evolved human being — was staggeringly complex and virtually unthinkable for today's

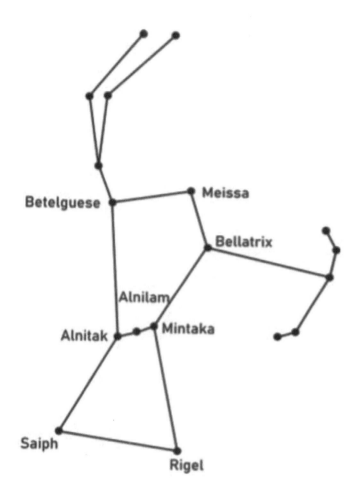

Betelguese
Meissa
Bellatrix
Alnilam
Alnitak
Mintaka
Saiph
Rigel

THE CONSTELLATION OF ORION, OR THAT OF THE HUNTER,
WITH THE THREE MAIN STARS FORMING THE "BELT"

scientific conception. We have seen that the level of action and forces involved in that grandiose plan have reached an extreme breadth, from the quantum level to our galaxy.

First, there was a need for a structural change in the DNA of the first primates on Earth in order to prime the process of evolution. When I wanted to understand a more nuanced way in which that extraordinary leap from the primate to a more evolved form and level of consciousness occurred, a sequence of files instantly appeared on the screen, like the ones I have previously

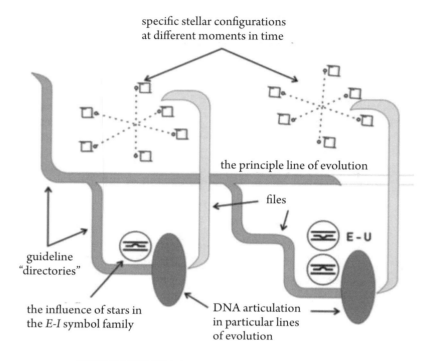

specific stellar configurations
at different moments in time

the principle line of evolution

files

E-U

guideline
"directories"

the influence of stars in
the *E-I* symbol family

DNA articulation
in particular lines
of evolution

SCHEMATIC REPRESENTATION OF SOME
EVOLUTIONARY PHASES IN HUMAN DNA

described, accompanied by various symbols. These files had certain guidelines. I understood then that they were related to and in fact represented a "folder" or, to make a connection with a modern understanding, a directory.

I had already seen in the previous images the symbols *E-I* and *E-U*, both of which were stars or a number of stars connected to each other at a specific frequency. As I said, they indicated an "alteration" of the linkage of a carbon atom in the primate DNA to create multiple possibilities that would form new structures within that DNA.

We also saw the huge alien ship, both in the configuration of the star-like alignment as well as it being near the Earth. We noticed, however, that when we came back to an aspect or phenomenon, asking to review a presentation again, other details or correlations were revealed to me in pictures that had not been included up to that point. This was important because it allowed me to then subdivide the subject on the basis of new details and through asking additional questions in order to get deeper into this knowledge.

TWO IMPORTANT SYMBOLS

In fact, I was pursuing two main directions: on the one hand, to clarify some details that I did not understand very well; and on the other hand, to try to get more information on the subject studied. I could only do this by repeating some images, sometimes even two or three times, in order to better understand that summary or to decode, as much as I could, the meaning of the images. The Apellos man was a discreet and agreeable presence that I felt was not in any way disturbed by the "maneuvers" I was engaged in. In addition, the increasingly secure and fast communication with the device I had access to was a pleasure, and I began to better understand the way of "conversing" with the highly advanced technology that was integrated into the construction of the holographic screen and the inter-dimensional helmet.

As a novelty to what I had learned before, I noticed that two of the symbols were present everywhere: the star symbol *E-I*, which always appeared when it was in a star configuration in the galaxy; and a symbol that resembled, graphically speaking, the number *11*, which represented a certain action at the quantum level in the atoms that make up the macro-molecule of DNA. As I pictured this, I understood that that symbol represented the ability to unite. In other words, when two aspects were different, they joined together and became one, and this process was represented by that symbol.

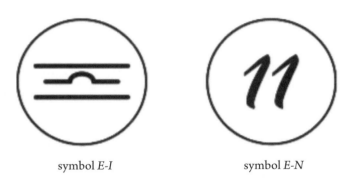

symbol *E-I*   symbol *E-N*

THE COSMIC VESSEL NEIBERÁU

The file complex on the screen was accentuated by the primate's image at different stages of development and with some symbols. At the top of the paper I again saw the representation of the group of stars in the galaxy, united in a specific way through certain lines and symbols, but this time I noticed a smaller circle at the end of such a line, a smaller circle than the circles that symbolized the other stars.

I also saw a second symbol beside the fixed symbol, over which I felt a strong emotion. Then, immediately, the symbol grew on the screen and turned into a clear and large image, representing the huge spherical cosmic space ship that I mentioned previously. Immediately, through a combination of frequencies and states in my mind, I understood that the name of the ship was NEIBERÁU. There is, however, a small variation involved because I also understand there to be a similar name known as NEIBERÉA.

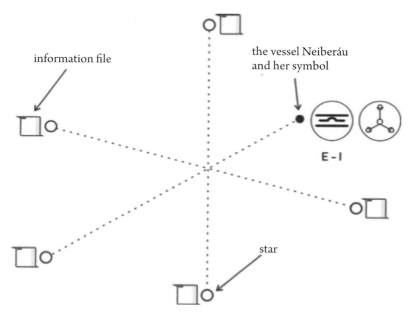

information file

the vessel Neiberáu
and her symbol

E - I

star

STELLAR ALIGNMENT TO WHICH
THE SYRIAN SHIP NEIBERÁU BELONGS

I immediately realized that a correlation can easily be made with a theme that is now widely publicized but misunderstood. The consonants in the names were stronger; and therefore, as a necessary connection, I think the names "slipped" into "N I B I R U" as an updated version currently used. [*]

Besides, the fact that the images did not blur nor disappear from the holographic screen when I thought of these aspects was further proof to me that this correlation is correct and is directly related to the huge alien ship.

---

[*] It is very likely that this explains a great confusion that has long been circulated on the internet or in other works concerning the "planet" Nibiru which, according to Sumerian tablets from 3600 years ago, visited with unusually devastating effects on the Earth. If we consider the author's words, then Nibiru is indeed the great Sirian ship Neiberáu. [Romanian editor's note]

What amazed me was the fact that that this ship occupied different positions in the galaxy, filling the corresponding "empty" place of another star in the essential configurations I was shown. I understood then that it was placed in an area of the galaxy so as to create the structures necessary to implement, in successive phases, the appropriate frequency to cause some change in the DNA of primates on Earth.

I then wondered why such a complex engagement was needed and how it was possible for those influences to propagate so precisely, from a gigantic level to a tiny level. Moreover, why did the cosmic energies generated by this specific stellar alignment not then affect everybody, such as all primates or other beings that existed then on Earth and not just a certain primate from those times?

The screen immediately "reacted" and pointed out that these were the only primates in which a special change was implemented while other primates remained "inert" to the same subtle influence. I immediately understood the idea, and I even thought that the old saying could very well apply here: "It is not for whom it is, but for whom it fits."

This selectivity seems to have been essential, and from the height of the extraordinary technological and spiritual advancement of the extraterrestrial beings that initiated the process of DNA modification in that primate, it determined a whole chain of gradual yet really quite fast transformations at the DNA level of other primates. The latter also served as receptacles for some subtle information that led to the appearance of man. I realized then that everything was an action of extraordinary programming and genetic engineering at the highest level, something which today cannot even be conceived of in similar terms, both because of the conceptual limitations of modern science as well as the lack of necessary technology. In the cosmic scheme of the stars that were involved in this immense plan to form a superior being who would become man, there was always the clear impression of interventions by superior aliens.

On the screen, I saw that next to each star was a symbol which the Apellos man told me indicated the overall scheme of timing and influence by very evolved entities from the subtle planes that would enable the star to interact in a certain way and at a certain point of time with another star, indicated by the line that unites them. When I understood this, the image on the screen changed and I could see everything from above. This seemed to represent that I had achieved a superior step of understanding, a superior look at that reality. I could not see the stars anymore but there were some kind of ties or "wisps" between the positions they occupied. It was a very complex subtle network between those focal areas, i.e. between the correlated stars. As I had first seen the subtle bonds between two electrons, so did I notice the subtle etheric link at the star level. Only then did I understand the profound truth that had been revealed to me about the quantum bonds between the electrons. I have noticed that the understanding of the entanglement phenomenon is only a small step in order to be able to understand the complexity of the links that exist between the stars in the universe, and these are far more spectacular than those links generated by gravitational forces.

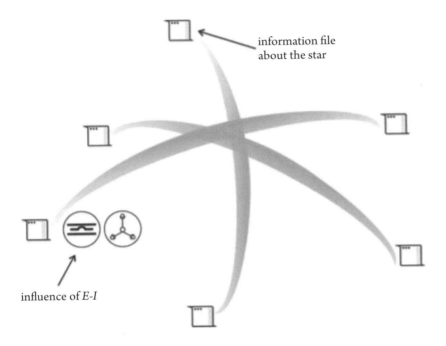

information file
about the star

influence of E-I

SUBTLE NETWORK OF "ENTANGLEMENT" BETWEEN STARS

On the screen, I could still see two different phases of primate evolution, presented in parallel, with two different star configurations of their position in our galaxy. In the "network" between what the Neiberáu ship and the stars were forming, the celestial object was always in the middle and being influenced by subtle energy. In the first stage, I saw that our place was occupied by our own planet, and at a later stage, I saw that that central spot was occupied by the Sun in our Solar System.

The Neiberáu was beyond the Moon, perfectly round and slightly smaller, shining brightly in the sky, but it was different in this respect from the Moon by its light blue color, as seen from Earth. I was presented with different images from different angles of Neiberáu's position and admired this special heavenly spectacle of the Earth apparently having two very "bright" satellites.

The beginning of this crucial moment in time was presented to me in sequential order. First, I saw the main command room inside the huge Neiberáu ship with its commander calculating the best possible configuration or network of stars that could specifically influence the DNA of certain primates from the Earth. I realized that he was particularly interested in determining the moment when that influence could be done with the greatest efficiency. I smiled because what I saw was very similar to actual astrology, but on a much more advanced level, and to me, this implied an astounding knowledge.

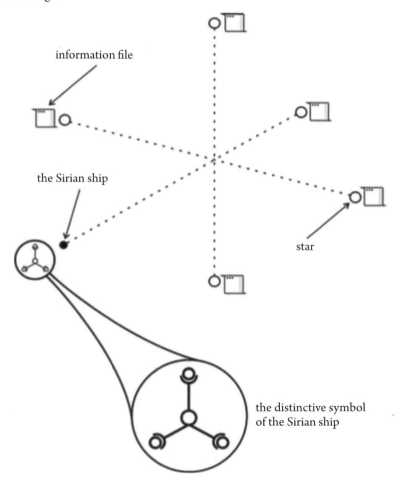

information file

the Sirian ship

star

the distinctive symbol
of the Sirian ship

**THE STELLAR CONFIGURATION
THAT THE SIRIAN SHIP WAS A PART OF**

The control board of the ship was complicated and extended over a large circle arc. Behind it were several beings, but telepathically, I understood that there were also other command centers at different levels of the ship, each one specialized in one particular direction of action: military, space jumps through cosmic chasms, and so on. The control room I was viewing, however, was the main one in which the most important decisions were made.

I saw how the main device onboard, which could be likened to a modern computer, could quickly manifest a myriad of stellar alignments in rapid succession. This was, in fact, a very large "crystal display" on which holographic information was projected.

The commander of the ship then chose a particular configuration and decided to move the ship to a certain place in the cosmic space near the Earth, maintaining a certain stationary orbit around the planet, just like the Moon.

Later, I saw and intuitively understood how the beings in the main command room promulgated the electromagnetic emissions of the ship to that of the star with which it wanted to create a link, thus giving rise to a so-called phenomenon of "galactic entanglement".

I was then shown the triggering of the entire network of subtle energy between the stars in the cosmic configuration that I had seen at the beginning; and then, the immense action influencing the area in the galaxy where the Earth is. After that, the simple structure of the DNA of that primate from Earth appeared on the screen. Finally, I saw the carbon atom and the resulting quantum modification, a factor which was essential to reorienting the evolution of a large group of primates from Earth towards a higher state of being.

THE CHRONOLOGY OF THE FIRST
STEPS OF TRANSFORMATION OF DNA

As I said, the first moment when the cosmic influence for triggering the plan to create the human being was implemented was around 432,000 B.C. More specifically, I was able to understand that it was 432,7(__) B.C., but the fineness of the frequencies and periods for the last two digits of that "distance" in time was too great for me to understand. This influence lasted approximately 10,000 years, corresponding to the time period for that stellar configuration. Transformation of primate DNA had begun to become increasingly apparent, and its effects increased over the next 50,000 years.

Later, that terrible war followed from space, and the Sirian shuttles began to descend on Earth to extract various materials, especially gold, needed to repair damaged parts of the Neiberáu mother ship. This was about 372,5(__) or 372,6(__) B.C. according to the audio frequency conversion.

Because they needed a workhorse tailored to the specifics of the planet, alien creatures on the ship decided to support the development of the primates and "work together" with them to extract the metals they needed.

This event was rendered as "Enki's descent on Earth" as the resultant frequency of the cumulation of symbols related to that decision were resonant with the symbol *E-N*.[*]

Then, not knowing what internal impulse was driving me, I wanted to find out more about that extraterrestrial being that was the first to trigger the radical transformations that would lead to the creation of Mankind. Soon, however, I was going to find out that the idea that sprouted in that alien mind — to use primates to help in terrestrial work and at the same time to help them evolve faster— was actually planned long before, highlighting much higher and more extensive dimensions of manifestation.

I was completely fascinated by the fact that I was seeing the very beginning of Mankind. Pragmatically speaking, thanks to the idea of Sirians using sophisticated technology on the primates existing at that time on Earth to achieve certain work, the foundations of the creation of a superior human being on our planet were laid. I have seen this in detail as well as the main faults which took place in the whole process. I also saw the motivations that led to the creation of the first human being and the nature that it had. I will come back to these issues later.

TENEKAU

As soon as I expressed my desire to know more about that Sirian being, I was presented with his image on the screen. He was wearing a blue coat with two stripes of a lighter-color on the edges. At the same time, the information file, which I unfortunately could not comprehend, appeared in a "writing" that did not belong to our planet, based mostly on signs and symbols. The Apellos man, who was patiently attending to my investigation, spoke.

"He was called Tenekau. Indeed — it can be said that, from a certain point of view, he was "the Father of Mankind", although this phrase is not exactly accurate. The plan for Earth was conceived of over eons at the causal level of the governing entities of this galaxy and of the universe we live in. It was hoped that there would be a certain manifestation of life in this area at a future time, but with a precision set by certain galactic conjunctions. Tenekau was chosen a long time ago for that fundamental role because his DNA structure resonated with what he wanted to get from primate DNA. He was born aboard the Neiberáu and was directed at that unique moment

---

[*] The author refers to the contents of the Sumerian tablets describing the Anunnaki "gods" who came to Earth (Enki and Enlil) as well as the origin of the human being and the way in which it appeared. For more information in this direction, see the books of Zecharia Sitchin. [Romanian editor's note]

in the history of Mankind, the moment when he looked at the primates and had the idea of transforming them and collaborating with them to ease the work on the ground. He has been constantly encouraged at the very subtle causal dimension to develop the plan of primate DNA transformation.

That moment coincides with what we might call the "Time of Tenekau", the moment when that remarkable extraterrestrial creature descended on the ground from the carrier ship that had come from the conflict in space and saw a large group of primates hiding with fear in the bushes. The holographic images showed me that picturesque moment in detail. I then saw how one of the beings in the group had the courage to get out of the bushes and even get a little closer to the ship, being curious. Tenekau stopped abruptly, watching him carefully. I think that was his "sparkle of genius" because he then had a special idea that led to the transformation and evolution of large primates into a superior humanoid being. As a result of a much wider plan, however, the process of forming a new humanoid being on the Earth began about 60,000 years earlier at the cosmic level through the stellar alignment I spoke of earlier.

While I was looking at those extraordinary images that had a great emotional impact on me, I understood that that ancestral moment can be considered the very beginning of the path to the formation of Mankind, the first scrutiny of the idea of the genetic transformation of primitive beings into a superior humanoid being. I was also able to feel the first emotion of Tenekau, his first thought and his first intention, all of which led to the impressive work of genetic transformation that was to follow. The transmutation of the new humanoid was astounding, and this would eventually lead to what we are today: superior, intelligent and self-conscious human beings.

I also felt a vivid emotion because I was a virtual witness even to the "first move" of the colossal chain of genetic transformations that were to follow, and that is why I wanted to insist on viewing those images as they presented to me a highly exceptional and significant moment.

Due to the kind of "biofeedback loop" I had with the holographic screen, it "followed" my desire, and Tenekau's image came to the fore. I saw him stop and look at that curious curiosity that was a few yards away. He bowed his head slightly to the left in a relatively meditative attitude, and that was the first trace of the idea that spurred into his mind his first intention of making a mental contact with those primitive beings. That idea then triggered a complex set of events that led to the transformation of primitive beings into higher beings.

Meanwhile, other crew members had begun to descend from the ship, bringing some equipment to the ground. After receiving his inspiration, the commander made a sign with his hand to the primates, and then joined the work of the others. But the images on the holographic screen showed me how his idea had already been arranged, being the last link needed to trigger the vast plan to form a new humanoid being in this galaxy sector.

In the beginning, Tenekau coordinated the entire plan only at the mental level. Only the primates who were curious and had a more bold spirit were chosen. After a certain period of time, I was even shown the way that initial plan was carried out. I saw Tenekau inside the ship, sitting in a kind of chair, leaning back, surrounded by certain sophisticated devices and mentally coordinating two items outside the ship, moving objects and doing various other tasks. One of them was lighter and even showed signs of a certain intelligence; the other primate was slower and more confused.

In the images I saw, Tenekau was a being that emanated a lot of bliss and deep respect for cosmic laws. I could tell from his outfit and the features of his face that his vast experience had revealed many spiritual mysteries and "carved" his formidable destiny, linked to that of the future of humanity. In a separate directory, he was depicted alongside the three distinct signs that characterized his name.

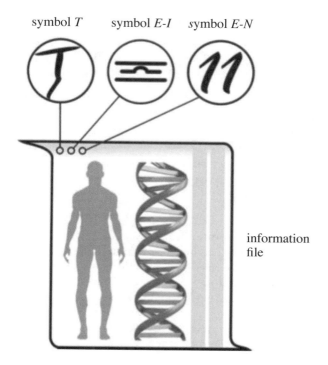

THE THREE SYMBOLS THAT DEFINE TENEKAU: T, E-I, E-N

THE SYMBOLS T, E, N, AND CHANGES IN DNA

In the spirit of my demand to know more about this first being who sparked the "spark" of humanity, the Apellos man continued to explain.

"Observe the similarity of the first symbol on the left with the letter *T* and also with the form of Orion's Belt."

Indeed. I had seen this before. In other words, displays on the screen in some areas are brighter and brighter and others less so and even darker, indicating the importance of that particular detail. In the case of Tenekau, the T-shaped symbol of Orion's Belt was emphasized in this way.

CORRESPONDENCE OF THE T SYMBOL WITH THE STARS IN ORION'S BELT

THE T SYMBOL FOR ORION'S BELT WHICH DEFINES TENEKAU

The middle part appeared brighter to indicate that Tenekau came from one of the planetary systems in the middle area of Orion's center.

As my mind was coupled with the information that had been received so far about the amazing way in which the DNA of the primates had been formulated in that area of Earth; and by the fact that I saw the technological elements of the Sirian beings interacting with these primates in the background, I wanted to see, in an almost reflexive way, how their DNA evolved from the first star influence on the carbon atom. Almost instantly, the image changed, focusing on one of the primates on the surface of the Earth, after which the structure of its DNA was revealed.

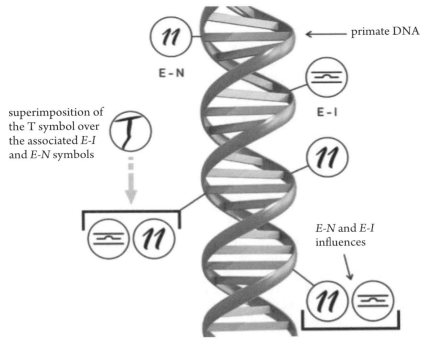

SCHEMATIC OF PRIMATE DNA WITH
ENERGETIC INFLUENCES OF E-I, E-N, AND T

I noticed that, in the molecular structure of the DNA, there were several areas to which the symbols *E-I* and *E-N* were independently associated, but there were also links where the two symbols appeared together. The *T* symbol appears to overlap the place where the first two symbols, *E-I* and *E-N*, are associated.

I have seen that *T* indicates a significant influence in the combinations that existed in the DNA of the evolved primate. The images showed me, in a way somewhat similar to what I had seen at the T-shaped tables in the Projection Room, a very powerful zoom inside of the DNA molecule: the isolation of an atom with the nucleus in its midst, after which I noticed the *T* symbol overlapping the atom. Such influence has created an excitation of the atomic nucleus which gave birth, through various core electrons, to a special hybridized electron orbit.[*]

---

[*] According to *Wikipedia*: In quantum physics, the hybridization process is a concept that involves the merging of atomic orbitals into so-called "hybrid orbits" (which have different energies, forms, etc. than those of the atomic orbits they come from) so that the pairing of electrons is suitable for the formation of chemical bonds. Chemical bonds are interactions that are established between atoms, [*continued on page 119*]

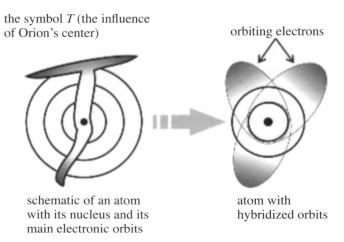

the symbol *T* (the influence of Orion's center)

orbiting electrons

schematic of an atom with its nucleus and its main electronic orbits

atom with hybridized orbits

HYBRIDIZATION OF THE MAIN ELECTRON ORBITS OF THE CARBON ATOM UNDER THE INFLUENCE OF THE T SYMBOL

After hybridization, electronic orbits faithfully copied the geometric structure of the *T* symbol. With time, I realized that there was a connection between the geometric orientation of the hybridized orbits and the shape of a symbol appearing in the hologram. Since these symbols represent subtle cosmic realities, it follows that the "writing" we see is galactic. This is not, however, just conventional writing or symbols. It is not like the Latin alphabet nor any other modern alphabet that was invented and then used by certain populations. This extraterrestrial "writing" involves symbols that represent cosmic, atomic, and molecular structures, a writing that links the various levels of Creation and expresses profound and complex actions.

hybridized orbit

superimposed *T* symbol over the orbital hybridization

T symbol indicating the effect of hybridization

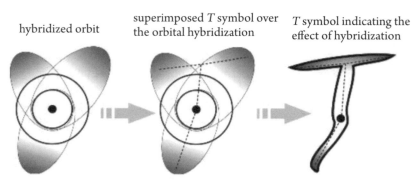

ORBITAL ARRANGEMENT ACCORDING TO THE INFLUENCE OF THE T SYMBOL

Starting from here, I later noticed that the nucleus of the atom resonates with the frequencies designated by the symbols *E-I, E-N* and *T*. Finally, I was shown the oxygen atom in the DNA with the hybridized orbits. Its hybridization resembled much of that found in the water molecule (H_2O), but instead of the two hydrogen atoms, there was a carbon atom. In the water molecule, a hydrogen atom is covalently bonded; and in the second semi-covalent, it is almost ionized. I saw something similar with the carbon atom in primate DNA. As a result of the various influences, both the oxygen atom and the carbon atom have a greater disposition to making covalent bonds as opposed to binding with other atoms. This could be seen, for example, at the hydrogen bonds between adenine and thymidine or between guanine and cytosine in the DNA macromolecule.

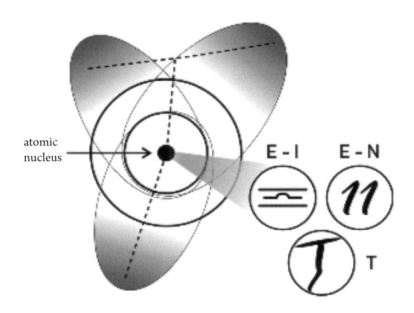

atomic nucleus

E-I E-N T

INFLUENCE OF FREQUENCIES DESIGNATED BY THE SYMBOLS E-I, E-N AND T ON THE ATOMIC NUCLEUS

[*continued from page 117*] groups of atoms, or ions. They are the power of attraction that manifests itself between atoms, binding them into molecules, ions or radicals. [note from the Romanian editor]

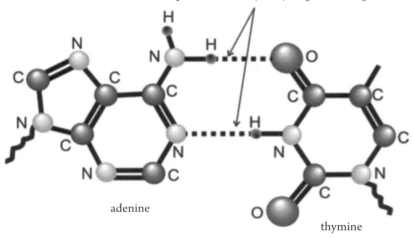

amplified sensitivity of hydrogen bonding

adenine

thymine

INFLUENCES ON CARBON AND OXYGEN HAVE CREATED AN ACCUMULATION OF FACTORS THAT HAVE INCREASED THE PREDISPOSITION FOR HYDROGEN BONDING IN THE DNA MACROMOLECULE

In the "translation", the bonds between the oxygen atom and the hydrogen atom resonated with the frequencies designated by the symbol T, and the two carbon atoms with their bonds resonated with the frequencies designated by the symbol E-I. Beyond the carbon atom is another atom, which we later identified while studying the structure of adenine nitrogen atoms. It links to the carbon atom or to the hydrogen atom, and we have noticed that it acts with the frequencies designated by the unit symbol E-N.

On the whole, I saw how primates from that area on Earth received, over time, those influences in their DNA which were from Tenekau. Over time, the effects of this action could even be noticed in their behavior. After Tenekau had withdrawn his field of influence and mental support from technological devices, some primates were no longer amazed or scared, but on the contrary, they even manifested a certain dominance of self and maturity, a clear sign of the guided evolution.

Pragmatically speaking, I saw a purely advanced genetic engineering project that was highly and thoroughly engineered, and this was backed up by the very special Sirian technology. In the images I have seen, there were devices in the background, some even large, that were brought with shuttles by the Sirian beings to Earth. Later, they were stored on the ground and assembled by the Sirian crew.

The largest object of this type was a sphere with a diameter of approximately ten meters with two huge branches, like two antennas at the top. In the middle of the sphere, I saw a kind of command room with an "ergonomic" chair in which Tenekau sat down, coupling himself to the very complex apparatus in the sphere. Intuitively, I understood that he was using that device to emit a field perfectly suited to the frequencies that were needed to influence primate DNA in order to help them progress in an accelerated fashion. There were other smaller devices around the sphere that looked like cylinders resembling containers. They were on a support at a certain height above the ground.

**THE FIELD EMITTER USED BY TENEKAU WHICH
WAS REQUIRED TO INFLUENCE PRIMATE DNA**

In the lower part, there appeared rays of white-yellow light that beamed to the ground as if they were lasers, forming turbines that facilitated extraction of the materials to be mined. As I saw those images, the extraterrestrial logistics operation extended over a large surface that probably covered several square kilometers. In the middle of it all was the "sphere of mental command" from which Tenekau coordinated the activities of primates so that they knew what to do.

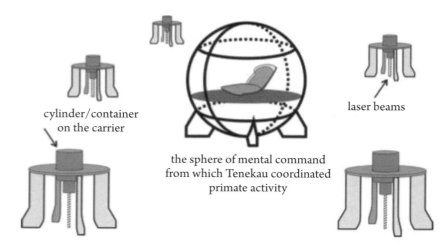

cylinder/container
on the carrier

laser beams

the sphere of mental command
from which Tenekau coordinated
primate activity

THE SPHERICAL MENTAL CONTROL DEVICE
SURROUNDED BY LASER CYLINDRICAL CONTAINERS

Tenekau's mental influence involved both the primates' work with those containers as well as their gradual transformation at DNA level through extraterrestrial technology. Gradually, primates began to remain in the areas where containers were extracted and where the mental control spheres were. Frightened at first, some left those areas, but I saw that, as their DNA changed its structure under the action of the modeling field, they did not run away and were no longer afraid.

THE HEXAGONAL SYMBOL

The implementation of frequencies designated by the *E-I* and *E-N* symbols had been achieved in the region we know today as the Persian Gulf. The frequency designated by the symbol *E-I* was used in the south, the one designated by the symbol *E-N* took place a little to the north, in an area situated to the right. As I have seen, images with the actual extraction of metals by the already transformed primates took place somewhere in a larger area to the north but also in the Persian Gulf area.

In the south, corresponding to the first transformations of DNA in primates, there was lush vegetation, but a little further north, in the wide fields where mineral extractions were done, I saw many cliffs, the landscape being quite arid. I kept my mind on the idea that preoccupied me from the beginning: the origin and evolution of the human being on Earth; and what appeared to me on the screen was an unfolding of this idea which I was not always able to understand or keep step with. Sometimes the presentation

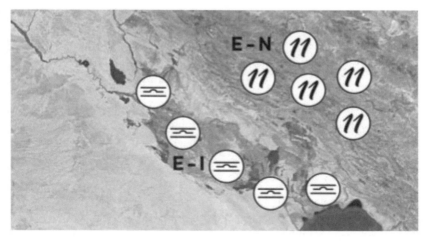

***THE PERSIAN GULF AREAS WHERE THE IMPLEMENTATION
OF THE FREQUENCIES DESIGNATED BY THE
SYMBOLS E-I AND E-N TOOK PLACE***

on the holographic screen was so complex that the descriptions and graphic renderings of the elements included here in this book were very difficult and would make reading very complicated. That is why I prefer to present the main elements as succinctly as possible and without going into too much detail. For example, how the action of the Neiberau alien ship, positioned in a certain network of stars, influenced the transformation of primate DNA

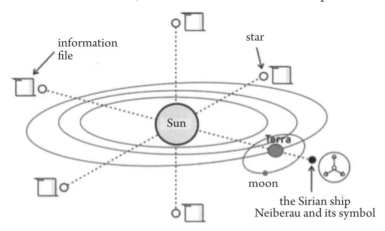

***THE NETWORK FORMED BY THE NEIBERAU VESSEL AND
THE OTHER STARS, WITH OUR SUN IN THE CENTER***

at that time on a mental and emotional level is quite remarkable but also very complex. When this aspect was presented to me, I saw a succession of directories with their specific undulating forms. As one of the files was brighter, I removed the other directories and chose the one which opened with the image of the star network and the Sirian ship, Neiberau, near the Earth. The main action of this cosmic network was then "targeting" our Sun. It has not been shown what phenomena happened at that time around this star, probably because I did not ask for it, but it is certain that there followed a time when the Sun shined brighter, radically influencing the transformation of life on Earth. The Persian Gulf zone, corresponding to E-I and E-N, dried out, and primate tribes living in that area began migrating north to an area that had become lush with vegetation, just above the area where metal extraction took place. The lush area, not very extensive, was between two large rivers.* When the image reached this point, the familiar symbols T, E-I and E-N appeared on the geographical detail.

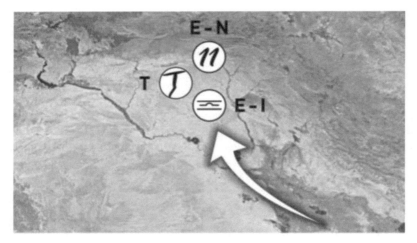

REPRESENTATION OF PRIMATE MIGRATION FROM THE PERSIAN GULF TO THE LUSH VEGETATION AREA

Besides the three symbols, however, I noticed the presence of a fourth. It sas not a letter but had a more complex graphic representation, similar to a hexagon with diagonal lines.

The general symbol designating the specific influence in that area was therefore composed of T, E-I and E-N in which E-I and E-N were bright and T

---

* It is quite possible that the author refers to the Tigris and Euphrates, rivers which are mentioned in the books of Zecharia Sitchin. The area that Radu Cinamar talks about is probably the area that was later known as "Eden", the cradle of the emergence of the first evolved human beings. [Romanian editor's note]

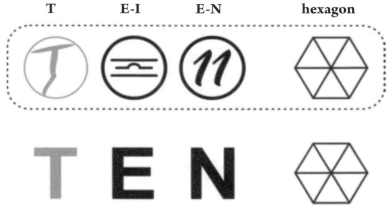

| T | E-I | E-N | hexagon |

small influence of
designated frequencies
by the symbol *T*

the symbol of happiness and euphoria
on some living primates due to
the presence of the Neiberau

REPRESENTATION OF THE COMPLEX SYMBOL: "T E N - HEXAGON"
WHICH INVOLVED THE REFINING OF EMOTIONS

was weaker. The appearance of three letter symbols was followed by a pause, and then came the fourth symbol, the hexagonal one, which I felt was a state of happiness and exaltation, the source of which was the Neiberau ship.

I understood telepathically that this euphoric state was associated with only one particular place, a certain area corresponding to that area with lush vegetation between the two great rivers. The primates who had retreated to that area, attracted by it like a magnet, enjoyed an extraordinary joyous overflow which was directly acting on their emotions, refining them. I saw how the state of joy and happiness created a certain cohesion in primate groups that continued to find creative expression beyond the period of influence that came from the ship. This allowed them to feel more refined emotional states than other primates.

At that moment, I asked myself how emotions helped the evolution of the people other than giving them an exalted state of consciousness, something which obviously could not be permanent. Almost immediately, the image of a portion of primate DNA appeared on the holographic screen as several pulsating luminous dots that represented that they were living in happiness. I understood telepathically that those bright dots were portions of DNA that resonated with a cumulative frequency that was designated by the complex symbol: *T E-I E-N* (T E N).

This "game" of frequencies began to form some new complex modifications within the primate DNA molecule, and at some point, they developed themselves emotionally. This fact is remarkable because the refinement of such psycho-mental aspects signifies an important leap on the scale of the evolution of being by opening it to the higher frequencies in the Macrocosmos.

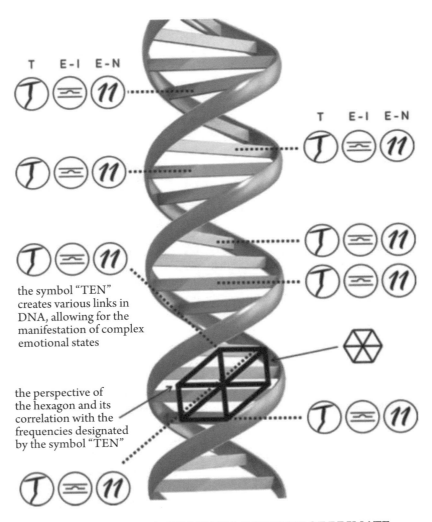

the symbol "TEN" creates various links in DNA, allowing for the manifestation of complex emotional states

the perspective of the hexagon and its correlation with the frequencies designated by the symbol "TEN"

THE REPRESENTATION OF A PORTION OF PRIMATE DNA INFLUENCED BY "T E N-HEXAGON" WHICH MEANS REFINING THE EMOTIONS

CHAPTER SIX

SPLITTING EVOLUTION:
THE E-N-L AND E-N-K BRANCHES

Using the headset, I continued watching with much interest, aiming to focus as much as possible. As my intention was very clear, complex images emerged on the screen that represented the environment of these "new" primates. Changes in DNA that were directly related to the *T, E,* and *N* symbols created the possibility of an increase in vitality. On the other hand, the feelings, emotions and thoughts of those primates were influenced by the new structures in their DNA which were directly linked to the hexagonal symbol. As I said, the hexagonal symbol was the complex influence that the Neiberáu had on primate DNA.

Sustained work on the planet, however, required better coordination between crew members and primates, even with evolved ones. The damage that the great ship had suffered was great, and in order to repair it, they needed some of the metals that had begun to be extracted from Earth. The difficulty was that alien beings could not work too much time on the surface of the Earth due to differences in the environment between their ship and our planet.

To summarize the presentation, I understood that Tenekau had received a suggestion from the group of physicians on the *Neiberáu* to create a hybrid clone that would be enriched with genes from the more evolved primates that had already made an evolutionary leap by reason of the subtle influence of energy represented by the T-E-N-hexagon. Tenekau agreed, and so began a complex process of "modeling" the DNA macromolecule, all of which would lead to structures with extraordinary potentials for cloning beings in the future.

From that moment on, I only saw the figure and body of that being into which Tenekau's consciousness had been transferred. I was able to identify, through the "play" of the frequencies and resonances that I had somehow been taught, that the transfer of Tenekau's consciousness to that being occurred about 371 B.C.

These elements may appear to be in the field of science fiction, but I can assure the well-intentioned readers that the technology underlying this kind of transfer, which is both physical and inter-dimensional in its nature, has already begun to be "deciphered" on Earth at present. It is true that the Sirians in the Orion Belt Constellation have been mastering this technology for half a million years or maybe even more, but this shows that evolution has no borders; and the fact that something is unknown to contemporary scientists does not mean that it does not exist or has not been used so far.

The being that Tenekau had designed into which to project his consciousness did not look perfect, but it clearly already had all of the "improvements" at the DNA level because it was always on the screen with the full symbol: *T-E-N-Hexagon*. I understood that that cloned being was, in fact, a composition of all parts of primate DNA that were originally influenced by *T-E-N-Hexagon*. That was the very special being that was compatible with Tenekau.

The *T-E-N-Hexagon* symbol was continuously associated with that being and was as tall as Tenekau, about 2.50 meters. Unlike Tenekau, however, who had no hair at all and whose head was slightly elongated at the back, this creature had a head similar to that of a modern long-haired human. The color of the hair was amazing. It was platinum white, shining very beautifully in the light. Intuitively, I understood that this being was basically a cross between primate DNA and extraterrestrial DNA, but it was a genetic engineering product and not a result of genetically crossing-breeding physical bodies. This was clear because there were no sexual organs. Then, later, I saw that being as he had left the lab and walked out among the other primates with a gentle meditative air.

I did not understand, however, why there were more such bodies in the other cylinders in the laboratory. The most plausible hypothesis seemed to indicate more "variants" of the original prototype which also were to be tested. Although I did not insist on this point, I was curious to find out more about the creation and evolution of that hybrid being.

A DECISIVE MOMENT

I was so stunned by what I saw that I lost my focus. The screen images then became blurred. Excited, I realized that I was watching "live action" events that took place hundreds of thousands of years ago, and that I was really privileged to get this information.

Regaining my composure quite quickly, I focused on the subject again, recreating the mental-emotional connection with the holographic image playback device. I continued to focus on Tenekau and the clone I had seen. After the images became clear, I noticed that they presented a reality in time that was a few years afterwards because I could see that there were now cloned beings among the primates. These cloned beings worked hard in several areas in the southern Arabian peninsula, being helped by primates who, in turn, were mentally coordinated by various crew members on the ship.

The holographic images changed, depicting the *Neiberáu's* huge command room, populated with a part of the crew. Then, another room was shown to me in the pictures which I immediately recognized as a medical room. I saw Tenekau talking to three of his fellow humans, and I also received telepathically the information that they were doctors on the great ship *Neiberáu*. There were other Sirian beings in that room with the characteristic insignia on their outfits which I could not decipher. I somehow realized, however, that they occupied high positions in the command hierarchy on the ship. They formed small groups in the room, discussing a particular subject with a lot of interest. I knew that this was an important topic about primates on Earth. At one moment, one of the beings raised his hand in front of himself, and a hologram appeared in the middle of that room, revealing some stellar configurations.

At first, I did not understand why those images were shown to me or what they represented. At one point, however, a star appeared in the image with the specific files, and their intersection focused on the *Neiberáu*. The image then grew, and I saw the Solar System, then the Earth, the ship, the middle area of the ship, and then a bunch of other creatures on the ship, including Tenekau. I did not understand the meaning of those images, and that is why I turned to the Apellos man. He smiled, looking at me as he spoke.

"What you have seen here is very complex. As is the case with astrology on Earth, it is working with planets, the Moon, the Sun, and other heavenly bodies but less often with other fixed stars. In the astrology known by those extraterrestrial beings, thousands of stars were taken into account, not just a few. When a birth occurs on a cosmic ship, the star influence is much stronger because it is in a place in space that is not related to the parents' home planet. One such case was Tenekau's. We were shown in the hologram image that, at the time of his birth, there were some star arrangements that had the same type of E and N structures which were found in primates on Earth. Tenekau grew up on the ship, taught on the ship, joined the military on the ship, and climbed the ranks. Throughout this time, he had the E and N type stellar influences in his DNA, also felt by primates on Earth over the last tens of thousands of years. When Tenekau descended to our planet with a ship to extract ores, he felt something "interesting" in the primates who were looking curiously at the ship. He resonated with the subtle stellar influences E and N which had already produced transformations in the DNA of those primates. I then saw images showing the connection between those DNA sections transformed by the stellar influences that existed in both the primates as well as that of Tenekau."

The Apellos man continued explaining.

"That was the reason that Tenekau was able to transfer his Consciousness to the clone. It could be easily accomplished because its genes were compatible with the primates. He realized the importance of those issues and sent a long report to his superiors on the *Neiberáu*."

I wanted to see that moment in detail and turned my gaze to the screen as the image cleared in seconds. A very large room was featured that was technologically oriented. Everything seemed to be done ergonomically, ranging from the layout of the objects to the forms of the technical apparatus which consisted mostly of different types of screens that were placed either vertically or horizontally.

The image presented Tenekau standing in front of a large screen that projected holographically many symbols, signs and images at a short distance in front of him. Seeing everything behind Tenekau's right shoulder, I realized that those were the moments during which he sent the vast report to his superiors. The images followed quickly, and I saw the moment when the answers came. Intuitively, I felt the very special subtle-energetic impregnation of that moment. Those moments were those that most definitely defined the destiny of humanity, the moment when the decision to create a new being was made.

The Apellos man helped me understand the new images I saw. He told me that Tenekau's report had the effect of a lightning strike on the upper echelon of the great ship *Neiberáu*. The commander, along with the ship's command staff, sent that report to the Wise Council on the mother planet. The answer was illuminating for all. Tenekau was informed that he was not randomly placed at that conjuncture in that place on Earth at that precise moment. He explained that all of this was planned long before on the level of the subtle superior planes; and that by his actions, he created the prototype of an evolved being that will exist in the future on this planet.

Tenekau then understood that, in reality, everything had been arranged and rendered so that he could synchronize and determine those decisions and actions he had committed. Even if his intention at the beginning was only to create a being with superior possibilities from the existing primates in order to help extract the ore they needed, everything was now making sense on a much deeper level. The order he received was for him to stay with his ship around the Earth and to support the necessary activities for the development and evolution of the primates that then existed in that area.

The problems arising from the spatial conflict continued to exist, but Tenekau was "detached" and received a direct order from that point on to support the natural evolution of the great primates on Earth who would, in time, become a thriving civilization. That order was given to him as well as to all leadership echelons on the *Neiberáu*. Upon receipt of that order, all of the crew and all the logistical resources of that giant ship were directed on the new mission. Only a small section of the ship would have to deal with the ship's military and security aspects in that area of the cosmos.

THE SIGNIFICANCE OF T

The images then showed a huge room where several alien creatures on the ship were studying the links between the stars and their possible configurations in order to implement certain energetic influences into the primate DNA to accelerate their natural evolution. The images on the holographic screen I was looking at proceeded quickly and stopped at a time when only two of the star structures were being studied. In front of those pictures were two symbols.

From the combinations of *T, E,* and *N* to the primate DNA, I saw that *T,* which was less intense than *E* and *N,* began to spin into two other symbols, representing two distinct families of frequency.

Then, on the screen, I was shown how the two frequencies combined, and their two symbols were united, resulting in a configuration whose intrusions were the very points in which the stars of the structure formed the necessary influence for the evolution of the primate.

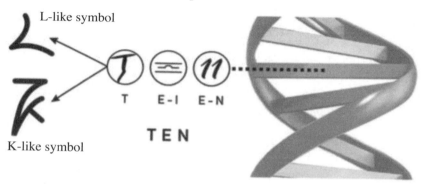

THE INFLUENCE OF THE FREQUENCIES DESIGNATED BY THE SYMBOL T-E-N IN THE PRIMATE DNA AND THE SPLITTING OF T, REPRESENTING TWO DISTINCT FAMILIES OF FREQUENCIES

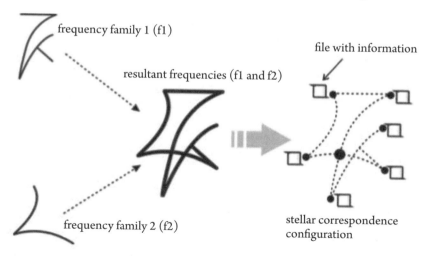

THE UNION OF THE TWO FREQUENCIES AND THEIR POINTS OF "STAR INTERSECTION"

At the primate DNA level, this splitting of T into two distinct families of frequencies represented the implementation of the ability to choose. The emotional states that these beings possessed allowed them to choose before engaging in a particular mode of action. It was no longer about instinct but rational feeling and choices being continually updated

Therefore, as we have understood from the succession of images, the frequencies designated by the E-N symbol influenced the frequencies designated by the T symbol in the DNA structure. As a result, consequently complex interfaces were born that gave birth to new families of frequencies. These frequency families have been designated by two symbols: a K-like symbol and a second symbol similar to the letter L.

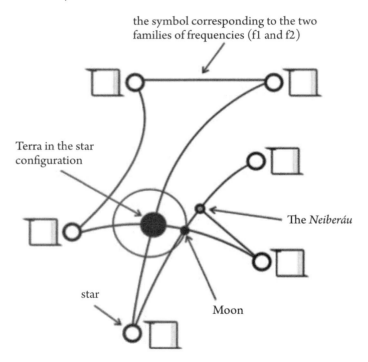

the symbol corresponding to the two families of frequencies (f1 and f2)

Terra in the star configuration

The *Neiberáu*

star

Moon

POSITIONING OF THE NEIBERÁU NEAR THE MOON IN THE STELLAR CONFIGURATION CORRESPONDING TO THE INTERFERENCE-GENERATING FREQUENCIES

As per what I have seen in a sequence of flashes on the holographic screen, the *Neiberáu* had settled among the planets of our Solar System to support this very important split in the future evolution of the human being. In some situations, *the Neiberáu*, to amplify these interfacing frequencies, is situated next to the Moon in a configuration that keeps it in touch with the overlapping frequency symbol.

THE SYMBOL K

The meaning of the *K* symbol is very important and, over time, it has come to define the genetics of the primordial primate of the Earth. In connection with its occult meanings, we then received some valuable information from the Apellos man. Especially for the Sirians, this symbol, which is similar to the letter *K,* is very important because it represents the connection between heaven and Earth. In other words, it signifies divine support, but at the same time, it indicates the support of other entities with a high degree of spirituality. I will subsequently elaborate in more detail different aspects of the symbolism of *K* as it was shown and explained to me.

The *K* symbol represents a wide range of frequencies that are directly related to divine influence and support as well as the spiritual help offered by entities that are right in the physical plane. In other words, we have the help of the subtle dimensions, especially from the etheric plane (which is close to the physical plane) on the one hand, and we also have the help that comes from the physical plane itself. The symbol as such signifies divine influence and support from the top down (refer to the vertical line in the letter or symbol "K") which makes the connection "between heaven and Earth." That is to say, it comes from the subtle planes as a downward manifestation to the physical plane. This influence is also supported, as we have said, by celestial entities of the subtle dimensions (refer to the top oblique line in the symbol "K"). The lateral line (the downward oblique line) represents the possibility of other influences supported by beings in the physical plane, such as the influence and help of the semi-gods who also had certain preferences or tendencies such as, for example, supporting a king, a people, or a group of human beings developing in a certain direction. All of this support starts from the middle point, but what does the etheric plane mean in this regard? I will offer a more detailed description of this very important symbol in the next volume.

DEFINITIONS BETWEEN E-N-L AND E-N-K

I then saw how the two distinct families of frequencies, in conjunction with the *K* and *L* symbols, were combined with *E-N*, resulting in the specific *E-N-L* and *E-N-K* families of the DNA of those beings. Of these, we saw how the beings designated by the *E-N-L* symbol had a larger and finer bio-field, whereas the beings designated by the *E-N-K* symbol had a somewhat more "restricted" bio-field.

Both frequency families existed due to the interference created by the frequencies symbolized by the hexagon, but the frequencies designated by the *L* symbol were more sustainable due to specific resonances.

After this splitting, I realized that the development of the beings represented by the *E-N-K* symbol was reserved for the physical plane while the development of the beings designated by the symbol *E-N-L* would encompass both the physical plane and the subtle etheric plane. This enabled some of the primates, those in which the *L*-designated frequency family was more present and more combined in the *E-N-L* format, to get more quickly familiarized to the frequencies designated by the hexagon symbol. Because of this, they evolved much faster. *E-N-L* had a faster development, as well as the fact that they lived for a long time near extraterrestrial bases, interacting in different ways with extraterrestrial beings, helping them or learning from them. The most advanced specimens even had access to those bases. In their evolution, hybridization in successive stages of extraterrestrial DNA was of great importance.

After a while, when the *E-N-L* beings began to produce, the embryo received the influence of the subtle fields emanating from the extraterrestrial bases from the very beginning, as well as the strong influence from the genetic mutations supported by the doctors of the *Neiberáu*.

PROCREATION SUPPORT ON THE E-N-L BRANCHES

After observing all of these elements of our origins on Earth, I then wanted to know how procreation was sustained on the *E-N-L* branch, which was clearly strongly hybridized with extraterrestrial DNA.

The image on the screen disappeared for a fraction of a second in order to instantly place the image of the Sirian *Neiberáu* ship within the network of its known star lines.

As I said, in the midst of the vast cosmic network they formed, there was always a heavenly body upon which the subtle influence was focused. For example, to initiate transformations at the level of primate DNA, the Earth was first in the middle. Later, in another stellar configuration, our Sun was in the middle in order to determine a new important stage in the evolution of the DNA structure of those beings. (see illustration on next page)

I was now shown another configuration with the Moon in the middle. It also showed me that the Moon was the fundamental element that determined the development of the sexes in the primates that would become human beings during their evolution on Earth.

On the holographic screen, I was then shown a projection that was a subtle "etheric duplicate" of the *Neiberáu* to note the existence of a great multitude of beings or, more preferably, souls as subtle ethereal manifestations. I also immediately realized by telepathic induction that they used the subtle body

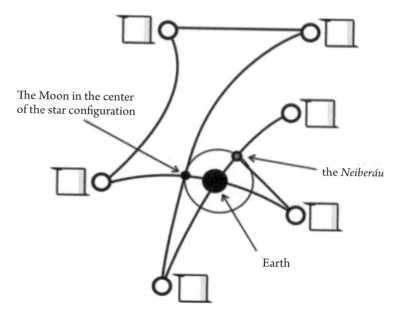

The Moon in the center of the star configuration

the *Neiberáu*

Earth

THE RELATIVE POSITION OF THE "NEIBERÁU" IN OUR SOLAR SYSTEM WHEN THE MOON WAS AT THE CENTER OF THE STELLAR ARRANGEMENT

of the ship to influence the development of the genetic combinations of the fetus belonging to the *E-N-L* branch. By doing this, the beings born on the *E-N-L* branch were supported, both mentally and ethereally, by compatible beings on the Neiberáu. This support from the huge ship was focused on the Earth at the level of groups of beings, tribes, or in some cases, just in a region. Besides individual capabilities, support depends only upon the compatibility between the primates and the extraterrestrial beings on the ship.

Over time, the *E-N-L* beings have evolved and even started to "break down" into secondary branches of the main *E-N-L* branch, forming new developmental pathways symbolized as follows: *E-N-L-A, E-N-L-I, E-N-L-O* and *E-N-L-A*. There are other combinations of this kind. I saw, as in the spectacular growth of a tree, the "splitting" of the main frequencies of *E-N-L*, or "the trunk," into several branches and secondary sub-branches or secondary frequencies, each with its own features, potentials and power.

The symbols in the secondary branches were not what I already knew or could recognize at that time (*A / E / I / O / U* etc.), but I gave these explanations only to make it as simple as possible to understand what was happening as the symbols I saw in the holographic images were far more complex and dynamic. In order to get an idea of their structure and the way they looked, however, I often stopped from viewing to write on paper and sketch these elements, associating them as best as I could with the letters that we know. Being curious about how those special primates from the E-N-L branch developed, I was able to see the complex ties and the extraterrestrial beings that began to come from the *Neiberáu* to the surface of our planet, having as their mission to support the accelerated evolution of those primates.

From the rapid succession of images, I realized that the *Neiberáu* had become a powerful focus of spirituality for over several thousand years. Her military mission has changed, focusing primarily on research to create and support the development of a new being and a new civilization. I also saw that the number of those on the ship almost doubled. As I said, there was also a military section to guard the space around the ship, but most of the creatures that inhabited the giant ship were oriented toward scientific research.

The images that appeared to me were sublime, but I could not enjoy them too much because I quickly noticed how that the supportive actions of the extraterrestrials was incomplete. Primates that evolved from the E-N-L branch, and which were supported by the method described above, failed to procure very much nor did they procure it fast enough. Even though *Neiberáu* researchers gave great support to awakening the consciousness in the population of the evolved primates, their number was still too small.

The deficiency was solved in a way that would mark the subsequent evolution of the human being. In the images I was watching on the holographic screen, I noticed an epochal event that happened about the Moon as a result of the positioning of the *Neiberáu* in a network with certain stars. This event, which most probably had a subtle etheric nature, was suggested in the images I saw as a star configuration with the very luminous Moon in the center. By influencing the Moon's movement and trajectory, the evolved primates were predisposed to be more sexually active.

On the other hand, the E-N-K branch continued to evolve at its own natural pace without any help or external interventions since the difference in vibrational frequency was still too high to allow for efficient hybridization with evolved DNA.

ADAM

The images followed quickly, showing some events that took place several thousand years after the initiation of the E-N-L branch. On a sort of "dynamic" map that was portrayed in holographic images, I saw that they coexisted on Earth at that time with many other types of primates that had reached different stages of evolution. Of all these species of humanoid beings, the E-N-L branch was clearly supported by extraterrestrial civilizations that oversaw the developmental processes of the new race on the planet, both by orienting individuals to develop in certain areas as well as by "seeding" them to boost the development of their DNA.

Women of the E-N-K branch procreated quite a bit, and as the men of E-N-L branch were still attracted to them, this could lead to a severe degradation of the E-N branch; and, thus the evolutionary rhythm of the human being could be diminished.

In terms of numbers of individuals, the E-N-K branch was dominant, and the E-N-L branch, which was rather small in number, had retreated to some of the most remote places on the planet, particularly to coastal areas and islands. I did not quite understand why the E-N-L beings had this preference for the coastal areas, but from what I saw, it was very clear that they settled only in such regions. Basically speaking, I have not seen E-N-L beings inside the continents.

The fact remained, however, that in the DNA of the beings of the E-N-L branch, the hexagonal symbol predominated, representing a certain family of frequencies that led to a clear elevation of them, thus enabling the more evolved E-N-L beings to become true emitters and powerful sources for other beings derived from other E-N-L branches and even for some beings in the E-N-K branch, contributing to the evolution of all. They represented a kind of highly evolved bio-field outbreak, and that is why the beings with whom they lived, even the lesser evolved ones, took over a greater or lesser part of that extraordinary influence and thus considerably improved the characteristics in their own DNA.

At each such change, I could see in the projections that were presented to me on the screen that there was another alien spacecraft besides the Neiberáu, and it was much larger than the ship with which I was now so familiar. This other ship was positioned in different areas of our Solar System: either near the Moon, Saturn or another planet, supporting complex genetic mutations created by stellar or planetary structures and amplified by the position of the ship.

After several thousand years, beings influenced by the higher E-N-L branch already had a structure closer to human nature. They had begun to lose their hairiness, became "brighter" with a more erect stature and began to manifest certain intellectual capacities. I have seen such evolved primates expressing inner happiness, having a certain elevated feeling, and being quieter than the others, even "meditative".

Genetic complexity began to manifest itself more and more. Some beings were born with blond hair, others with no hair, some of them had blue eyes, others had green eyes, and so on, the changes being made in the embryo right from the start, just after the procreation phase.

This happened until, one time, I saw that the planets in our Solar System were positioned in a specific way, along with a gigantic spacecraft. I was then shown how, from a more complex extension of the *E-N-L* branch, a highly evolved embryo was targeted to fulfill a highly sophisticate genetic transformation that would take place over a few thousand years. The images focused on those moments, giving details from the embryo's conception.

Then there was a very important event which eventually became a myth. Through repeated cross breeding, an embryo was naturally developed by a female of the *E-N-L* branch that was compatible with the subtle etheric body common to the Sirius civilization. Up until then, the beings of the different branches of the *E-N-L* line could only be "mentally" and subtly influenced by an extraterrestrial being. It was now possible for that being to become the prototype of future man and for an alien soul to actually incarnate in that body.

Usually, this is done through a conscious assumption by the evolved soul of the alien being — before he leaves his physical form — to reincarnate into a coarser body. Essentially, the extraterrestrial soul assumes one of the physical bodies of an *E-N-L* on Earth in order to gradually determine the necessary changes in the DNA by the very high vibrational level of his consciousness.

Once this process has begun, the souls of alien beings who have become entangled in bodies of the *E-N-L* line remain in the astral plane in the vicinity of the Earth and then continue to reincarnate here, respecting the natural laws of life and evolution.

On the one hand, the balance between what is allowed to intervene in such a "modulation", and on the other hand, the cosmic laws that govern cosmic order and evolution, is something that resembles walking on a tightrope at a great height. You must have a profound knowledge of Universal Laws and also be fully humble and devoted to the Divine Will, understanding and perceiving the direction of one's actions so as not to oppose them, especially when it comes to a galactic project involving conscious life. Otherwise, failure is guaranteed and will happen in short order.

There must therefore be a certain science of merging technology with the divine laws of Creation, and this is known to beings who have reached a high degree of spiritual evolution. In my opinion, as I have been able to see and understand from the pictures presented, those from very advanced civilizations had performed a sacrificial act, because a return to a lower plane and a purely inferior physical form through successive incarnations, as some of those souls have assumed, cannot be neither easy nor enjoyable. At that stage, however, it was a quick spiritual way of achieving the correct and natural transformation of humanoid beings from their origins into a more evolved being

This was the first time that all conditions were met for the birth of the first human being. If, in the past, as in the case of Tenekau, there was a transfer of consciousness into a clone, this was a natural evolutionary process of a new species. I then saw the beginning of the process of incarnation of a highly evolved extraterrestrial being, highlighted on the holographic screen through a more intense luminous ray which had penetrated into the embryo of a woman of the *E-N-L* line. Through repeated transformations of the embryo at the DNA level, a body was created that was compatible with the souls of advanced alien beings. I understood that this was the first human being to be very evolved on Earth, and it belonged to the *E-N-L* branch.

Of course, , as one can imagine, this "birth" was not an ordinary one. I was shown in detail how the future of this being developed, step by step, through a very advanced technology that included connections with subtle superior dimensions. I was curious to see the inside of one of the round-shaped alien laboratories that were built on Earth and where the genetic development of the new humanoids of the *E-N-L* branch was accomplished. I saw there a kind of ovular sac , filled with a semi-transparent and slightly gelatinous liquid, where the embryo extracted from the *E-N-L* female was placed.

Embryo development was fascinating. In the beginning, white spikes were emerging that looked like nerve endings. They then merged, forming more and more complex and compact structures, probably based on a code and already established structures of subtle-etheric fields. The ovular sac was in suspense, but around it, I saw other complicated devices that emitted rhythmic bright flashing lights that were like lasers shining on the sac. I deduced that it was most likely a specific process necessary for the creation of the physical body into which the "spark of life", the soul of that highly evolved Sirian, was then lowered.

I saw in detail the rapid process of his body's development. Where there were luminous flashing lights, a small vortex emerged from a viscous liquid, from which a thin white thread-like element extended. Later, it grew more and branched out to unite with other such threads. Everything was very dynamic and contained many nuances, the description of which would take require too time and space to tell.

I was very curious to see what was at least the approximate year in which this extraordinary event for Mankind took place, a sort of "foundation stone" for this human being in particular and for the whole of humanity in general. As soon as I showed such genuine interest, I heard the "play" of frequencies in the special helmet I was wearing, doubled by some specific symbols that followed in the top right of the holographic screen.

As far as I could understand and decode, the time period was approximately 368,000-367,000 B.C. This was the period in which the first human being appeared to be perfect, after several thousand years of successive transformations that took place in the DNA of the primates. There were other physical bodies of *E-N-L* beings around, but of them, only this body was somehow "infused" with perfection.

Esoteric and Christian mythology present this as Adam. That being yet existed in the logical sequence of the evolutionary transformations that have taken place; surely, not within the metaphorical Eden Garden (though later, that was indeed the area on the north side of the Persian Gulf in Iraq where Adam was) and not accompanied by Eve, the snake or the famous Apple. These were probably subsequent metaphors, directly related to the possibility of procreation, for at first, Adam was androgynous.

So, through a divine act and as a result of a very complex and ancient epoch of time — as I have shown in an exceptionally clear and highly summarized way — Adam (as the soul of a highly evolved extraterrestrial entity) was incarnated by emitting that intense ray of light from the ship that was there, as was mentioned previously.

I was shown on the screen the moment when this very first human being was born. This was the first superior conscious being in the framework of the successive transformations towards a new race of intelligent beings, all of whom were born on Earth at that time of the project's development in connection with the creation of the human being. The name given has remained almost unaltered in time: Adam.

I can confess with an open soul that I have never seen a perfect being such as the Adam who appeared to me on the screen. Due to the special interaction between me and the holographic screen — through the inter-dimensional helmet that reflects the advanced technology of Apellos — I was able to feel with great clarity the extraordinary features of the first human being whose legacy has remained for a long time afterwards, serving as the foundation of the so-called "modern" man. Although the process was much more complex than that and did not adhere to a linear evolution, we can still say that, to some extent, the root of our DNA started from that first extraordinary being who was Adam. In this regard, biblical text is accurate

The telepathic and intuitive transmission I was receiving, which also included my senses, became so clear and intense at one point that I was almost overwhelmed with excitement, unable to master a faint trembling of my body. I was shown and understood clearly that the soul who incarnated into the body of Adam was a perfectly spiritual Sirian. On the physical level, however, Adam's DNA contained a certain percentage of primate DNA on Earth as the embryo came from a woman in the upper E-N-L branch. Adam's level of consciousness was so evolved that, when he first opened his eyes, I was able to see that he was already in a deep trance state in which he remained for a long time.

In the brief summary of his life, I noticed a few "gaps" that have not been elucidated upon; meaning, that for some time, Adam was not in the Persian Gulf area; but for the rest of his long time on Earth, he remained in approximately the same area. His existence represented an almost continuous meditation and introspection as well as the attention to preserve that extraordinary purity of the body and soul necessary for the efficient transmission of DNA for the genetic changes that they wanted.

Even if some might be horrified and others find it blasphemous, this is the truth about Adam's existence. Perhaps I have an advantage by the fact that this very advanced technology is not wrong and that, moreover, we had access to the summarized elements of those times in a fairly rapid but especially precise and interactive rendering. This is why I have decided to present these aspects of the true origin of Mankind and some important moments in its real history, convinced that at least some readers will be able to intuitively feel or even verify what I have revealed here by other means.

For example, I understand that the successive moments of Adam's "awakening" are probably hard to accept, but I will still state them here exactly as I have seen in the pictures presented to me. The first was the moment when Adam opened his eyes for the first time, being immersed in that gelatinous liquid. Then, in the next flash, I saw how that gelatinous substance leaked slowly as his naked body remained in the alveolus. I was then shown the moment when he got up from the alveolus and stepped out of it. After that, I saw different situations where he was engaged in meditation or doing other activities, but he always seemed to be a self-contained, silent, and even mystical being.

It is interesting to know that the evolution of the primates to the present day human being has not been achieved only physically. In the case of the first cloned beings, in which there was a transfer of Tenekau's consciousness, it was just about the body being used as a vehicle. This was necessary to support the spiritual evolution of the primates so that their souls could be embedded in increasingly specialized vehicles. If the Sirians and advanced civilizations who participated in that project had proposed to do only clones, they would have succeeded in doing so quickly. The stakes, however, regarded the evolutionary development of those primates' consciousness so that they could evolve. That is why Adam's "birth" is very important as it is the first natural incarnation of an evolved soul into a body of clay, that is, the "biological raw material" of the planet. By this, it is understood that his DNA also contained the basic structure of the DNA from the primates on Earth, and it is this from which the "modeling" of his body began.

Adam's incarnate manifestation was necessary to allow divine nature to manifest: firstly, by descending from the vertical planes, and then expanding horizontally by multiplying the DNA of that particular being. Expansion was accomplished by many seedlings in the feminine beings in the E-N-L branch. The beings born through this procedure could be perfected into bodies which were able to incorporate alien souls from different civilizations that supported the development of the new species on Earth. In other words, starting from the DNA of that very pure human being, which was actually androgenous, various possibilities of embryonic development were then explored through genetic engineering.

The androgyny of Adam reflected more like it was an exceptional harmony of body and mind which could easily be noticed, and it did not include sexual differences. I saw him in all the splendor of his perfection: he was a great creature and about 2.5 meters tall, similar to the extraterrestrial beings around him. His waist was thinner than that of the normal male; his skin was white and he had long silky silver hair. His eyes were large and almond-shaped, like deep waters, and his features impressed me by their perfect refinement and harmony. The general impression created was that of a man, but he had some feminine features that made him very refined.

From the specific sounds I heard, which my cortex had somehow translated, I deduced quite easily that Adam lived for a long time, which I approximate to be more than 750 years. *

Due to the extraordinary purity and harmony of his physical body, this was possible by reason of the very evolved nature of his DNA. In a sense, it was his "main mission" to serve as a "DNA matrix" for the beings that would be derived from his DNA, to which various other types of DNA were added in order to gradually deliver the complex but stable formula for the new civilization that they wanted to create. From this perspective, we can understand the biblical text that says Adam "begot" sons and daughters. The meaning is that his gene has been spread into several feminine beings that have spawned bodies with the ability to be "inhabited" by souls of evolved extraterrestrial beings who have assumed that mission.

THE SYMBOL N, THE "MARK" OF REPRODUCTION

Even though Adam was created, being a perfect matrix of the new species, he could not procreate. Likewise, no other beings, even those born of Adam's genes, could procreate in the beginning. Most beings born, being hybridized with Adam's DNA, were androgens. Over time, through the increase in the number of beings born in this way, sexual differentiation was achieved. It is quite possible that the esoteric and Christian tradition regarding "Adam and Eve" referred to precisely that stage of human evolution in which Eve represented the moment of the splitting of the sexes, and this includes a direct connection with and incidental occurrences concerning some very special events that involved the Moon. It was then that the enigmatic, mysterious and reflective character of femininity defined itself in the new being created upon the Earth.

Starting from here, it is now easy to understand the expression that the woman was born "from the rib of the man"; meaning that "Eve appeared from the rib of Adam" because the appearance of the two sexes (male and female) was, in fact, nothing but an extension of Adam's DNA base. For example, there

---

* In the *Bible*, it is stated that Adam lived 930 years. [Romanian editor's note]

was no "primordial" female being, namely Eve, the original representative of the female sex. I did not see anything of this kind in the summarized history on the holographic screen, but instead, I telepathically understood what the word "Eve" was referring to, as I just explained.

The special moment of the splitting of the sexes in the new beings was displayed by the symbol *N* which rather looked like a kind of *H* because, when it was displayed on the holographic screen, I saw two vertical lines with a larger point in the middle.

the point represents the manifestation of the divine will

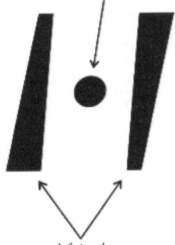

segments defining the necessary sexual
polarization in the evolution of the near-human

THE SYMBOL N AND ITS GENERAL MEANING

His significance was that of an increased sexual polarization that applied to both extraterrestrial and human beings. On the one hand, the souls of extraterrestrial beings who assumed the task of forming the superior man "separated" from their civilization in the sense that they became associated with the planet Earth for the mission they had assumed: to create a new civilization here. This was the first vertical line (see above illustration). On the other hand, many of the humanoid beings on our planet whose DNA had already undergone certain transformations separated from the inferior structure of other families of humanoid primates. This was the second vertical line. The point in the middle of the *N* symbol signifies the Divine Will which made that transformation possible. That point also represents a fundamental moment of celestial mechanics when certain stars, in their relative motion, aligned, creating a massive influence on the planet Earth.

As the number of humanoid beings that were born under these influences increased, more and more extraterrestrial beings had to be incarnated on Earth. The development of the new civilization obviously depended upon the evolution of consciousness in the new bodies.

As for the spiritual evolution of the beings, they were not yet so evolved as souls to be able to incorporate themselves into the pure bodies of the beings derived from Adam's genetic structure. To bring about the evolution of the entire humanoid civilization on Earth, many extraterrestrial souls, originating from various other civilizations in our galaxy, began to "migrate" and incarnate on Earth.

The advanced alien civilizations involved in this cosmic project exercised these tremendous possibilities; but this, of course, happened at a cosmic rate of time; that is, over a period of several tens of thousands of terrestrial years. In this way, the evolution of the human being of the *E-N-L* branch was quickened in the positive sense by precisely utilizing that chance at the cosmic level. At the same time, those extraterrestrial civilizations had to make sure that a large enough number of individuals of the new species had come in order to secure its self-preservation on Earth.

A NECESSARY EXPLANATION

I feel compelled to make a point here because ignorance and, in particular, the bigotry of some individuals can very easily block the fair understanding of things. From what has been presented so far, especially in connection with Adam, one might understand that man would not be "a creation of God" but would only be a product of scientific operations of genetic manipulation and cloning; and further, that the human being — and implicitly Adam —is only a kind of "experiment" conducted at the discretion of extraterrestrial civilizations who have nothing better to do than play "master and slave".

Such an interpretation would highlight the lack of spiritual maturity in correctly understanding how the human being was created. I think we can readily overcome the infantile idea that "God created a man of clay", modeling him with His hands. I think that, even for the most bigoted, such a "reality" is too pathetic and unethical to be argued as a good argument.

First, the presence of God must be correctly understood and perceived at an intuitive level as being unknowable and transcendent; or, on the contrary, it can be understood from the perspective of the surrounding reality in the sense that God is everything we see and experience through our senses and our minds. If these two "variants" were not valid at the same time, it would mean that God would not be omniscient and omnipotent. But, because God is precisely all this and much more than that, He is present everywhere or, in other words, in all things. Therefore, God's action must not be "manual" in order to create "something" — a thing or a being — because His presence and energy penetrate everything and can accomplish everything. When acting with a certain purpose in His Creation, God acts through His "proper" tools, all of which are His creations in a well-established spiritual hierarchy.

Just as a matter of mathematics or physics is solved by well-established theorems, laws, or rules of calculus, which are the working tools in these exact sciences, God also acts and accomplishes His divine intentions through his "tools"; which are usually beings and entities that fulfill the role of being "emissaries" and "perpetrators" of divine plans. This is a reality that transpires from every action that is observed in Creation because everything always works perfectly and without cracks, even though it often seems to us — in the face of the subjectivism we manifest — that things do not go as they should and as we wish.

In the case of the creation of the human being — as a distinct humanoid race on Earth — things happened the same way. God acted through His "instruments" that were best suited to accomplish this very complex plan, instruments which in the case at hand referred to several very advanced alien civilizations. These were mainly the Sirian civilization, controlled by its Supreme Council; the Arcturian civilization; and the Pleiadian civilization who, in turn, were guided by celestial supernatural entities to accomplish the divine mission that has been entrusted to them.

We are talking about extraterrestrial civilizations that have reached a high degree of spiritual and technological development and who very well understand the divine laws of the cosmos, both physically and subtly. All of their actions were divinely integrated and enjoyed the support and inspiration of the great beings in the superior celestial hierarchies, for as I have seen and subsequently understood, the creation of the human being in this way — and even the formation of the planet Earth and the Solar System over eons of time — were based upon certain intentions and clear and profound ideas with a "great pulse in time" that is occluded and unknown to the majority of beings. Therefore, everything that has happened with regard to the appearance and evolution of man on Earth is not a particular fad, play or experiment of any extraterrestrial civilization but was and is totally the Will of God , expressed by the very high level of consciousness of the main extraterrestrial civilizations that have assumed this mission and then took part in the creation of the human being on our planet.

GENOME REINVENTION

I was excited by what we were hearing and by the incredible accuracy of the presentation in the holographic images that underlined the crucial moments of the formation and development of the human being. Everything that is in the texts of the various spiritual traditions or in historical writings has been presented only allusively or metaphorically as regards the origin of man, but I now saw, in reality, an admirable and very clear summary. It was, however, very condensed and difficult to track due to the complexity of the information, requiring a great deal of concentration and emotional stability in order to allow for a coherent and intelligible unfolding of the images.

It is not so easy to truly "digest" seeing the first human being, the "ancestor" from which you might have been derived from, much later, through an amazingly complex chain of transformations, syntheses and nuances that defined the structure of DNA over time. It is a kind of ancestral connection, a time arc that sensitizes us and makes us aware of the deep resources we have. What I saw there brought the necessary light on our origin as human beings, clarifying many unknowns and question marks.

Although the development of the images was difficult to track, the effort required for this was largely offset by the amazing value of the information.

HYBRIDIZATION OF THE TWO
MAIN BRANCHES OF HUMAN DNA

Adam was the first conscious human being, belonging to the E-N-L branch, which was created on Earth and had most of the characteristics of perfection. From the images I saw, many other beings were born after him with approximately the same DNA structure, highly evolved and following the same "reproductive" pattern. In my estimation, their number was a little over a thousand. Then there was the time of sexual differentiation for these special beings, after the very special energetic event in which the Moon played the most important role. Due to the special star alignment, there were some "cosmic implementations" at that time on the Moon, after which the satellite of our planet acquired a great transformational role on the Earth.

On the other hand, as I said, "Eve" represented that important "element" related to the fact that human beings, after the event on the Moon, could be born sexually; that is, the astral souls that were to follow and incarnate on Earth were able to choose between the two sexes, male and female. There was no longer just one type of being, the androgynous ones, but because of the genetic combinations repeated over several thousand years, it came to that significant leap in which the DNA of the primates became sufficiently improved to allow for the incarnation of evolved souls from the astral plane. As we saw in the holographic images, future genetic combinations involved genetic engineering in which DNA was enriched with other specific DNA fragments taken from other extraterrestrial populations which accepted this kind of "hybridization" of the future human being on Earth. From what I've seen, I estimate that there have been more than twenty types of extraterrestrial DNA that have been involved in genetic engineering operations.

As I have said, what happened in Adam's case with the Sirian DNA was made step by step for other beings after him, using DNA from other extraterrestrial civilizations; thus, beings could be born on Earth that originated from other planets.

I was shown both of the bodies developed inside those special laboratories as well as the synthesis of DNA combinations which involved hybridization. Thus, the DNA of the new human being had a common basis in the DNA of primates on Earth, a significant part of the Sirian DNA, as well as other "fragments" of extraterrestrial DNA from other civilizations.

Contrary to what one might think, we did not see "zombie beings" which usually result from inferior or gross genetic engineering such as is happening on our planet today. Those hybridizations of new DNA that were created, however, were very refined and gave birth to bodies in which the evolved souls could and wished to incarnate.

SYNTHESIS

I stopped watching for a few minutes at this point because the volume of information and data was too large. I felt the need to relax a little and, helped by the man from Apellos, made a general recapitulation of the first stages of evolution of the human being so that things would be as clear as possible to me. I even made a sketch which proved useful later in the sedimentation of knowledge. Therefore, after the appearance of Adam, the population did not recover because the beings that appeared were androgynous. Little in number, they were very harmonious and spiritually evolved and this resulted in a combination of natural development and genetic engineering with the help of the highly advanced technology of extraterrestrial civilizations that monitored the process of human evolution. Of those beings, Adam was the first to assemble the most appropriate combination in the structure of DNA, balancing almost perfectly, an androgynous characteristic.

Only later, when a sufficient number of evolved beings who had lived for quite a long time was a certain point reached where the process of multiplication by sexual reproduction (represented by the symbol N) began. As I said, this was due to a special event in direct connection with the Moon. After the split in the two sexes and after they began to procreate, a slowly evolving species of human beings (from the original *E-N-L* branch) appeared whose DNA was mainly of extraterrestrial origin but also combined with some of the DNA of primates on Earth. Another species of human beings (associated with the symbol *E-N-K*) was somehow "left" to develop on its own, naturally, especially so as to maintain the strong resonance with the specific energy of the Earth.

Thus, from one of the fundamental combinations of frequencies, *E-N-L* (which contributed to the development of *E-N-L* branches such as *E-N-L-A*, *E-N-L-I*; *E-N-L-O*, and *E-N-L-E*), a branch which we can call, for example, *E-N-L-X*, appeared as Adam. After the "birth" of Adam, even more complex sub frames manifested such as *E-N-L-I-L*, *E-N-L-I-L-A*; *E-N-L-A-A*, *E-N-L-A-I*, etc. All of these represented nothing but diversifications of frequencies, starting from the fundamental one (*E-N-L*), some of them having "insertions" from Adam's DNA, and others from the DNA of the androgynous beings that followed him but which came from other extraterrestrial DNA lines other than Adam's Sirian DNA.

On the other hand, the beings associated with the *E-N-K* symbol developed in parallel, but more slowly, because they did not have as much of an "infusion" of extraterrestrial DNA as was the case of the *E-N-L* beings, and most did not even have any at all. However, due to the presence of the developed *E-N-L* beings, even the *E-N-K* branch developed faster as compared to the development which would have occurred only through natural selection.

Of all of these phases in the evolution of the human being on Earth, it seemed to me that the most important one was that of the splitting of the sexes; or, in other words, the one in which the beings from the DNA of Adam began to procreate.

The meaning of that fundamental stage was then deciphered and depicted to me very quickly, with great clarity, by the symbol associated with the modification produced on the Moon: the middle circle (see diagram on page 143) representing the original androgyny, that of the first beings who embodied both the masculine and the feminine aspects.

Then, the two branches on the side represent the phenomenon of the splitting of the sexes which was determined in the physiology of the human being by the modification produced on the Moon which, in turn, led to the diversification of the *E-N-L* beings. These were different, measuring over 2.5 meters, but they had a relatively thin body, harmonious and refined. Their physical beauty was doubled by an extraordinary spiritual value and refinement of consciousness. They had a very sharp intellect and also showed great paranormal powers, thanks to their highly evolved DNA.

Compared to them, *E-N-L* beings — who came from primates whose DNA was mostly "earthly" and secondarily extraterrestrial — were shorter than *E-N-L* beings, did not have the same spiritual and intellectual endowments, but instead were more vital, and their bodies more muscular and more endowed with physical exertion. Over time, however, even though the *E-N-K* beings were thicker and their mental potentials were not as developed as in the case of the *E-N-L* beings, they nevertheless displayed certain abilities but to a much lesser extent than in the case of the *E-N-L* beings.

For a certain period of time, the two main branches (*E-N-L* and *E-N-K*) coexisted and gave birth to the so-called "mythical" civilizations from the immemorial times of our planet, but in reality, they were as true as possible. It is true that, in time, some sub-branches of *E-N-L*, due to the interference with the *E-N-K* beings, "lost" certain capacities and traits, but even so, they were exceptional beings, their genes still being pregnant and powerful. Through these mixtures, their average height decreased significantly. On the other hand, the legends of the "semi-gods" are mostly born of true events, and they refer to human beings with hybrid genes (between *E-N-L* and *E-N-K*) who had special powers and traits, being the fruit of the union of beings from the *E-N-K* branch with evolved extraterrestrial beings or with beings developed from the *E-N-L* branch.

The so-called "semi-gods" had *E-N-K* bodies, but their genes belonged to the *E-N-L* branch due to their combination with extraterrestrial DNA. Through repeated sexual crossings, some very tall beings had been developed, up to 3-4 meters; and, generally speaking, that was the period of the "giants" on Earth, some of their skeletons being discovered relatively recently in several areas of the planet.

Unlike the large mass of *E-N-K* beings, the "semi-gods" had special abilities, being able to interact effectively with alien technology, having access to their ships and having amazing physical capabilities. Families of these extraordinary human beings (either pure *E-N-L* or *E-N-L* hybridized with evolved *E-N-K*, i.e. "gods") continued to remain on Earth even in times closer to the present, but they gradually disappeared as *E-N-K* beings multiplied greatly and populated virtually all areas of the planet.

Even after this personal synthesis, however, I felt confused and a little tired; so, at the advice of the man from Apellos, I took a short pause to relax. I was served with a "made in Apellos" drink which had a light green color and a phosphorescent appearance. Up to that time, I had never drank anything more pleasant and invigorating. And when I say invigorating, I mean an effect appeared a few seconds after the liquid was swallowed. It was amazing because I almost immediately felt a very pleasant force spreading throughout my body, and my mind became very clear and lucid. In my enthusiasm, I felt that I would be able to continue watching for days in a row without getting tired. Smiling, the man from Apellos told me that it is indeed a revitalizing drink which provides great strength and force of concentration, obtained by

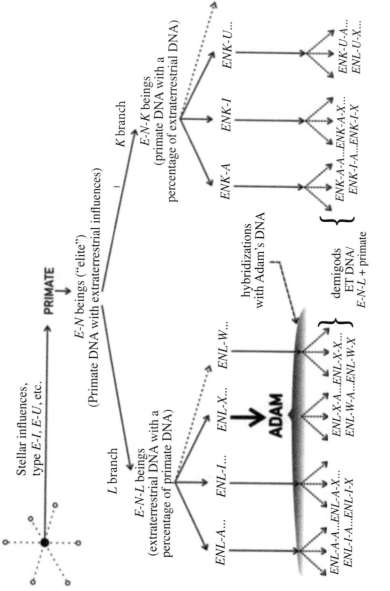

GENERAL SCHEME OF THE FIRST STAGES IN THE EVOLUTION OF THE HUMAN BEING

combining special plants whose nutritional values have been amplified several times by certain processes of technology at the cellular level. As I was already feeling overwhelmed, I asked him to return to the viewing room because I was already eager to continue with the amazing history of the origin of humanity on Earth. The man from Apellos agreed, adding that he would now request a new summary from the holographic projection device to make the concepts even clearer.

"SPECIALIZATION" OF THE GENOME

After this summary presentation of the main branches in the evolution of Mankind, I returned to the beginning periods to specify certain details. As I said, it all started and developed in the northern part of the Persian Gulf, encompassing in particular the areas of Iraq and, to a lesser extent, the areas of Iran and Saudi Arabia.

It was primarily the Sirian civilization which had assumed the role of "parent" in the creation of more beings in our galaxy — among them the future human being on Earth — having collaborated in this respect with several other very advanced civilizations, among which one of the more important ones were the Arcturian. They were considered the "doctors" of the galaxy because of their exceptional knowledge in the field of spiritual development of genes, life and evolution.

I was shown in a few pictures that the Arcturians deal in our galaxy with the state of harmony, well-being and spiritual health of many civilizations, especially those in the early stages of evolution. Knowing the "theme" of the genetic project on Earth, which I will talk about later, they suggested that the strain of human DNA must withstand a very high degree of complexity of genetic combinations and also indicated the frequencies that were needed to make it happen in order to get this extraordinary versatility of the macromolecule of life.

Fleetingly, I was shown some of the "design" assemblies of the DNA molecule and of the human being made up of members of the Arcturian, Sirian, Pleiadian and other two civilizations whose names I did not understand. Arcturians pointed out the main civilizations in the galaxy that they had to connect with so that genetic engineering would produce a strain of Earth's DNA that could be very easily linked to other extraterrestrial DNA strains.

At first, the DNA that was to characterize the new being created on Earth was designed to have twelve "branches." I was shown the whole structure of the initial macromolecule, and its complexity was extensive. But, over time, some of these branches or "branches" of the original DNA were "undone" by the trunks and individualized while others were "hidden," and all this happened due both to specific external actions as well as the conditions that existed on our planet in its various phases of existence.

We can talk about several stages that took place with the passage of time. At first, it was specialization so that DNA would encompass and support as many frequencies as possible. This was the E-N gene derived from primates existing on Earth. Their DNA was mostly modified by stellar influences directed to Earth.

I also saw that, at one point, one of these primates broke off on a branch of their own, their members living in the waters of the oceans, becoming amphibious beings over time and evolving in that environment. They were later guided by certain extraterrestrial civilizations that adapted to the waters of our oceans because that was also their natural environment. I noticed that the amphibian beings derived from the E-N primates were guided in particular by one of the Pleiadian civilizations who lived underwater. This is a little known aspect in the contemporary world.

With regard to the E-N gene from the ground level, through the subtle energetic interventions of the Neiberáu ship and the genetic ones realized by Tenekau and the team of researchers, it gradually developed and split into two main branches: the E-N-L and the E-N-K. They developed over time, and through diversification, each formed sub-branches. Following the "birth" of Adam, the E-N-L branch became a specialized nursery for the "incarnation" of extraterrestrial beings who had accepted the mission to help ground the new race while the E-N-K branch has grown more slowly and mostly naturally, with certain occasional "infusions" of extraterrestrial DNA or through combinations with higher beings from the E-N-L branch.

The specialization continued on certain sub-branches of E-N-L (derivatives X, Y) when, in fact, the necessity of "amplifying" sexuality also emerged to allow the reproduction of the beings born in this form. However, this strengthening or fixation of DNA in the physical plane also meant a kind of "breaking" of the easy connection with the subtle upper planes which represented the connection with the extraterrestrial beings that supported them through the network of devices on the ships that monitored the process of DNA development on Earth. By this, the DNA of the new being was "hardened" a little, and the physical nature created the need for a rapid multiplication.

Seeing those images, I was somewhat puzzled because I thought that, instead of evolving, the human race could take the path of involution due to the attention that was predominantly procreation oriented, but I was immediately corrected by the man from Apellos.

"It is improper to speak of an 'invasion' as you think. Rather, it is a 'specialization' that was needed to achieve a certain goal, that of diversity of DNA structure. If you gather from the street a thousand people, almost everyone has different concerns: one is a computer scientist, another is a carpenter, another a driver and so on. You cannot create a thousand people, all of them alike. That would be meaningless. You have to offer multiple possibilities because this is the creation game itself. If we were to make an analogy, your oil, for example, serves many purposes. At first, it is a uniform mass; then it 'specializes,' depending upon the required direction: one part is refined into several types of fuel of different qualities, another for certain solvents, another for certain paints and dyes, another for plastics and so on. It is therefore a necessity in the physical plane where the initial causal energy 'specializes' later on in several directions."

I was puzzled, however, and that is why I asked the following.

"Okay; but in the concrete case of the evolution of the human being, why was this specialization necessary?"

"It was necessary for many souls in the astral plane to incarnate here, in the physical plane. Over the course of tens and even hundreds of thousands of years, these 'specializations' or 'branches' have become increasingly clear. Now you have the mongoloid race, the black race, the red race, the white race, the yellow race and there are even some subdivisions that are not yet well understood by your scientists. Also, the process of creating several civilizations is first of all a natural process, and then an artificial one. It was a galactic necessity, and the extraterrestrial civilizations involved did not support the decay of the being but rather its 'specialization.'"

"Then," I said, "why wasn't it about 'specialization' right from the start?"

As the man from Apellos turned his eyes to the screen, I felt him mentally interacting with the technology at the subtle level. Immediately, holographic images appeared which showed, in a kind of synthetic collage, the first phase of the creation of the new being; that is, the E-N stage. Then followed the E-N-L and E-N-K branches which we could distinguish by their physical characteristics. In several hundreds of thousands of years, due to the multiple combinations with the E-N-K branch, which was following its own evolutionary path at a much slower pace, the E-N-L branch has, to some extent, "fallen."

In the first stage (symbolized by E-N-L and E-N-L-X), we saw only Sirian extraterrestrial beings involved. Then, in a very clever and ingenious way, I was shown that, after a certain time since Adam's appearance, there was a kind of balance between the number of beings in this branch (E-N-L) and the number of souls in the astral plane who were capable of incarnation into those physical bodies due to their having become sufficiently evolved to receive and sustain the evolved consciousness of souls from advanced extraterrestrial civilizations.

I was then shown the need to increase the number of beings enshrined in the physical plane through "specialization." That was the time when the Sirians proposed to other advanced civilizations to participate in that grand project and begin to "specialize" or to individualize a branch from the main strand of the DNA already formed; that is, to add their frequencies to those inherent in the structure of the DNA molecule of the human being. This is how E-N-L-X sub-frames started to appear, such as E-N-L X-Y and so on. At the same time, as I said, the E-N-K branch evolved at a natural rate and without "massive infusions" of extraterrestrial DNA.

Here, the review stopped. I thanked the man from Apellos, and at his invitation, I resumed the thread of the gradual evolution on the branches of which I was particularly interested. I did not succeed the first time, but I was helped; and then the images were "aligned" approximately to the time period I was investigating.

DIFFERENT DIRECTIONS OF EVOLUTION

In time, through the development of DNA, the E-N-L branch, representing different hybridizations of primates with a significant proportion of extraterrestrial DNA, allowed the incarnation of extraterrestrial beings while the E-N-K branch had a slower evolution as it was mostly done by the auric influence of E-N-L beings and of ships that have followed one another in various orbits around the Earth. In other words, the fact that the E-N-K beings lived around evolved E-N-L beings allowed a certain beneficial influence on their part and, in time, even on the DNA level. However, the genetic information of the E-N-K physical body was not sufficiently evolved to allow the embodiment of a more refined consciousness, such as that of the souls of extraterrestrial beings who supported the E-N-L branch.

The L branch (E-N-L), however, had developed the capacity to receive such souls. This was shown to me in the form of intense and fast rays of light which descended from the large spherical ship, entering the body of an E-N-L female. It was a short time in which the evolution of E-N-L beings reached a high level.

Surprised even more, I asked the man from Apellos, who was watching me carefully, why the K branch did not also benefit from the spirits of evolved extraterrestrial beings. He replied immediately.

"Because their bodies, due to the specific structure of the DNA, were characterized by a coarser energy and those extraterrestrial spirits could not be incarnated in them. You cannot put a barrel through a kitchen pipe, no matter how hard you try. Each object or being in the Universe matches only some objects or beings which are similar but not all. That law applied in that case, too.

"And the differences arose from this cause?" I insisted.

"Obviously. Basically, the K branch had a slower evolution while the L branch evolved rapidly due to the high vibrational level of the consciousness of the spirits that were incarnating in their bodies. If the evolution of the *E-N-L* branch took place in several tens of thousands of years, the evolution of the *E-N-K* branch took hundreds of thousands of years.

"Okay. Then what is the place of homo sapiens? How did he get there? It does not seem to come from the *E-N-L* branch."

"The chain of genetic changes and the evolution of new beings on Earth has been complicated, as you can see, but there is a guiding thread nonetheless. At first, genetically manipulating about 20% of the DNA of primates with 80% of Sirian DNA has created several successive generations of highly evolved beings. Among them was the one you call "Adam," the most "finished" variant of DNA possible on Earth, a truly exceptional being, from which the future *E-N-L* sub frames developed. Starting from this, for a long time, the percentage of new beings increased by reason of genetic manipulations because this is what the Sirians wanted. This planet, however, has on its surface beings with mostly local affinities, not just extraterrestrial. They wanted to obtain a being that had the basic structure of the great primates on Earth but in a highly evolved form. On the other hand, the *E-N-K* beings, who were closer to the primates and more adapted to life on this planet, evolved much slower. They were smaller in height than the *E-N-L* beings but had stronger muscles and a more vital structure. The civilization we now call homo sapiens is a bridge between most of the *E-N-K* branch and the remaining parts of the *E-N-L* branch or hybridizations between them. At present, most of human civilization is of type *E-N-K*. This is because *E-N-L* beings have withdrawn from the physical plane. You will be able to see this later, and you will understand why it was so. In recent years, however, the structure of the *E-N-L* typology has begun to grow dramatically due to a galactic event that is beginning to feel more and more powerful on Earth."

Hearing this information, I became more attentive, but before I could ask a question, the man from Apellos read my intention and spoke.

"The mind will explain that to you later."

I reflected for a few moments on this news. I understood that, at least now, I could not find out any more, so I set out to emphasize knowledge about the subtle differences between *E-N-K* and *E-N-L*.

NUANCED DETAILS ABOUT THE EVOLUTION OF THE BRANCHES E-N-L AND E-N-K

I was especially concerned about the very high level of evolution that *E-N-L* beings had during that period, of which not even the dust of memory remained. I wanted to have a global view of their evolutionary transformation and I focused my attention to see such a summary on the screen. I had discovered that this was a very good method of dealing with the many subtleties and variations that have existed in the process of human evolution over the last 400,000 years.

Everything was an extremely advanced genetic engineering project, basically a project to train another race. At first, the evolved extraterrestrial souls could incarnate in some of the E-N-L bodies that were sufficiently prepared for it. It was an impulse given to the evolution of the new race in order for it to reach an ideal stage of development from which the process of incarnation was stabilized for highly evolved beings. The bodies of the E-N-L (branch L) beings were already evolved and had practically no characteristics of those specific to primates, even though they were born from them.

As I said, the E-N-L beings were tall, very balanced and harmonious in body; their hair was long, silky, often silvery-white, and their eyes were large and almond-shaped. In several tens of thousands of years, their bodies became very good receptacles for the evolved and even highly evolved extraterrestrial beings who wanted to incarnate during that period on Earth to help the process of creating the new race of human beings.

On the other hand, the E-N-K beings (branch K) had not evolved so much; but instead, they could reproduce without any problem. This explains, in a way, why some of the beings on Earth benefited from extraordinary technology and were highly evolved, engaging in interplanetary and interstellar travel while, in other areas of the planet, other human beings still carved stone and hunted, being dressed in the skins of animals. It was not until after the Atlantean period and its fall that humanity became somehow more "uniform" and the E-N-K branch was able to rise higher; but I will talk about this when I present some elements related to the existence of Atlantis and its decline.

TENEKAU's "INHERITANCE"

An interesting fact that caught my attention was that, after projecting Tenekau's consciousness into that cloned being I mentioned, which was also an evolved version that preceded Adam's appearance a few thousand years ago, I did not see Tenekau's physical body. Instead, I noticed that his specific frequency, rendered by the symbols shown, was found in many other beings that followed up until the time of Adam's appearance.

I was amazed at this, and then the man from Apellos told me that, after completing his mission on Earth – which was coordinating the extremely complex process of transforming the DNA of the primates – Tenekau had evolved as a being in the etheric plane without it being necessary for him to have a physical body. Thus, in the DNA of Adam and the beings after him, I could see the symbols T and E-N but also the hexagonal symbol.

Thus, something of Tenekau's genes had been further transmitted, meaning that he had left a "genetic inheritance" but not through physical coupling, but rather auric, his spiritual influence being determined in primates over time. Later, the Sirian civilization from the Orion Constellation, of which Tenekau was also a part, made many efforts to make that subtle impulse permanent.

I was shown that, after Tenekau initiated the "epic of the human being" and after he had passed on to a higher existential level in the etheric plane, three more extraterrestrial beings were successively designated by the Sirian sages, originally from the Sirius A system, to continue the project of accelerated transformation of human beings on Earth. From the images I saw, these beings covered a period of about 12,000-13,000 years after Tenekau as their structure allowed them to have an extremely long life. Thereafter, the E-N-L specific DNA was found to be strong enough to branch out and combine without the danger of losing its initial baseline information.

The first to take on the task of continuing the project was Karaan, a Sirian man who, like Tenekau, came from the constellation of Orion's Belt. As far as I could tell, he was part of the high-level military leadership of his civilization and had close links with two of the Pleiadian cities with which he collaborated intensely on Earth at that time.

According to him, the wise people of the Sirian civilization from the Sirius A system decided that the project would be led by a representative of this civilization who was named Nasamar. He was a very gentle and wise man, specializing in scientific research, but he was not part of the military rank. I felt a strong sympathy and spontaneous attraction towards him due to the exemplary way in which he knew how to combine the continuation of studies and the application of genetic engineering in the case of human DNA with the aspects of long-term organization and design of the activities.

Unfortunately, Nasamar led the project only for a short time because a tense situation in a certain sector of the galaxy — close enough to Earth which involved, it seems, a large armed conflict — necessitated his replacement with another leader whose name was Jama-al. As we have seen in the images presented, he had a very high degree in the military hierarchy, being recognized and respected for his talents as a strategist and for his diplomatic knowledge. He was a tough man, coming from a civilization derived from that of the Sirians, but I could not figure out either the star system or constellation that he came from.

Jama-al also proved to be a very practical being because, from the pictures I saw, I realized that he was correctly fulfilling the mission entrusted to him on the ship near Earth: to carry on the project of transforming human DNA; but in parallel to this, he used certain resources of the planet to build a large number of small and medium-sized warships.

The images showed me how he created small urban centers throughout North and East Africa. These were like small semi-circle towns where human DNA was extracted from beings belonging to the E-N-L branches with genetic engineering being done on those samples.

An interesting aspect that I noticed was that the three project leaders who followed Tenekau did not know why the Sirian Council of Wise People wanted human evolution on Earth. However, as it was known that the Sirians were not wrong and that they were permanently connected with the celestial governing entities of our galaxy, the three great leaders accepted the mission to carry on the work started by Tenekau, realizing that it is was a very important plan at the cosmic level. They accepted the mission that was first given to them as a spiritual mission.

As I said, Jama-al had not only undertaken the continuation of the project of evolving human beings but also the development of a very efficient battleship construction industry. He extracted from the soil of our planet many types of ores, focusing on gold and titanium, but especially quartz crystals which were later processed and integrated into the construction of those ships.

Jama-al was also the commander of the cosmic ship which was then in an orbit near the Earth. He was also a military leader of the highest order, something that today could be associated with an admiral or the marshal of an army. From the summary provided in the images, I saw what at one time represented a simple diagram depicting our Sun, the star Sirius A and the direction in which the constructed ships had left. This was oriented about 30° to the right of the line joining the two stars, after which they probably passed through a space-time vortex because their direction was tilted abruptly by about 16° towards Sirius A, and then again at 90° towards the final target. Depending upon the astronomical distances used as a standard in those representations, I estimated the area of the conflict as being about 6000 light-years away from Earth.

THE COMPLEXITY OF HUMAN DNA

The "game" of genes and their crossing and of combining different types of DNA and genetic manipulations within the limits allowed by the Laws of Nature has been a relatively long and very complex process. As I could see, stabilizing a change in DNA has been done for a long time, by repetition. On Earth, some of the genes were no longer sustainable; and then, being rejected, they were "distributed" on other planets that could support them. Other genes continued to develop naturally, and others were combined in various ways.

Over 300,000 years, the active and attentive process of the evolution of the genes of the new human being has made its DNA very complex. From what was presented to me, I understood that the simpler the structure and more uniform DNA is, the faster it is subject to degeneration because it lacks the vital energy needed for complex combinations.

The evolution that led to the current complexity of the DNA of the human being, however, was not a linear process, but rather a discontinuous one. The genetic differences from one area of the Earth to the other were very large. We have seen, for example, areas of modern-day Africa where primitive people lived, carving spearheads, but also populations with amazing technology, levitating ships and buildings of great refinement, living on a large portion of land from the Pacific Ocean in the southern hemisphere. There were also, however, "transition" areas where people had reached a certain level of well-being and high living standards.

Based upon a non-intervention treaty that was established more than 300,000 years ago, however, these different areas of the Earth did not support trade nor other exchange because they constituted experimental fields for each extraterrestrial civilization which were interested in the project of the new human race. It seems that the decisions of territorial independence and unilateral action in the respective territories were very strictly respected as no one was allowed to intervene in the "garden" of the other. This lack of connection between populations in different areas of the Earth has even led to a degree of isolation due to the need for them to develop and evolve in a "specialized" manner in the direction of the genetic influence experienced by the respective extraterrestrial civilization to which that territory or area of the planet had been assigned.

As I said, it should not be understood here that the term *experiment* had anything to do with slavery or oppression of the population. I didn't see anything like that. The terms *experiment*, *laboratory* or *nursery* used here are to designate a reality that was and which I have seen sequentially in pictures, about how the human race appeared and evolved.

It is true, however, that over time, some of the extraterrestrial civilizations developed a warrior nature and in one way or another tried to oppress the populations of the Earth or at least some of them. From what I could see, only some races were influenced by the race of evil reptilians and manifested such behavior; and there were four other inferior civilizations who were welcomed by them, but even those manifestations happened on relatively narrow territories and with numerically reduced populations such as, for example, in Africa and in an area of modern-day Oceania where at that time there was a larger continental area, undivided and without so many islands.

Even within the same genetic branch (*E-N-L* or *E-N-K*), there have been variations over time in the evolutionary process. Evolution was not linear, but at different times, it recorded ups and downs, depending upon the geographical and climatic context, the contribution of extraterrestrial civilizations, or even the choices made by the members of these branches of evolution of human DNA.

THE EVOLUTIONARY JUMP OF THE E-N-L BEINGS

The civilizations of E-N-L followed one another quite quickly, only rarely being more than 15,000 years old. As we have seen, the ones that lasted the longest were the Mu civilization (about 40,000 years) and the Hyperborean civilization (about 35,000 years), during which there was an important spiritual leap for the E-N-K beings through the cross-breeding. The civilization of Atlantis (about 25,000 years) had developed quite a bit, and it followed a whole series of other civilizations of the E-N-L beings that preceded it.

Finally, each gene "exhausts" its time of active manifestation in a plane (of existence) because it has the natural tendency to evolve but not horizontally as before, not by extension and variation, but especially vertically. That is, it registers an important qualitative leap, passing into a higher dimension of Creation. Generally speaking, this happens when the gene in question has reached a high level of maturity and complexity which allows it to assimilate the high energy frequencies from a dimension higher than the physical plane such as, for example, that of the etheric plane.

From the point of view of Mankind, this was the case for the E-N-L beings who, due to the ease with which they could combine their DNA with other types of DNA, have been refined enough over time so that they get very close to the threshold of "withdrawal" from the physical plane so as to remain only in the etheric plane.

We are not talking about an "extinction" of the species or of the DNA in question because the resource base is large due to its complexity and the amazing possibilities that have been developed over time. We are talking, however, about a special refinement at the genome level so that the general frequency of vibration of most E-N-L beings resonated more with the general frequency of vibration of the etheric plane which caused these human beings to gradually disappear from the physical plane, choosing to remain in the subtle etheric plane. In fact, the highly evolved extraterrestrial beings who incarnated in E-N-L physical bodies began to remain in the etheric plane and even above it, while most E-N-K beings remained on the physical plane, on our planet. It was like a "separation" which separated the two adjacent planes (the physical plane and the etheric plane), but the dramatic nature of these events reached the highest levels after the fall of Atlantis.

Naturally, the withdrawal of the E-N-L branch — a sign of which was the withdrawal of Shambhala into the etheric plane about 27,500 years ago — did not occur suddenly but rather gradually over a relatively long period of thousands of years. Also, it did not mean that all E-N-L beings on Earth disappeared because small families of such beings, who had not yet reached the appropriate level to move to the etheric plane, continued to remain in the physical plane, serving as virtual "intermediaries" who transmitted high occult teachings to the E-N-K beings who had already formed the majority of humanity. Of these beings, I noticed that they were especially the pharaohs, the high priests or the sages around whom small groups of E-N-K beings had formed, slightly more evolved than the others, thus forming "schools" or just currents of spiritual revival.

I was interested in that occulted area of transformation of the human being because I found it very complex and interesting with regard to the destiny of humanity, a destiny which we now indirectly share. I was shown that the break-up of Atlantis was the final point of departure from the stage of evolution in the physical plane of the E-N-L gene and its multiple derivatives because it had reached the end of its period of existence. In about 350,000 years, the E-N-L branch had exhausted about as many variants or sub-frames as possible. After the sinking of Atlantis, what remained of the L branch (E-N-L beings) evolved in different directions on Earth, some groups becoming more developed than others. They created certain bases, being connected to the extraterrestrial beings that evolved from the initial group.

Communication, however, was no longer direct because the frequency of the physical plane of the Earth had greatly decreased and there was no longer "compatibility" between it and the frequencies of the etheric plane. As a result, the E-N-L beings that had already retreated into the etheric plane no longer actually lived on the surface of the Earth, but they "descended" from time to time from the etheric to the physical plane to maintain the connection with the few E-N-L beings that were still in the physical plane. As I said, every gene has certain "resources" that, when consumed, cause that gene to "age" or, on the contrary, to be restored, refreshed, and revitalized, but always in the direction of evolution. This is especially true at the level of the physical plane. In one sense, the withdrawal of a gene from the evolutionary scene occurs, analogously speaking, much like the withdrawal of a banknote from the financial market. In its place remain the newer notes which are not so worn. This very intelligent summary was presented to me in the images on the holographic screen, clarifying even certain nuanced aspects of the evolution of the human being and its branches, such as transitions from one stage to another in the transformation of DNA, influences of different natures, or even changes to another condition of existence, as was the case with the E-N-L branch.

THE SUPREME BRANCH OF E-N-K

The problem with the resorption of the E-N-L branch from the perspective of terrestrial evolution was that everything that those beings had achieved over time had to be taken up, in summary, by the E-N-K branch which was, in turn, diversified in several directions. In this "dowry transfer" of knowledge was also included spiritual knowledge which had reached a high degree of refinement in the *E-N-L* beings. That is why some *E-N-L* beings that remained in the physical plane, as well as some of the more evolved *E-N-K* beings, were supported by direct "counseling" from the extraterrestrial beings who were part of certain advanced civilizations involved in the process of creation and the evolution of the human being. It was important that at least some of that invaluable knowledge and experience — accumulated by *E-N-L* beings in the context of living within many civilizations that appeared and then died out — would be saved for future generations. For a time, the "assistance" of extraterrestrial beings was realized directly in the sense that they were even physically among humans: explaining, detailing and showing what needed to be understood and memorized. Those teachings, however, were not given to anyone but to the few *E-N-L* beings that remained on Earth or to the more evolved *E-N-K* beings. In most cases, they were or became leaders, then transmitting to the masses only a small part of the knowledge they directly gained from the extraterrestrial beings they were connected with. The motivation was obvious: most *E-N-K* beings did not have a high enough level of consciousness to understand those teachings correctly. Thus, with the passage of time, several elitist social categories have been differentiated: great leaders (such as pharaohs, kings or emperors); priests (who had an important initiatory role, transmitting the knowledge of the "secret sciences" further, i.e. to those who were trained); and hermits, prophets or saints (which were a special category and especially appreciated by advanced extraterrestrial beings). In fact, at that time period, about 25,000 B.C., the *E-N-K* branch had the first really important "start" in the evolutionary plan, thus taking over a certain part of the "inheritance" of the *E-N-L* beings.

The same thing happened in the case of the cataclysm that led to the sinking of Atlantis. Some of the Atlantean scholars knew what was to come. That is, they knew that the great continent would be sunk, so they wanted vestiges, knowledge and much of their culture and science to remain for posterity. That was first and foremost a decision made on their part, an act of will that was completely altruistic, for the benefit of the human race in the future. To achieve this, they wanted to extend their reach to the area of Central America, especially to what is called Mexico and Guatemala today, then to Egypt in northern Africa, to the north of Europe in the area of Iceland and even further to the east of that continent. The "seeds" of their knowledge had to be spread to many places on Earth to be sure that the dowry would not be lost forever. For a certain period of time, all three main types of beings lived together in such centers of spirituality: *E-N-L* beings, more evolved *E-N-K* beings, and certain extraterrestrial beings, but they separated afterward and each race followed its own path of evolution.

In every place on Earth where such centers, occult schools of esoteric sciences and highly philosophical systems of thought began to be built, the emphasis was on preserving the ancient knowledge of *E-N-L* beings and further developing such teachings. Simultaneously with these initiatives, the great "galactic relays" that are the pyramids began to be built, and it was decided that they would also support a certain line of spiritual development in addition to their consecrated role of serving as "galactic communicators". Thus, when Atlantis sank, there were already many such powerful spiritual centers on the planet with spiritually evolved beings, but there was also a very large number of less evolved *E-N-K* beings.

I will present more broadly and in chronological order some of the main moments of the evolution of Mankind as they were presented to me in the holographic images, pointing to their main characteristics but also to the errors of interpretation that have been transmitted up to now or even the intentional concealment of important events that have served as true "marking stones" throughout human history.

CHAPTER EIGHT

SHAMBHALA

The so-called "mythical realm of Shambhala" is actually an obvious reality and quite close to us, denied only by those who have not had access to the truth about it or who have no spiritual affinities to understand this important topic. In a way, it can be said that Shambhala even existed on Earth, at least up to its great "resorption" from the surface, about 27,500 years ago. I presented some elements about this sacred land in the "center of the Earth" in the previous volume of the *Transylvanian Series* where I described the magnificent constructions that I have seen from a distance.*

A NECESSARY SPECIFICATION

Many people probably ask themselves, "Okay, but if Shambhala is a reality, then where is it actually? Is there a specific place for this land? Is it really at the center of the Earth?"

We must first understand that these are specific questions for something that exists in the three-dimensional physical plane, characterized by certain laws of space and time, but they do not make sense when referring to a reality from the etheric plane which is characterized by four dimensions (three spatial and one temporal). Theoretically, in order to have access from the physical plane to something in the etheric plane, there is no specific space. Something in the etheric plane — the realm of Shambhala in this case — can be accessed from anywhere in the physical plane, but for this it is necessary to raise the frequency of vibration in the consciousness of the observer.

Shambhala can be found in the "center of the Earth" because spirituality is much more sustained in that area, and it does not appear only in isolated centers or places on the surface of the planet. It would be a mistake, however, to understand that Shambhala actually existed concretely "in the middle of the Earth" because then the question might arise: If it is in the center of the planet, then how is it possible to reflect on the surface, in this, the world we live in?

Things must therefore be understood correctly. The world of Shambhala represents a frequency of manifestation of consciousness and energy that is very high and has to do with Earth, with the existence of life here; but it cannot be said that it is above or below the surface of the planet because this would only be a limited approach to the situation. Being manifested in the etheric plane, it is not obligatory for it to be in or out of something in the physical plane. People who do not have adequate esoteric knowledge cannot understand

---

* *Inside the Earth - Second Tunnel*, 2019, Chapter 7.

these subtle realities and will tend to apply the laws of classical physics that they know to solve or investigate realities from higher subtle planes, but this is not possible. The only way to solve such "mysteries" is to raise the vibrational frequency of the individual; that is, the spiritual evolution of the being and implicitly transforming it to a higher level of consciousness.

There were times, however, when the Shambhala realm was easily accessible, even from the surface of the planet. One could easily move from the physical plane to the etheric plane, and some of the most well-known of such "passages" were in the mountain areas. Tens of thousands of years ago, this was a common thing. E-N-L beings had fast access to Shambhala thanks to their high level of consciousness, and even some of the E-N-K beings could reach this realm because there were quite a few points of confluence between the physical and the etheric plane on the surface of the soil or on water.

THE FORMATION OF SHAMBHALA

An image summary of Shambhala's history on the holographic screen showed me that it was beginning to form at the time a spiritual brotherhood was born. As I saw in the pictures on the holographic screen, rudiments of its formation appeared during the period 100,000-120,000 B.C. but without a clear orientation. It was about the existence of territories in which only E-N-L beings with a high degree of spiritual realization lived. I realized that only those highly evolved beings could live in those areas because they lived easily in both the physical and the etheric planes; that is, both in the 3-D and in the 4-D plane. Because of them, those etheric realms were "paired" with the physical plane, and E-N-L beings could move from one plane to another at any time which was allowed to other evolved types of beings, such as extraterrestrial ones, but not to the E-N-K beings. The level of evolution for most of the E-N-K beings was primitive, and they preferred the veneration of the "gods" who, in the vast majority, were in fact their own, belonging to the developed E-N-L line. As far as I was aware, Shambhala was formed by a kind of "spiritual selection" between the beings who could pass into those areas surrounded by etheric dimensions, characterized by high vibrational frequencies, and the beings who did not have access to there by reason of their insufficiently developed level of consciousness. In other words, some people could penetrate and remain in those etheric "areas" while others could not.

For a long time in these areas, the physical and etheric planes "coexisted" because the general frequencies of the two planes were quite close. On the other hand, the connection between the physical and the etheric planes was also possible thanks to the existence of multiple hybridizations between the E-N-L and E-N-K branches, each on different stages of spirituality which gave birth to the so-called "demigods". Those human beings successfully managed

166

to make the transition from one plane to another and thus could transmit information to and from the area of the etheric plane to the *E-N-K*.

Higher etheric frequencies were the germs of formation of what would later become the "realm of Shambhala". In those areas, a sacred spiritual side of the Earth developed because the *E-N-L* beings who lived there had a high degree of understanding of spirituality in its deepest aspects. After several tens of thousands of years, due to the repeated subtle journeys, certain strong subtle connections were created between the various territories inhabited by the *E-N-L* beings, those being etheric zones elevated in vibrational frequency. These have amplified their subtle connections with the areas inside the Earth through those "bridges of subtle energy connections" that we have already talked about.

Thus, connections were made with all areas of spiritual refinement on the surface of the Earth and within it. In this way, Shambhala was born precisely by the unanimous decision of the *E-N-L* beings living in such elevated realms in order to maintain an identity separate from the territories inhabited by the *E-N-K*.

Apparently, Shambhala is now known as a big city, but in reality, it represents a multitude of areas in the etheric plane which are characterized by a high spirituality. As I said, it initially consisted of several "areas" of the physical plane in which the etheric plane could also develop. When the conditions on the surface of the planet — both physical and spiritual in nature — worsened, the union of those ethereal zones into a harmonious bonding led to the "withdrawal" of Shambhala into the etheric plane which actually meant the dramatic diminution of the connections with the physical plane, as I will show below.

THE SPIRITUAL MISSION OF SHAMBHALA

The first intentions of Shambhala for the settlement of a planetary spiritual mission came only after the Great War of the Tarshians, so after 50,000 B.C. and the especially terrible conflict that I might as well call "The war for the conquest of Shambhala," that became the main cause of that sacred realm.* Of course, at that time there was not yet a name to designate it, such as "Shambhala" or another variation; at least I did not notice such in the images. The wise *E-N-L* beings who lived in those territories and had a "double" in the higher etheric dimension understood that life on our planet needed support because the conflicting forces were beginning to be very strong. The inhabitants of Shambhala began to act in this respect; and although the struggles in the physical plane for the next thousands of years did not cease, they were no longer as intense and destructive.

* See Chapter 9 of this book.

Later, from what I saw, the time period between 30,000 B.C. and 26,000 B.C. was marked by long and painful wars, but unlike the terrible confrontations between the extraterrestrial civilizations on the Earth, about 100,000 years ago, the wars of the mentioned period were fought only between human beings, especially between human being hybrids that came from the union of the *E-N-L* and *E-N-K* beings, but also those coming only from the *E-N-K* branch. They were supported, however, by certain extraterrestrial civilizations, especially after the "division of the regions of influence" at the Great Planetary Council of 27,000 B.C. The participation of the *E-N-L* beings in those wars was quite weak, numbering less and less. The conflicts were bloody and took place especially in the area we know today as Europe, but I did not focus on this aspect, merely "wandering" through those times. The atmosphere was tense, and I felt the clash of the war situation, seeing images of people fleeing and even specific sounds of combat weapons.

As a result of that tense situation and the obvious decline of spirituality throughout the planet — due to aggressive population growth of *E-N-K* beings and the gradual diminution of the number of *E-N-L* beings — it was decided at the Great Planetary Council around 27,000 B.C. that the areas where Shambhala existed would be delimited and separated from the rest of the zones and frequencies on the planet so that most spiritual teachings and knowledge on Earth would be concentrated in Shambhala.

Shambhala's "withdrawal" took place in two stages. In the beginning — after the decision taken by the Great Planetary Council — there was more of a "demarcation" of the rest of the population which was mostly *E-N-K*. Accordingly, access would be even more restricted in this realm. Later, in the final stage, Shambhala completely "resorbed" into the subtle etheric plane. This happened, as far as I was aware, in approximately 25,500 B.C.

With that resurrection in the subtle plane — which was the result of the decision taken by the Great Planetary Council — Shambhala was formed as a spiritual center for the support and evolution of humanity on Earth. Until then, Shambhala did not exist separately, but we can only say that there were "areas of profound spiritual manifestation in the etheric plane" which intersected with the physical plane of the Earth. Most of the beings now populating Shambhala are actually beings from the former advanced civilizations, mostly belonging to the *E-N-L* branch. As those beings were genuinely spiritually oriented, they were recognized as such by the rest of the populations on the planet; and Shambhala therefore became the protector and spiritual supporter of the Earth.

RESIDENTS OF SHAMBHALA

Even though it represented a reference pole of spirituality and the support it could offer to Mankind, Shambhala was no longer so easily accessible by human beings, not even to the hybridized *E-N-L* and *E-N-K* beings, all of which correlated with the diminishing vibrational frequency of the consciousness human beings on a global level. Generally speaking, Shambhala is revealed only when an area of the Earth or a being becomes sufficiently spiritualized so as to resonate with the high frequency of vibration of this sacred realm.

Shambhala's exit from the physical plane — where the aid it provided could be much more effective — was to be followed by another "decisive blow", breaking the last pillar of spirituality and the advanced technological level from the surface of the planet; and by that, I mean the destruction of Atlantis. The sinking of Atlantis also meant the "sinking" of our planet into a deep spiritual darkness which has been perpetuated thousands of years since.

Gradually, however, and at the same time driven and supported by Shambhala, new centers of spirituality began to appear on Earth which developed in different regions of the globe. The problem was that the difference between the frequency of the physical plane of our planet and the frequency of the etheric plane had become far too large to easily allow for — as was the case long ago — the "experiential exchanges" between the two planes. As I said, a human being from the physical plane can only have access to the realm of Shambhala when they reach or at least approach its vibrational frequency level.

As for the inhabitants of Shambhala, they are practically an "extension" of the *E-N-L* gene, but among these beings, there are some that continue their evolution on the hybridized *E-N-L* and *E-N-K* branches, as well as those *E-N-K* beings that have evolved sufficiently from the spiritual point of view. I have also seen that the realm of Shambhala is open to extraterrestrial beings who have reached a high degree of spiritual evolution; and moreover, collaboration with them is closely linked to the future destiny of Mankind.

SUMMARY

As usual, and as I especially wanted to go deeper into the subject, I made a summary on the holographic screen at this point which helped me to digest the information better. I also knew that it was often possible to get some extra details. The images on the screen were reconfigured and focused on the decision to form a spiritual center of the planet. The decision was made after 50,000 B.C. by Hyperborean *E-N-L* beings who decided to further support the *E-N-K* gene because human civilization, being formed in the majority by this category of beings, needed and still needs great help.

Around 30,000 B.C., Hyperboreans, who have been in contact with other ethereal focal zones on Earth inhabited by *E-N-L* beings, noticed that the etheric plane no longer had "adherence" to the physical plane. They then proposed that the "areas" of the etheric plane in the vicinity of the Earth which were deeply spiritualized to unite in order to form a strong realm, a spiritual center for the support of humanity, consisting mainly of *E-N-L* beings.

In the etheric plane, the union of the different etheric zones which "intersected" with the physical plane on the surface of the planet was made quite easy by manifesting a common will of those *E-N-L* beings. This was possible because everything that existed in the those "areas" in the etheric plane, being "built" on the same spiritual rules, were attracted and united in accordance with the law of universal affinity. This resulted in an etheric unity that was common to all the etheric areas of the Earth that displayed a high spirituality. Thus, a spiritual center of the planet was established which came into being by uniting the respective "zones". Initially, the new realm was called Anagon, and this happened about 25,500 B.C., after the total withdrawal into the etheric plane. Later, probably due to the influence of the different cultures belonging to the subsequent civilizations, as well as due to the imprint of time, this center became known as Shambhala.

CHAPTER NINE

THE GREAT TARS WAR

The period of about 100,000 years ago was very "black" for humanity because it involved a devastating conflict between many of the alien civilizations that existed on Earth at that time. I would even say that it was the most terrible confrontation I have ever seen in relation to the Earth, but it was entirely from extraterrestrial sources. All the belligerent parties were extraterrestrial and disputed their territories or power of influence. It was a very difficult period and a period of "rupture" because many civilizations then separated from the Galactic Alliance to which they had joined.

THE DRAMATIC INFLUENCE OF MALEFIC REPTILES

Due to the very advanced technologies and the nature of the weaponry used, life on the surface of the planet had much to suffer, and in some areas, which are now under water, it was completely eradicated. I saw terrible images of this conflict which took place both in the Earth's atmosphere and outside of it, in cosmic space. I was struck by the fact that the intensity of the fighting was so high that a significant part of the sky of the planet, as seen from the ground, was almost red.

The confrontations were of unheard of harshness. Huge explosions left enormous debris on the surface of the Earth. I also saw how, afterwards , they "extracted" those residues by "crushing" and then absorbing them into giant ships, like containers. At those times, in my mind, I called them "scavenger ships" but they were probably huge transport ships. Strangely enough, that terrible conflict was not an atomic one. I saw only a few detonations reminiscent of nuclear explosions, but they were of less intensity than other deflagrations that took place at that time.

The main source of misunderstandings was complex in nature. It involved a race of evil beings in our galaxy with reptilian features. In the economy of the universe, the reptilians seem to have a special destiny because they appear at key points in the evolution of races or civilizations, even if their actions are unconscious in this aspect but directed only for selfish, controlling and oppressive purposes.

From the presentation I saw, reptilian beings live long lives; and in order to develop, they seek to find a suitable "land" from which to "feed", that is to say, the evil reptilians seek to conquer planets and civilizations in order to exploit them and achieve their goals but do so in a manner that they do not have to worry too much about them. Being quite technologically advanced, they aim to infiltrate those star regions and systems of the galaxy where there are already advanced civilizations but not as much as their own. Primitive civilizations or those at the dawn of technological progress do not interest them because they target those who already have a certain potential but can be conquered relatively easily but still have some use afterwards, depending upon their level of development.

From this point of view, it can be said that the reptilians are pragmatic. If the respective civilization is primitive or at a too weak level of development, this implies or requires a consistent effort on their part to "pasture" them, and they do not want to work so hard. On the other hand, if they conquer too much and too quickly, that outweighs the possibilities of occupation and control. That is why the evil reptilians show amazing patience, being specialized in infiltration through subversive actions. They corrupt and conquer an advanced civilization, but not necessarily through arbitrary destruction, looting and then leaving that planet, but rather and especially through undermining, intrigue, and corruption.

In other words, they are not brutal predators in most cases, but they work at more refined levels, through hybridization and by introducing genes with low vibrational frequencies. They know that if they can corrupt enough DNA in a race, it will eventually retain their specific trace whereby they will then always have a point of support and action in that civilization. The greater this specific imprint is imprinted on the DNA of a race, the better for the reptilians because they will then be able to influence it more easily when it comes to decisions and actions.

CORRUPTIONS BY HYBRIDIZATION

Their plans are therefore, less violent, immediate or with large scale cosmic struggles. A more long-term strategy is employed by infusing the DNA of some races with their own DNA. In time, they know that this action will corrupt our race, at least to some extent, and such weaknesses may be used later for their own purposes.

In this way, the evil reptilians end up corrupting even advanced civilizations in an indirect way. As I said, they always aim to orient themselves towards those civilizations that are not very developed but which still belong to cosmic alliances or have entrances to developed civilizations. By applying the hybridization method, they simply infiltrate the germs of evil into that civilization or alliance of developed civilizations, placing their hybrids in important places and thus creating gaps in the security and good understanding of that alliance. It is a very subversive but effective way of spreading their evil influence in the galaxy. This was also the way they acted on Earth.

Using infiltration through some of the civilizations that are members of the Galactic Alliance and even a civilization that descended from the original

Sirians but settled in a star system other than that of the Sirius A star, they transmitted elements of their own DNA to the human population.

What surprised me somewhat was that the infiltration was not a massive one but rather a subtle path. We have seen that, through certain actions of hybridization, their genes initially corrupted the DNA of a small number of human beings. That corruption, however, later spread to a large number of beings, taking the form of negative ways of thinking and action. They have manifested themselves mainly through misguided beliefs which, through repetition from generation to generation, have created gaps and perverted connections within human DNA.

This subtle way of perverting was later used by people to achieve certain onerous purposes. It can also be found today in different forms, one example being communism. This system as such has inoculated a way of thinking, a concept and a way of psycho-mental behavior which, over time, has determined a specific resonance in human DNA. This explains why, even after thirty years since the fall of communism in our country, there are still typical communist ideas, tendencies and actions that represent the manifestation of that negative resonance, deeply infiltrated into the DNA of the population. The predominant subtle energy, sustained for decades, has materialized that ominous change in the DNA macromolecule.

Thus, in ancient times, the reptilians first planted some bad seeds which then proliferated and developed, over time, to the level at which their influence on human DNA could no longer be denied or annihilated. It is true, however, that this corruption does not occupy a large percentage of the DNA macromolecule, but as we have seen, it represents only about 2-3% or even less; but even so, some tendencies, habits and actions chosen in contemporary society show us what negative effects can occur as a result of the resonances induced by this very dangerous civilization.

BREAKING AND RESTORING ALIEN ALLIANCE

Corruption and infiltration of reptilians, even among advanced civilizations in the Alliance, led quickly to manifesting claims on certain territories, both on Earth and in our Solar System, which they wished to have under their control.

I saw and understood, in a clever combination of images, that some of the elevated beings of those civilizations began to manifest certain intentions and tendencies other than those respecting universal harmony, orienting themselves towards goals, and in particular, individual goals and those concerning power. In other words, they began to decline spiritually because the path of temptation is very sinuous and deceptive, and the evil reptilians know very well the tricks by which to influence beings in this sense and even whole civilizations. The problem was that those extraterrestrial beings, representing some civilizations in the Alliance, began to forcibly delimit some territories of influence which they took under occupation. Following the outbreak of the conflict, the Alliance broke up over a period of time and divided into several smaller alliances according to affinities and interests.

That was a very turbulent and trying period for humanity. As we have seen, it has been necessary for over twenty thousand years for things to return to normal and to restore a certain equilibrium, both in the planet's ecosystem and in the existence of Mankind since then.

At the same time, the original Alliance was restored to a certain extent. The images showed me summarized renditions of fleets or instant shorts from diplomatic meetings between representatives of civilizations which varied in the number of members. It was the only way I could figure out what actually happened immediately after the conflict.

THE ROLE OF THE ORIGINAL SIRIANS

About 70,000 years ago, the Sirians in the Sirius A system decided to strengthen the Alliance of which they were also a part. They did not use armed intervention in the great conflict of the Alliance although, practically speaking, they were the ones who sponsored it. The Sirians then only played the role of mediators.

Being somewhat puzzled about this, I asked why they did not intervene in that conflict in order to end it or at least to diminish it. The man from Apellos explained to me that, to the extent that he knew, the war between the extraterrestrial civilizations involved not only the Earth but also had as an element of dispute and a delimitation of certain areas of interest in the galaxy for different forces and groups within it. The situation was tense on several planets, and that is precisely why the Sirians sought to protect as much as possible the galactic sector we were part of. Probably, if they had actually intervened in the conflict, it would have increased the hostilities; and at some point, the situation could have become uncontrollable. On the other hand, they wished to set free the course of events and individual choices in accordance with cosmic laws and principles, intervening only where the ignorance of some civilizations could bring great damage or irreparable disturbance in the natural course of things and of the divinely integrated plans.

The Sirians never wanted to escalate the conflicts, even if they could have won them quite easily due to the extraordinary technological advances they possessed. They preferred the alternative of peace and evolution in accordance with the laws of universal harmony, seeking to respect as much as possible the free will of the civilizations with which they came into contact. Only in the conditions in which they are attacked and have to defend themselves, as we have seen in the case of the great confrontations with the reptilians, do they use their very advanced combat capabilities. In the terrible extraterrestrial space war of about 100,000 years ago, they were limited to only supporting the diplomatic path, mediating certain relations between the alien civilizations in conflict.

As I said, the seeds of evil consisted of the influence of the evil reptilians. After the conflict was over, the Sirians wanted a strengthening of the Galactic Alliance they were part of. Their decision was determined by the need to prevent, as far as possible, the conquering corruption by the reptilians of other civilizations within the grouping of extraterrestrial civilizations. This had already happened to a certain extent, and the negative influence of reptilians had been felt in many areas on Earth.

The strengthening of the Galactic Alliance implied a closer collaboration and support between those civilizations that formed it. It was an eminently beneficial alliance, and I was told that there were others in other sectors of the galaxy. The beneficial alliance, consisting of Sirians, Pleiadians, Arcturians and several dozen other civilizations, had a counterbalance in the sense that the Reptilians also formed an alliance with several civilizations oriented to the conquest, exploitation and control of some planets or even star systems.

That is why the Sirians wanted to amplify the collaboration between the civilizations within their alliance, thus bringing together different vibrational frequencies against the reptilian force and the evil and very subversive alliances they formed. Therefore, it was important to prevent one of the less developed civilizations of the Galactic Alliance from being captured or conquered by reptilians, all of which would have repercussions both for the Galactic Alliance and for the genetic "laboratory" on Earth.

ALIEN "OBSERVER" CIVILIZATIONS

I have been shown, however, that there are also neutral civilizations who do not wish to be part of any cosmic alliance. These are called "observers", meaning they are only interested in observing the course of events and processes that take place over a period of time on a planet or in a particular area of the galaxy.

After declaring their neutrality status, they are allowed to attend the theater of operations, based upon a cosmic law of evolution. Generally speaking, these are highly evolved civilizations which use such situations created at a galactic level only in a somewhat philosophical sense, as an element that can contribute to their experience. For example, I was shown at that time two such huge ships witnessing civilizations who were assisting remote events, in a kind of "sovereign silence". Due to the way the images were, slightly translucent and somewhat blurred, I understood that the observers were assisting everything from the etheric plane, probably so as not to disturb the physical space around the Earth. They do not only consider the actual and immediate events, such as conflicts, but for a period of time, they have followed the evolution of life on Earth with interest and the development of the DNA of the human being and the implications that flow from such.

TARS CIVILIZATION

Returning to the period after the terrible interlocking of the Alliance civilizations, in the period of time between the years 90,000-72,000 B.C., I saw many battles and tensions on the surface of the planet which then involved human beings. Those conflicts culminated in a terrible and huge war on the territory of today's Europe, about 50,000 B.C. This war represented a decisive moment for our planet and for the beings from its surface because it involved a certain "break" between the planes of existence, especially between the physical plane and the subtle etheric plane.

At that time, there was an advanced civilization of human beings on Earth called Tarsus, but I also heard small differences in the frequency of this word which I understood as *tarsei* or *tarasei*. I considered, however that *tars* is the basis of the word; and so, the inhabitants of that time, from that region of the world, can be referred to as the Tarsus of old, the ones I will refer to below.

The configuration of the land in the northern hemisphere, as I saw in the holographic images shown to me, was slightly different from what we know today in the sense that Sweden, Norway, and Finland were united with Europe. Instead of the large surface that in our day is covered by the sea, there were only lakes and a few large rivers. The Tarsus civilization advanced even further south, towards Poland, Ukraine, Romania and even slightly to the east, capturing some of today's Baltic countries. In other words, the territory was spread very wide.

For the most part, the Tarsites were *E-N-K* human beings, but they had a much slimmer, more vital and more harmonious body than that of contemporary humans. At the beginning of their civilization, many thousands of years ago, that is by 70,000 B.C., they were *E-N-L* beings, but due to repeated combinations with more primitive *E-N-K* beings, their DNA underwent major transformations with strong *E-N-K* accents. From a certain point of view, we can say that they were a civilization of demigods; that is, hybrids coming from a combination of *E-N-L* beings with *E-N-K* beings.

At that time in that area, which covered much of central and northern Europe, the many frequencies of the etheric plane intersected in many places with the frequency of the physical plane, thus resulting in many space-time portals which could be easily passed through from the physical plane to the etheric one and vice versa. The colossal armed confrontation between the populations in the mentioned area , which were mostly Tarsus populations, also signaled a "rupture" of the planes of existence for Earth, that is to say, a much more severe separation between the physical and the etheric plane. Until that time, the conjunctions or the intersections between these two planes of existence represented something natural. If, for example, an E-N-L being in Africa wanted to reach northern Poland, it could happen in a few moments through such a portal which was, in fact, a specific "union" or "touching" between the physical and the etheric plane.

THE ORIGIN OF THE CONFLICT

As I was shown, the cause of the immense conflict around 50,000 B.C. consisted of frictions between the different beliefs shared by the Tarsus populations. I have said that, at that time, the connections between the physical and the etheric planes were numerous, creating many portals from one plane to another on the planet's surface, but especially providing access to the sacred realms inhabited by wise E-N-L beings which were to be later established in the realm known as Shambhala. Over time, however, some groups of the Tarshish population began to want an expansion of the population of their territory, also involving many crossing zones between the physical and the etheric planes. Thus appeared the first armed conflicts which, at first, were relatively minor.

The insistence upon these struggles and wars and the quantity of them destabilized the natural existence of the bridges between the physical and the etheric. The frequencies corresponding to the etheric zones began to separate more and more from the physical plane, and this gave rise to great dissatisfaction and misunderstandings because many possibilities were lost which were previously valid due to the coexistence with the etheric plane. These included higher knowledge, much easier access when moving from one area to another, contacting higher beings, higher states of existence and many others. Each faction of the population involved in the conflict therefore wanted an acceptable area to continue their existence, many of them wanting the Shambhala territories for themselves. Since then, the situation has been unfortunately similar to what we encounter today: different states and ethnicities claiming territories belonging to other states and ethnicities, inevitably leading to tensions and conflicts which often degenerate into wars.

That was actually the time when the Great War broke out, through a kind of "unification" of all the hostile outbreaks that had been going on for many years in different areas of the Tarsus territory. Different factions and groups of populations had fought in different parts of Tarsus territory, but gradually, through the portals between the physical and the etheric planes, they became concentrated in a single convergence zone. This further intensified the misunderstandings between the factions of the population which began to form numerous ad-hoc alliances. At one point, things became so complicated that no one knew who they were actually fighting with or who they were allied with.

THE WRATH OF THE ARMED CONFLICT

It was a terrible, huge, and devastating war. A huge army, led by factions hostile to the Good, forced entry into some entrances into Shambhala, attacking through several access areas located, in my opinion, in the southern and central areas of Poland. There, however, they were struck by a strong defense of the common areas of transition between the physical and the etheric plane. The conflict zone then spread to huge territories, as it did in the small areas, encompassing part of Ukraine and northern Romania, the entire territory of Poland, and also the southern part of Sweden.

The terrible conflict involved a huge number of warriors, perhaps millions. It was a virtual slaughter, especially since it was not a medieval battle with swords, bows and spears. The Tarshish were elite warriors, very powerful and with weapons that lent some characteristics and powers specific to the etheric plane with which they had very frequent contact until then. That was another reason why the war broke out: the illusion of losing power can give birth to monsters in thought.

I also saw, however, other groups of E-N-K beings, less developed but also very powerful, that had conventional weapons such as axes, spears or bows. Not even the E-N-L beings stayed away from that terrible confrontation, using far superior technologies such as some highly advanced armament attack aircraft. I saw, for example, how they emitted some kind of "jets" like a bunch of lasers which branched out near the surface of the Earth and produced huge damage, both materially and in terms of human lives.

I have watched a few fight scenes, and I can say that, by scale, the intelligence and the energy involved in that human conflict was even more terrible than the war that was started by the alien civilizations around 100,000 B.C., both in the vicinity of the Earth and on its surface. Even though the level of destruction in the case of the extraterrestrial conflict was much higher, and the nature of the weapons used by them was far more terrible and destructive, the unimaginable ferocity imposed by the combatants involved in the Great Tarsus War was out of the ordinary. It was basically like generalized insanity.

AFTER THE WAR

The conflict was so violent that it deeply affected the morale of all parties involved. It was so painful and shocking that, after its termination, some defenders of peace among the E-N-L beings decided that it should be "engraved" in the memory of Mankind in order to prevent this from happening again. The images then showed me, in the "translucent" and slightly blurred mode, specific to the reality of the subtle etheric plane, the presence of giant columns designed to serve as warning broadcasters. Dizzying constructions by reason of their size, I was shown that they contained a kind of "telepathic wave transmitter" whose purpose was to prevent any such devastating conflict in the future by issuing specific frequencies that were to be activated in the event of such a threat.

Those who survived remained in those areas, gradually laying the foundations of a new civilization: the great and powerful Hyperborean civilization. During those sequences, the man from Apellos intervened, and operating some commands on the holographic screen, changed the course of the images, bringing into the foreground a mountainous region and some tall and very powerful inhabitants who lived there a few thousand years after the Great War. From the frequency the columnar structure was emitting, I immediately deciphered that they were called Tharos, probably a throwback or alteration of the old term *Tars*. Telepathically, I understood that the meaning of that name was "invincible".

The images then showed a place near a cave which the Tharos guarded with great devotion, and subtly, I understood that it was one of the areas of passage from the physical plane to the land of Shambhala. I was surprised, however, by the intervention of the man from Apellos, but I quickly understood the reason: he wanted to show me that the entry was in Romania. Of course, this is not the only entrance as there are such penetrations to the realm of Shambhala in the territory of other countries, but this represents one of the rare permanent intersections between the physical and the etheric plane which was not affected by the Great Tarshish war.

At first, the image was presented to me as a view from a great height from where I could even see the curvature of the Carpathian mountains. Then, some specific indicators and symbols appeared on the right, indicating the place of entry into Shambhala. I then realized that the entrance is somewhere on the mountain that is today known as Ceahlău.*

The Great Tarsus War of 50,000 B.C. destabilized many areas of transition to the etheric plane, later leading to the separation of the etheric plane from the physical one. It was a rearrangement of the dimensions, a recalibration of them, and here I refer in particular to the physical and etheric planes. Due

---

* Ceahlău Mountain is a very curious and interesting location in the Moldavian region of Romania. Every August 6th, the shadows of the mountain and early morning (from approximately 6 a.m. to 9 a.m.) mist create the image of a holographic pyramid that approximates the Great Pyramid at Giza. Pilgrims visit the area during this period and the Romanian Orthodox Church sites this locale as where *The Transfiguration* took place. *The Transfiguration* is from the *New Testament* and is where Jesus becomes the Christ. In other words, he transforms from a regular human being into the Christ.

to the nature and intensity of the emotions conveyed by the combatants during that period, the energies involved were huge so that even the astral plane around the Earth was affected. The incredible violence, as well as the ferocity that characterized it, remain engraved in the etheric memory of the Earth as an important reference point for humanity. The negative effects on the planet's existential plane made that armed clash a sad memory and a kind of crucial reminder that such a somber event should never be repeated.

As a result of the very bloody war that took place at that time, numerous hybridized beings that came from the E-N-L and E-N-K branches could no longer support the connection between the physical plane and the etheric plane, and they consequently separated. I was then shown in a few summary images that, after the end of the war, the few remaining beings, especially the upper ones in the E-N-L branch and those in the upper E-N-K branch (that is, some of the "demigods" who represented hybridizations with E-N-L beings) later developed an elevated spirituality in that area which thus became the birthplace of the great Hyperborean civilization.

CHAPTER TEN

HyPERBOREA

Just as in the case of Shambhala, historians and archeologists place Hyperborea among the so-called "mythical" civilizations as there is almost no clear material evidence of its existence. In reality, as I viewed the exceptional images that were presented to me on the holographic screen of Apellos, I could see the very vivid reality of the Hyperborean civilization in distant times.

ETYMOLOGY AND LOCATION

The name *Hyperborea* is of recent origin, only a few thousand years old, and comes from ancient Greek. In fact, the roots of Hyperborea are very old as they extend to about 70,000 B.C. The population that lived in that territory represented the old Tarshish, the ancestors of the Hyperboreans. The meaning of the word *Hyperborea* is known to almost everyone: the northern land, those who lived in the northern part of the ancient world.

This idea was correctly transmitted because the region in which the extraordinary civilization of Hyperborea developed advanced far to the north. After watching the events as they were shown to me, I did some brief research on the internet to see any differences between what is being circulated and what was in reality.

With the exception of small errors related to locale, the other elements, although few in fact, express the truth but only in a very general reference frame. I think the lack of information is mainly due to the fact that the age of this civilization is very ancient, and the knowledge about it has simply been lost over time.

Texts and stories of the ancients mention, for example, the territory of the Hyperborea as being north of the Danube or bordering on the Black Sea, but this is not entirely true. From what I saw, Hyperborea encompassed a vast territory in a somewhat "vertical" strip of land, from today's Transylvania upward into what we know to be western Ukraine today, also capturing a small part of the western Baltic countries. A significant part of the territory was on the present surface of Poland, ascending to the south of Sweden. I did not see, however, that the Hyperborean territory had reached the Black Sea. Even so, Hyperborea occupies a vast territory.

COAGULATION OF THE HYPERBOREAN
CIVILIZATION AFTER THE GREAT TARS WAR

The Tarshish represented the first spiritual line which would later define Hyperborea. Their civilization existed and prospered between 70,000 and 50,000 B.C. From what I saw and understood, there were many spiritual directions and beliefs at that time but none prevailed. As I said, at the end of that period, a terrible war took place which practically destroyed the Tarshish civilization and gave rise to the development of a new civilization which was the Hyperborean civilization.* It was only after that great war that the territory of Hyperborea was better defined and the civilization unified into a common spiritual creed.

Thus, in the history of Hyperborea, there were two great periods: before the Great Tarsus War and after its end, which also meant an important change at a subtle level for our planet. Before the war, that is, during the period 70,000-50,000 B.C. which was dominated by the Tarshish, I could see an amalgam of races derived mainly from the E-N-L branch and only a few from the E-N-K branch.

After the terrible confrontation, the respective territory on which Hyperborea was to be later settled remained almost uninhabited for a fairly long period of time. Later, as I saw in a rather rapid flow of images, the population of that area began to grow and to become individualized in the sense that it became a civilization of its own, a kind of administration to the degree that the E-N-L beings who were leaders, because of their high spiritual level, managed to unite all the factions of the population into a strong civilization and a common spiritual orientation. This was due to the fact that, especially in the distant past of humanity, the leadership was eminently spiritual. At that time there was no other type of leadership because the administrative leader of a wider territory was at the same time a priest, and this fact gave an extraordinary force to the population and oriented it positively.

I also saw that, after 50,000 B.C., the territory of Hyperborea featured a "nursery" of DNA development which led to the population of that area having a vast range of breeds, even more diversified than before. Unlike the 20,000 year period prior, the new Hyperborean population was united and coherent in aspirations and thinking, just as, to use a close analogy, the Christian countries of Europe in the Middle Ages were under the spiritual authority of the Pope. Part of the old Tarshish, who were initially E-N-L beings but also included combinations of E-N-L and E-N-K in the form of "gods" as a result of the numerous combinations with E-N-K beings, became an E-N-K majority, known as good craftsmen, especially with weapons of combat.

---

* See Chapter 9 (ed.)

This is why they were defending the southern part of Hyperborea, living especially in the territory of Transylvania today and further northward, towards Ukraine. This gene was "inherited" by the E-N-L branch and transmitted further. It propagated very rapidly, much faster than the E-N-L gene had been after the so-called "Hyperborean DNA" was established. On the other hand, the branch of beings E-N-L whose DNA was easy to modify continued to refine. Its "extensions" have led to numerous variations of DNA and, implicitly, of different types of E-N-L beings.

GENE BREEDING

Something very interesting then happened. According to my estimation and based upon the synthesis of images I witnessed, about 27,000 years ago, the E-N-L gene had evolved so much that it had reached about the same level as that of advanced alien civilizations. When that balance was reached, an understanding was created between humans (the E-N-L branch) and certain extraterrestrial civilizations in order for some of their elevated souls to be reincarnated into the bodies of E-N-L beings in an understanding of coexistence, collaboration and mutual support.

Generally speaking, every great civilization that existed on Earth was located in a precise area of the planet without any admixture of other civilizations. This included, for example, the Mu civilization, the Lemurian civilization, and a civilization of E-N-L beings having a strong Sirian influence which existed on the great island later called Atlantis — to name only a few of the great civilizations of the very distant past. The there was also the Atlantean civilization itself, this following the Sirian civilization on the same island

All of these were mostly represented by beings from the E-N-L branch but at different stages of their genome development. They did not mix with other civilizations; but in the case of the final period of the Hyperborean civilization, due to the evolution of the E-N-L beings and the understanding that took place with several extraterrestrial civilizations, the possibility of hybridizing the DNA of the E-N-L human beings was created in the sense that the souls of some evolved extraterrestrial beings were incarnated into the bodies of E-N-L beings. Until then, only the souls of E-N-L beings were incarnated in E-N-L bodies, but once a sufficiently refined level of their DNA structure was reached, the physical bodies of some of the E-N-L secondary branches became able to support the high vibrational frequency of the consciousness of advanced extraterrestrial beings. It is true, however, that the E-N-L beings with these characteristics were quite few compared to the majority of the Hyperborean population which was composed primarily of evolved E-N-K beings.

It can thus be said that, in the Hyperborea of those times, there was a kind of "gene nursery" which led to an "increased flexibility" of human DNA. The evolved *E-N-L* gene allowed for the incarnation of advanced extraterrestrial souls which later combined with the human body. If not for this, their DNA binding would not have been possible. For example, a Sirian soul incarnates into a male *E-N-L* being and a Pleiadian soul incarnates into an *E-N-L* female being, both within the Hyperborean civilization. Their child was also an *E-N-L* being, but she had within her DNA essential information from both the original DNA of the Syrian being and that of the Pleiadian being.

The majority of the hybridizations were realized on this principle. The basis upon which these hybridizations were built remained the *E-N-L* gene, but the complexity of the "loops" of other extraterrestrial genes on this basis was astonishing. There were numerous hybridizations between *E-N-L* human beings who were already evolved and other *E-N-L* beings in which alien souls were incarnated.

WITHDRAWAL OF THE E-N-L BRANCH

Thus, at that time, the old Tars territory, which had virtually become the territory called Hyperborea, was inhabited by many types of populations. This resulted from the ease with which many souls on other planets were able to be incarnated on Earth; and they had the physical bodies of *E-N-L* beings as they could support the evolved extraterrestrial consciousness. I could see in that vast territory almost all the typologies of populations: white, black, Métis, yellow, Mongolian and even other types which were derived from these but were still distinguished by certain features: skin color, eyes, hair, and particularities of face or body, sometimes quite different from what we know from today. It was a conglomerate of races even more alive than can be found in our times in the great metropolises of the West, both in diversity and in the number of individuals, yet their proportion was balanced.

I think that the last period of relative harmony on Earth was before the withdrawal of the *E-N-L* gene due to it having exhausted its resources. The retreat of the *E-N-L* branch was quite slow at first. It started by 27,000 B.C. as *E-N-L* beings evolved, only remaining in certain areas and no longer spread throughout the surface of the planet.

The withdrawal of *E-N-L* beings from the physical plane, however, accelerated considerably after the fall of Atlantis. I could even say that the last *E-N-L* "act" was Atlantis because, after its sinking, the Earth remained populated only with beings from the *E-N-K* branch with the possible exception of some *E-N-L* beings hybridized with *E-N-K* beings. At the level of leadership or great rulers, only *E-N-L* beings could be found, such as the pharaohs of ancient Egypt or the great kings of the Middle East. Until the fall of Atlantis, the *E-N-L* beings in Hyperborea, knowing that it was time for their withdrawal from the evolutionary chain as it had reached its maximum, wanted to open and further refine the *E-N-K* branch, which had a more "rigid" DNA, in order to drive the evolution of Mankind. For many *E-N-K* beings, that period meant a surprising evolution, a special purification, and this was precisely because of hybridization with highly evolved beings which left the seeds of complex resonances in their DNA.

The *E-N-L* branch thus carried out a complex evolutionary cycle on Earth and was about to withdraw to a subtle plane superior to the physical one, partly due to special climatic conditions which were increasingly manifesting, more so in the northern areas of the planet. Starting in about 25,000 B.C., the temperatures on the surface of the planet began to fall which led to the *E-N-L* beings, who already had a large resonance with the etheric plane, remaining more and more in this subtle plane with increasingly reduced links with the physical plane.

This required a need for "crossing zones" or portals to the etheric plane so that the connection with the remaining beings in the physical plane would not be interrupted. Mountain areas or stretches of water were preferred, but such crossings between one plane and another could also be encountered in forests or even in the fields. In the beginning, these areas were easy to find because they penetrated much of the planet's surface, especially in the Northern Hemisphere.

As I said, in the distant past of the planet, the physical and etheric dimensions were somehow "twinned" in the sense that they had quite a lot of points of convergence or portals through which beings could easily pass from the physical to the etheric plane and vice versa. I was shown, however, that beginning with 25,000 B.C., the number of these transition zones had decreased significantly. Additionally, some of them were in the territories in which the *E-N-K* beings were established. Although they knew of the existence of such portals in their territory, the *E-N-K* people could nevertheless not go "beyond" because their own vibrational frequency did not allow for it; that is, it was too low to support the passage to a larger dimension than the physical one.

THE END OF A GREAT CIVILIZATION

In its active state, the Hyperborean civilization continued until about 14,000 B.C., after which it died out. Its rudiments, however, continued to exist in certain areas of the former Hyperborea, even further north, but from what I saw, they formed just very small communities. The rest of the population migrated rather quickly, especially to Atlantis and also south to Transylvania, where it settled in the mountains. Since then, after several millennia, a part of the population descended to the south of the continent, giving birth in time to other great civilizations closer to the present day. Another part, however, migrated eastwards to Asia in distinct stages, also laying the foundations of great civilizations. As I mentioned, the cataclysm that led to the sinking of Atlantis greatly disturbed the state of the planet, both physically and subtly. Many links between the physical and the etheric plane were interrupted while others have been completely suppressed and, generally speaking, it was shown to me that the two planes separated so much due to the massive disturbance in both the physical and subtle structures of the planet. That separation between the physical and the etheric was even more pronounced than the separation that took place after the Great Tarsus War. It became more and more evident and also caused a dramatic drop in the vibrational frequency of the physical plane of the planet which became even harder.

Inter-dimensional energy portals have become a rarity with the passage of time, and communication with the higher beings in the etheric plane of the Earth and with those in Shambhala has become increasingly difficult. This state of affairs has become even more complicated since 5,000 B.C., when dark forces began to intervene in the evolution of Mankind, taking advantage of the huge breach that appeared in the Earth's energy network. Some extraterrestrial civilizations which were already contaminated by the reach of the evil reptilians began to weave a very complicated network of intrigues and plans for total control of the planet. They were based mainly on the significant decrease in the vibrational frequency of the physical plane as well as on the lowest level of consciousness of humanity, composed almost entirely of *E-N-K*.

ROYALTY AND DISPOSAL OF THE HYPERBOREANS

All of this was presented to me in a simple way and with intelligent links that combined edifying images with symbols or signs of connection between different factors, beings or objects from those presented on the screen. In this way, it would be as easy as possible to understand. I did not cease to marvel at the extraordinary intelligence that almost instantly synthesized all the information I requested, presenting it in a form appropriate to my understanding and also suggesting subtleties or other branches of investigation. Generally speaking, due to the limited time I had at my disposal and the immensity of the information, I studied gradually. What was shown to me in the first phase were general aspects of the requested subject, without going into details. Interestingly enough though, having access to that information, I rarely felt the urge to find out more about one or more of the other directions that the information might lead to. Although I could go into detail with any aspect I would have liked and which was within my sphere of understanding and interest, I only rarely did such. Instead, I preferred summary presentations.

Explanations were of a practical nature because I was trying to store as much information as possible, even at a general level, reserving the possibility for the future of getting into some details of interest. In any case, the synthesis of images was admirably done in real time, even with much more information than I could understand, at least at the level of symbolism. In parallel, I was also helped by the telepathic transmissions that my cortex translated as acceptable, thus enriching the general knowledge of the requested subject. The images appeared in a flowing stream and were intelligently linked to certain graphic representations or even rushes of colors which indicated either the direction of a certain phenomenon or tendency or the nature that characterized them. For example, when the migration to south and southeast Europe was indicated, it was represented by images in three different planes with super positionings. I saw, for example, groups of people and even domestic animals, especially sheep, going through different forms of terrain. In parallel, in the background, I saw a kind of land map showing the continent and part of the Mediterranean; and over them, in tandem with the movement of people, a yellow flow was super-imposed, like an undulating wave, indicating the length and time of travel to their destination.

At one point, it split in several directions with a smaller thickness, almost like a fan, and one of them headed further east, stopping near the Mediter-ranean shore on the territory of what is today's Turkey. I was then shown, in quick succession, the building of a large settlement in that area by the fol-lowers of the Hyperboreans in the form of a city that, in time, became a big city, very well developed and even endowed with certain technology. I saw, for example, that the fortress was illuminated during the night, but I did not identify the sources of light, of which there were apparently more than one. In any case, they did not come from fire. Around that area and in connection with it, several symbols appeared in the hologram, some of them moving and with different colors. Snapshots of the life of that city and the beings, buildings, or interiors were sometimes highlighted suddenly; then withdrawn, making room for other aspects.

I understood, of course, that this place was important, but I did not know what city it was until I got used to the frequency of the area; and then, telepathi-cally, I immediately understood that it was Troy. This mental understanding came packaged with another set of information which correlated with the holographic images. Thus, I understood the subtle connection with the city of Troy, in direct correlation with the evil influence of some extraterrestrial civilizations and the way in which their members on Earth attracted acolytes among the E-N-K beings. This influence intended to destroy any "rays of light" and Troy at that time was the last bastion of resistance. I will return to this topic later.

CHAPTER ELEVEN

Planetary Council of Teotihuacan

After more than 300,000 years since the beginning of the project to create a new intelligent human being on Earth — by combining extraterrestrial DNA with the DNA of the great primates that existed at that time — the DNA of the *E-N-K* branch became complex, thanks to the multiple combinations that have taken place over time, either with DNA from other extraterrestrial civilizations or with *E-N-L* human beings.

THE REMARKABLE EVOLUTION OF THE E-N-K BRANCH

This was achieved by mutual understanding between the representatives of extraterrestrial civilizations who were interested in hybridizing the new race of beings that had spread all over the globe. But, while the *E-N-L* beings were carefully "cultivated" and their evolution was assisted by the beneficial extraterrestrial civilizations, the *E-N-K* beings were somehow left to develop on their own. This plan had been previously established so that diversity could be achieved within the same breed. The experiment showed that although the *E-N-K* branch developed much more slowly, being left to natural laws, it was precisely through this that it acquired a special vital force, being linked much to "Earth" and to Nature. Some of these beings, however, have been hybridized with extraterrestrial DNA, thus creating an even greater complexity of their traits and capabilities; but for the most part, the *E-N-K* branch has been left to evolve on its own. Therefore, the qualitative hierarchy of the beings that existed at that time on our planet was based upon the small group of *E-N* beings with mostly Sirian DNA. They represented the "elite" in the sense that their genetic structure was so evolved that, at that time, they could only be combined with a very small number of other extraterrestrial beings, also highly evolved. From the group of *E-N* beings came, by "specialization", the refined *E-N-L* and *E-N-K* beings. The latter evolved in their natural rhythm because, at first, the difference in vibrational frequency between *E-N-L* and *E-N-K* was too large to allow for natural and efficient combinations between the individuals of these two branches.

As I said, however, some combinations between the *L* and *K* branches were possible and have occurred over time. The resulting DNA was a secondary branch of *E-N-K* beings with a more refined consciousness, doubled by a good vital root on the planet. These were powerful beings, capable of great efforts, but at the same time having a higher level of consciousness than most of the population of *E-N-K* beings. Those higher and stronger *E-N-K* beings were the so-called "demigods" mentioned in ancient literature.

At the great meetings of the representatives of the extraterrestrial civilizations who visited the Earth, however, it was established that the higher branch which had derived from the *K* branch would not be sustained any further. I did not quite understand why such a decision was made because, at that time, I became very interested in those Councils of extraterrestrial beings. A valid hypothesis, however, would be, as I said before, that representatives of extraterrestrial civilizations wanted the *E-N-K* branch to be closer to Earth's specificity without too much extraterrestrial influence in its specific DNA, as could be seen, for example, in the case of *E-N-L* beings.

TEOTIHUACAN — THE MODEL SIRIAN CIVILIZATION

The first high level recognition of the evolution of *E-N-K* beings took place about 28,000 years ago. At that time, the "demigods" were admitted to the superior decision-making council on the planet that met at that time in the place we now call Teotihuacan, in Mexico. Known as the Great Planetary Council, it consisted of members of the advanced alien civilizations that were on Earth as well as representatives of the *E-N-L* branch. The city of Teotihuacan was built by the original Sirians, known as the Lords of the Galaxy in the Sirius A system. Considered to be the true parents of Mankind, they represent the main civilization that assumed the role of overseeing and guiding the long process of formation of the new race of humanoid beings which has become the humanity of today. The construction of the city was done before the meeting of the Planetary Council, during which time the Sirians, together with the Pleiadians, established a certain line of action for that part of the world on the continent of America today.

Teotihuacan is a faithful replica of a Sirian city, but other extraterrestrial civilizations from the Alliance, especially the Pleiadians, participated in its building. What has been discovered today, with the main pyramids and the wide road that is exposed to visitors, is only part of the huge city that was built about 30,000 years ago.* It was gigantic, with many branches that made it look like a real metropolis. I was even shown the initial project as a three-dimensional holographic scheme, and after that, I saw the city already built and populated, especially by Sirians and Pleiadians. For quite some time, the city was home to their representatives, and to a lesser extent, to other extraterrestrial civilizations.

The city was conceived and realized as a city with circular symmetry, from which several branches were also arranged circularly. To these, as I could see,

---

* The author refers, without a doubt, to the two great pyramids within the city: the Pyramid of the Sun and the Pyramid of the Moon, as well as to the main road, Calea Morţilor. About this ancient city, also called the "City of the Gods" or "The Place Where the Gods are Born", nobody knows anything, not even the Aztecs who lived in it for over a millennium. It is not known who built it, why, and especially when it was built.

it was reached by means of teleportation devices. The basis for the design and construction of the city was the Sirian one, but its design respected the affinities of cosmic energies in direct and precise correspondence with the stars and planetary systems of many extraterrestrial civilizations in the Alliance. The Sirians wanted to do just that so that the Alliance would become more united and more motivated to act in unison in order to develop the human race on Earth.

In designing the city — which I saw in a combination of holographic images, both in the three-dimensional and the etheric plane, through the headset that was offered to me — a certain complicated star structure was considered which was to "preside" and energetically support the longevity of the settlement and its subtle radiation. I was even shown how the extraterrestrial beings who designed the city were running the future of that specific star structure in the future, looking for new configurations and thus establishing a longer period of existence for the city. I will return to this when I describe how the pyramids in Egypt were designed and built.

In the case of such megalithic plans, the advanced extraterrestrial beings knew very well that the shapes and dimensions of the construction of the future city were in direct connection and resonance with the movement of certain stars, already in a precise arrangement. Emphasis is naturally placed on the durability of those constructions. For example, they look for specific and important star positions, arrangements or configurations, all of which are going to last for a long time. They are then certain that over that period the respective construction will be supported by the specific subtle energy emitted by that star configuration. The appearance remains valid only if the other resonant elements are respected, such as the structure of the buildings and the pyramids, their dimensions and other characteristics of the materials, all of which must be in consonance to the detail with that star configuration or with others that present affinities with it. For example, I saw that the Sirians were attentive even to what stone slab they placed at a certain intersection. It had to be of a certain type of rock, different from the other stones, and cut at a precise angle in order to resonate according to a certain detail of the complex stellar structure.

I was amazed by certain features of this ancient city because I had not encountered them before. The first one I mention is the feeling of greatness, of the gigantic distance over which it spread. Then, there was communion with Nature. The vegetation was practically an integral part of the city's construction, "living" with it. I did not, however, even see a strand of grass that exceeded the edges imposed by the space of the stone slabs, very well polished and joined together. The leaves, the lilies, the shrubs, and everything else came exactly to the edges of the stone areas, never beyond them, as if the vegetation had "known" how to perfectly respect those boundaries. It then occurred to me that it was probably a specific technology whereby the vegetation was somehow "mirrored" and made to go back to the forest or jungle, but I cannot be sure.

The cleanliness in the city was incredible and I could not even begin to figure out how this was possible. I saw no dust, no mud, no marks or other debris. When I looked, everything was so well done that I felt like I was looking at a diagram on the computer, and yet, I saw extraterrestrial beings walking through that city and performing various actions. I have also seen aerial vehicles and even small and medium-sized vessels, landing or taking off from the central market and also from a region some distance away from it.

DIRECTIVES OF THE PLANETARY COUNCIL FROM 26,000 B.C.

From many points of view, that "multicolored" encounter of the extraterrestrial civilizations that "shepherded" the DNA in the formation of the human being was a turning point for the evolution of humanity on Earth. The territories were then delimited, agreements and understandings were established, and certain codes of inter-racial behavior were imposed and crucial decisions were taken regarding the future of human beings and life on our planet. That council impressed me in particular with the size, complexity and value of the decisions made regarding the destiny of humanity.

Generally speaking, such aspects are little known, and if they are revealed to people, they tend to respond with derision. This is mainly because the common man does not have access to such direct information and also because he tends to think in accordance with the norms, laws and ideas that are currently being conveyed. Of these, the most annoying and often repeated are the ideas that "we could be alone in the Universe", that "science has pretty much solved everything that has to be solved so far" and that "contemporary civilization is the most developed that existed until now on the planet." For those who are intelligent and have good sense, however, such statements are just the fruit of ignorance and the manifestation of a very arrogant vision.

As for myself, I have the belief that some of those who are truly educated can intuitively understand what I am presenting here. Even though my reports are a serious test for current conceptions, this information illustrates a whole series of confusing, unclear or erroneous elements about the history of humanity and its origin. After all, all I do is to present as accurately as possible what I have witnessed and discussed personally on this topic, all of which is very broad and complex. It is up to the reader, however, to decide whether or not he can accept the information that is thus made available to him.

I will now return to the aspects related to the main decisions taken at that Great Planetary Council and to emphasize their nuances. The admission of the *E-N-K* beings into the planetary coordination forum and the recognition of the level of evolution that they achieved also had to do with the fact that the representatives of the Great Council showed an even deeper interest in them than the population of a planet with a new race of beings.

Indeed — the initial plan was the creation of a new, intelligent and complex human being developed in the Universe. After more than 300,000 years, this plan had already developed and evolved quickly, and even unexpectedly, if we think about the natural course of things and if we consider it on a cosmic scale. That is why the Great Planetary Council from Teotihuacan from 26,000 B.C. virtually signifies the beginning of the "withdrawal" of the extraterrestrial upper races from the involvement in the life of the new humanity.

The main purpose of the initial project was to create a higher grade of human being and to populate the planet with this newly created being. Since the E-N-K branch had shown a surprising fertility and adaptability to different types of external influences due to its DNA, it had somehow acquired the right to take over the planet and evolve freely here.

By contrast, the E-N-L branch, although more evolved than the E-N-K branch from a spiritual point of view as well as other characteristics, was nevertheless more fragile in terms of genetic structure and vitality, to the point where it could not sustain a continuous and energetic development of a new race of beings. Moreover, as I said, the E-N-L beings had already begun to withdraw from the physical plane, and their existence was gradually replaced by myths and legends. The L branch, however, has made an important contribution to refining part of the K branch.

Accordingly, the Sirians and the other main extraterrestrial civilizations involved in the project of creating the new being on Earth considered that the E-N-K gene was strong enough to carry out the project which could now follow a natural path. Sovereign surveillance by these extraterrestrial civilizations continued to exist, in particular to stop attempts at self-destruction of civilization by devastating wars at the planetary level or by the use of terrible and very advanced technologies, both by humans and other extraterrestrial civilizations who expressed a certain interest in life on this planet. This small group of very advanced extraterrestrial civilizations did so, however, with a high spiritual knowledge and without intervening where the course of destiny had to take a certain form for humanity.

THE "SPECIALIZATION" OF HUMAN DNA

After the "segmentation" of human DNA took place, in the sense that certain extraterrestrial civilizations began to create more "nurseries" for it in different parts of the Earth, the DNA of the human being spread out in different directions, somehow losing "total power". In other words, the E-N-K beings from these secondary branches — which were E-N-K-A, E-N-K-I, E-N-K-U...

etc. — gained the same strengths and power as the *E-N-L* line because their DNA "specialized" over time in one specific direction, induced and developed in particular by an extraterrestrial civilization.

Each of the extraterrestrial civilizations that participated in the "nursery" program of human civilization on Earth proportionally contributed their DNA to the complexity of human DNA, thus "shepherding" a certain population of the globe as assigned by the Great Planetary Council from Teotihuacan who had designated "areas of influence" for each extraterrestrial civilization that was involved in the project.

Basically, their representatives took over close supervision of the evolution and development of the human beings that populated the Earth at that time, mostly belonging to the *E-N-K* branch, within the territories they occupied. This is why we can see very different influences and characteristics in races and even populations in certain areas of the planet. For political reasons, however, I was advised not to present details of this in this book.

DEMIGODS

One of the important decisions taken at the Great Planetary Council of Teotihuacan was that the *E-N-K* branch be allowed to start self-governing. In other words, *E-N-K* beings would have their own territories and even be invited to be represented at that Great Council at certain times to contribute to planetary discussions and decisions. By this, the fact was recognized that they had evolved enough to have a relatively high degree of responsibility and that they could integrate well into the spiral of progress at the planetary level. It was clear from what I saw in the pictures, however, that the *E-N-K* beings were listening to the directions, advice and directives that were given by the sages of extraterrestrial civilizations who were guarding the entire planet and who they considered to be their "parents".

I noticed that the elevated members of the *E-N-K* branch of the Council were very harmonious, powerful, and independent beings. I was attracted in particular to the special magnetism they radiated, and I focused on these aspects as they related to their participation in the Great Council of the planet. Immediately, I was shown a sequence of representative images, and to the right of the screen, I saw a rich display of other directories. I preferred, however, to pursue the sequence of images because the particular study of those files would have taken more time than was available to me.

Combining the images with the telepathically intuitive transmissions that I received through the inter-dimensional headset, I realized that the *E-N-K* branch had evolved remarkably throughout, characterized in particular by the complexity of their DNA structure. This made for amazing possibilities for combinations with other DNA. In addition, it conferred on those beings a special radiation, a bodily and magnetic beauty that easily produced fascination. Moreover, as we have seen, the E-N-K delegation consisted only of "demigods", both men and women. As they were closer to our tendencies, manner of being, way of perceiving things and manifesting ourselves, I was very attracted to those images because at a certain level, the E-N-K delegation produced a strong impression amongst the other extraterrestrial beings.

The most representative were the women of E-N-K. They had an extraordinary impact and showed a kind of irresistible attraction that undoubtedly stemmed from the complexity of the structure of their DNA and especially from a special common "something" unique to the human being that was created on Earth. If I were to make a comparison, however, I would say that their radiation was most similar to that of the women in the Pleiades. Many representatives of other extraterrestrial species and civilizations were "courting" them, precisely due to their extraordinary fertility and ability to give life to a level of high complexity. In this sense, there was a kind of "rolling" of many extraterrestrial civilizations who, from time to time, came and "redid" their genetic dowry with the most special E-N-K beings.

DIVERSIFICATION OF DNA IN E-N-K BEINGS

More than 100,000 years ago, the planet was divided into several territories, each with its own specific population which was supported, protected and helped to evolve by one or more extraterrestrial civilizations. Accordingly, each such area on Earth had a "soul" or ego which was the specific ego of the respective population.

The representatives of the governing civilization came from time to time and "ran" their own DNA with that of the population in that territory because the resonant frequencies in the structure of the DNA macromolecule of E-N-K beings were so great that it easily facilitated such combinations. So it was that each population or civilization on Earth had its "gods" who, in those cases, were the evolved extraterrestrial beings who supported the specific development of a branch of human beings.

This fact was important because, in this way, certain extraterrestrial civilizations could fortify their "tired" or degenerate DNA, gaining a new impetus for existence and evolution while others seeded other civilizations on other planets from DNA samples that were taken. This was especially so from the E-N-K beings, thus helping the evolution of various civilizations in the cosmos. I was shown the structure of the DNA of beings on several planets in the galaxy which were all based on the DNA of the human being. Practically speaking and no matter how paradoxical it may seem, we can say that, in a certain way, we are the "parents" of many civilizations in the galaxy.

After the great extraterrestrial space conflict in the vicinity of the Earth, the *E-N-K* branch has somehow "drifted" because, for a long time, there was no clear order of extraterrestrial territories and influences.

As the Galactic Alliance was then restored, things started to return to normal, but it was only after the Great Planetary Council that the territories of alien influence on the *E-N-K* populations was able to be re-established and reoriented but according to new rules.

The exceptional characteristics of human DNA from those times caused the Planetary Council to include the presence of *E-N-K* beings in the decision-making chain at the planetary level and also to offer them freedom of expression and autonomy because the level of evolution that the *E-N-K* beings had reached justified that decision.

It is true, however, that the spiritual aspect, inner perception, refinement of consciousness or higher understanding was not very developed in *E-N-K* beings in comparison to the members of certain extraterrestrial civilizations or to the human beings of the *E-N-L* branch. The *E-N-K* beings of that time, however, those who represented the "demigods", were incomparably smarter and more evolved than the contemporary man as well as being full of superior qualities. As we will see, the invasion occurred when even these evolved *E-N-K* beings began to withdraw from the Earth's surface, especially starting with the last period of Atlantis, culminating in its total immersion.

MATURATION OF MEN

Another very important decision taken during the Great Council of Teotihuacan was the beginning of the sequential withdrawal of the permanent extraterrestrial presence from the life on Earth. The supervision was thus transferred gradually from direct involvement on the surface of the Earth to a careful monitoring by technological means from the physical plane but also from the etheric plane. By their wisdom, these highly advanced extraterrestrial civilizations knew very well that a civilization must evolve "on its own feet" in order to have the chance for a proper understanding of its future and the future of the Universe. Besides, this is a natural law that governs all kingdoms: the child reaches an age at which, being quite mature, separates from his parents in order to follow his own path in life. This had to be accomplished in stages, however, because the process of creating the human being had been and is based upon high knowledge, patience and wisdom. Even so, there was the unfortunate event of the decline and sinking of Atlantis which I will treat separately and which is an example to understand how unstable and delicate things can become in the context of the evolution of beings.

CHAPTER TWELVE

Atlantis

Beyond the current controversy surrounding the existence of the old continent of Atlantis, there is also the question of where it would have been. The clues are vague and the searches difficult. Some discoveries are noteworthy, however, except that the international media, as well as the scientific community, do not react in such cases, hoping that everything will fall into derision or oblivion. The recognition of such a discovery would shed light on all that was believed to be true about humanity's past evolution, epochs of development, ancient civilizations, and technology at that time.

SOME CLARIFICATIONS

Most opinions converge on the placement of Atlantis in the Atlantic Ocean, and this is correct. One of the oldest representations, in Athanasius Kircher's view, gives a good idea of where Atlantis was, but it is incomplete.[*]

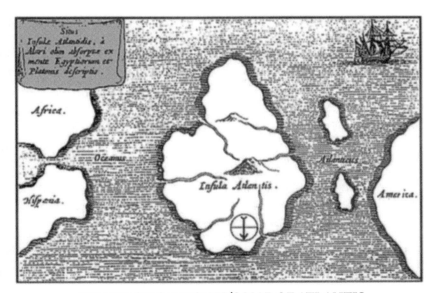

ATHANASIUS KIRCHER'S MAP OF ATLANTIS

---

[*]Athanasius Kircher (1602-1680) was a German Jesuit scholar who published around 40 major works, most notably in the fields of comparative religion, geology, and medicine. He correctly established the link between the ancient Egyptian and the Coptic languages, and some commentators regard him as the founder of Egyptology.

**THE ABOVE DRAWING SHOWS A LOCATION THAT
IS CLOSER TO THE GEOGRAPHICAL REALITY
OF THOSE TIMES REGARDING ATLANTIS**

There are, however, some observations to make. As I have seen in the pictures on the holographic screen, the surface of Atlantis was relatively large, almost like a continent, occupying the center of the Atlantic Ocean; but the northern part of the island was a little lower, parallel to Philadelphia today. On the other hand, the island's shape was more decidedly triangular, and from this point of view, Kircher's drawing is better. Also, in Kircher's drawing, only two islands surrounding the great continent-island which was Atlantis are correctly represented, but those under Africa are not mentioned, one of them being slightly smaller than present-day Sri Lanka. A proportional representation of what I saw in the images is on the opposite page.

Subsequently, after the first fragmentation of Atlantis, there were indeed a few island strings around the central island which could be considered as its "suburbs". For example, the Azores are remnants of the upper islands that were part of Atlantis as well as the Cape Verde Islands which are actually areas of the slightly larger island that existed to the right of Atlantis. The Canary Islands, however, as they are presently constituted, have no connection with the territory of Atlantis.

On the other hand, the Bermuda Islands are currently fragments of the large island to the left of Atlantis. Several vestiges can be found on the bottom

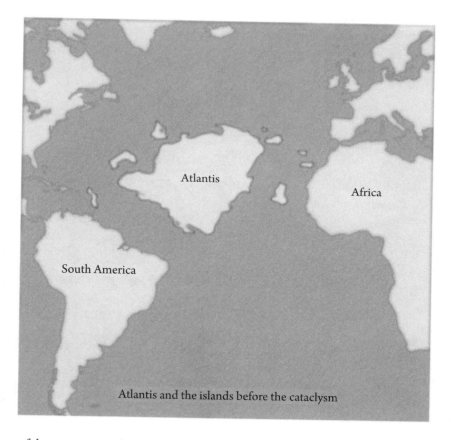

Atlantis and the islands before the cataclysm

of the ocean around some of these islands. For example, in the area of where Bermuda is today, huge pyramids were built, and in the Azores, there was a developed city.

In the northeastern part of Atlantis, towards Europe, there was even a "fan" of small islands which are not shown in Kircher's drawing but do appear in the second drawing. Only small fragments remain (the Azores), reminiscent of the great civilization of many thousands of years ago.

THE FLOWERING CIVILIZATION OF ATLANTIS

Interestingly, when Atlantis was in its infancy, most of its population and life was concentrated on the coasts of the islands and the "continent". In the middle of it was a lot of vegetation which aesthetically surrounded the great pyramids there, the gigantic spaceport and other buildings that appeared as very tall towers. Most of the activity occurred, however, in the

Overview of Atlantis

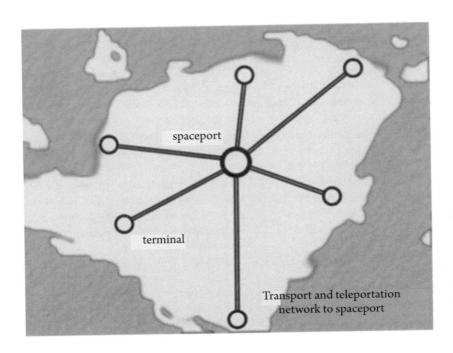

Transport and teleportation
network to spaceport

coastal areas of the island where the bustle was very high, both on the ground and in the air.

Many regions on the great continent were circular with what appeared to be rays leading to the center of the island. When the image zoomed in on them, I noticed that the rays were in fact a type of tubes with a fairly large diameter, probably to facilitate rapid transport.

Atlantis was known not only for its highly advanced civilization and culture but also for being a central area of connection between the Earth and beings on other planets. There was a complex mix between beings on Earth belonging exclusively to the E-N-L branch, and many other types of beings on other planets in our galaxy. In this regard, this was not too much different from some of the science fiction movie scenes that have appeared on the market so far, although this might seem unbelievable to many readers.

Atlantis was highly evolved compared to the rest of the continents, much like we are today in comparison to a tribe in the Amazon or New Guinea. It not only had connections with beings from other parts of the Earth; but as I said, it represented an important point of connection with other civilizations in the universe, being an active part in trade and cosmic diplomacy in this region of the galaxy.

In the middle of the island, there was a huge spaceport with a very intense activity of both Atlantean and extraterrestrial ships of many types and sizes. Watching the images on the screen, I noticed that they largely correspond to other stories about Atlantis which have been presented over time in books or on the internet. Earth had become a very important center of cosmic transit, meaning that extraterrestrial activity, especially diplomatic and commercial activity, was very intense. Many ships of various sizes and shapes came and went from our planet, using different platforms and terminals on the big island, but the largest and most important spaceport was the one in the middle of the Atlantean continent.

I could also see in those images a kind of "subtle x-ray" of the Earth where its magnetic field was somewhat different from the current one. I was shown, in a very ingenious way, that over a fairly large area above Atlantis, the terrestrial magnetic field had many vortices which made it appear that there was a "third pole" of the planet. It was a natural phenomenon due to a massive deposit of specific metallic rocks which exist below the surface of the Earth and correspond to that area. This is why, even in the modern period, the strange phenomena that occur in the Bermuda area are still noticed.

The existence of this "third pole" of the Earth's magnetic field allowed for the entry to and exit from the atmosphere in a very easy way for extraterrestrial ships as well as those from the Earth. This created a sort of "corridor" in the aerial activity whereby the friction with the air was much smaller and the action of gravity was weaker. For the ships of advanced civilizations, this aspect was of little importance as their technology was not dependent on such forces, but at that time, Atlantis had many other connections with developed middle civilizations whose ships depended upon those aspects. The technology of such civilizations had not, for example, reached the level of very advanced propulsion systems based on elements of a quantum nature or special forces fields, and they did not possess the knowledge necessary to sufficiently generate resistant "energy shields" around their ships in order to cancel out the frictional or inertial effects.

THE FINAL SINKING OF ATLANTIS

Before the great cataclysm that led to the extinction of Atlantis, the sinking of the continental shelf had already begun, but the process proceeded slowly, over several tens of thousands of years, culminating with its total disappearance under water around 11,500 B.C. This date is shared by many visionaries, esotericists, clairvoyants or beings with special powers; and as far as I was able to calculate and interpolate the frequencies shown in the images on the holographic screen, the time point indicated is correct, maybe within a margin of several decades. The continent, however, began to sink dramatically and crumble into islands about 1,000-1,200 years before the final cataclysm. The last deluge was faster and even more terrifying due to devastating earthquakes which not only occurred in the area of the Atlantean continent but also in many other areas of the planet. What remained relatively intact from the old continent was its part from Africa, but the rest was scattered on larger or smaller islands.

One of the very interesting aspects of the disappearance of Atlantis is that of its sudden destruction. Plato says it happened "in one day and one night". In reality, the destruction of the continent took place in stages, and only the final phase was abrupt. In the first phase, what was once a huge island continent "broke" into a few "slices" which have become islands. As a result, Atlantis quickly transformed into an island area, thus losing cohesion.

As an important remark, I can say that what was perceived as sudden was the phenomenon of breaking the connection between the physical and the etheric plane which, until then, was quite solid in Atlantis. At the beginning of the destruction, the beings from the etheric plane did not very clearly notice the sinking of parts of the physical continent, but at one point, due to the dimensional split, those from the etheric plane found that they no longer had support, as if the rug was being pulled out from beneath their feet, and the etheric plane was beginning to dissolve.

They could no longer relate to the physical plane as they had been used to before. For example, as I witnessed in some images, they were going in a certain direction to reach a city on land; but they saw sea water instead, knowing there had to be something else.

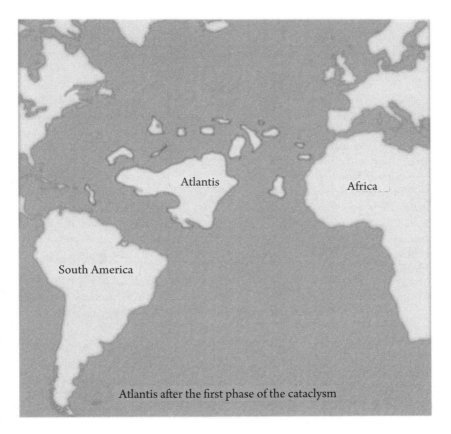

Atlantis after the first phase of the cataclysm

Therefore, that part of the etheric plane that remained without support was re-absorbed into the dry territories of the physical plane because, at that time, being close to it, the etheric plane also needed to "lean" on something. Even today there are such alignments between the physical plane and the etheric plane; much less than in that period, but they still exist. For example, if you go through a forest and pass through a dimensional chasm, you can enter the etheric plane, but that does not mean that it is compulsory to wake up suddenly on the top of a mountain or in the middle of a lake; but it usually respects characteristics of the surrounding space where the passage was made. There are differences in the landscape, but they are not blatant, at least not from the beginning.

Atlantis therefore did not die "in one day and one night" as has been said. Her submerging went a long way and went in stages, her last vestiges disappearing into the water about 13,500 years ago. The notion of "sudden" could be the break from the etheric plane or the last cataclysm that was sprinkled with disasters.

If that cataclysm had taken place naturally, a duration which would have corresponded to a period of millions of years, the sinking of Atlantis might indeed seem like it took place "in just one day and one night". That is to say, it was pretty fast.

The forces and energies involved at that time were huge and they deeply destabilized the energy structure of the Earth's crust, also causing large disturbances in the corresponding etheric plane. The sinking of Atlantis was also due to major changes that occurred at the Earth's crust level during that period. I saw the holographic images depicting the rearrangement of the Earth's crust. Basically, it "rotated" and then arrived at its current structure.

After that massive rearrangement of the crust, which took place around the third polar axis that passes through the area of Atlantis, the very strong magnetic vortex that characterized that axis decreased in intensity, and as a result, the potential energetic connection with the etheric plane diminished. Interestingly, this truth was already exposed by Charles Hapgood, and I knew his theory referring to the displacement of the Earth's crust as a result of the "drift" of the poles.[*]

I was amazed but also glad to find that it was, in fact, perfectly true.

THE TWO ATLANTEAN CAMPS

The commercial, scientific and cultural exchanges that Atlantis had with many other extraterrestrial civilizations made the Atlantean civilization evolve very quickly. From what I saw on the holographic screen, their golden color was yellow, which is not surprising, especially since the symbol of their civilization was the Sun, often represented on their clothing in the chest area. After reaching an advanced level of spiritual and technological development, however, due to the phenomenon of the diminishing connection with the etheric plane, segregation occurred in their civilization. A part of the population evolved, reaching a higher frequency of consciousness by maintaining the connection with the etheric plane, and another part remained rigid in thought, having limited beliefs which were shared by some members and even some wise people.

I understood this when I was shown the general energy field as a sphere, both emotionally and mentally, of the last period of this civilization. I noticed that it split so that from the global yellow that characterized it as a subtle hue, two distinct subtle colors appeared: one had a light blue hue, and the other was red-orange. There were two different frequencies: those more oriented to red-orange belonged to a high level of society and scientists, and those who were part of the subtle field of light blue represented the sages and the "spiritual category" of society of Atlantis.

---

[*] *The Path of the Pole*, Adventures Unlimited Press, 1999.

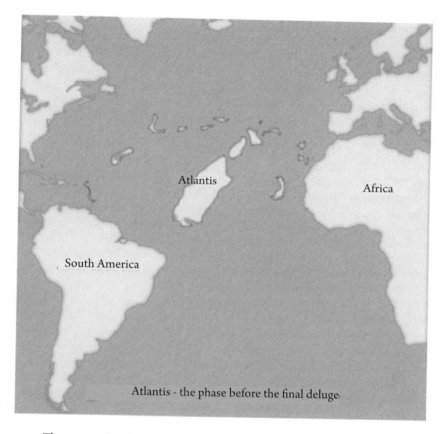

Atlantis - the phase before the final deluge

The separation into two somewhat antagonistic categories of thinking and feeling among the Atlantean population had become increasingly evident. As a result, many of those who belonged to the blue category went to other parts of the world a few hundred years before the final cataclysm, giving birth to other centers that were developed in areas where the connection with the etheric plane remained for a while longer. Gradually, due to the withdrawal of the blue faction, Atlantis began to be dominated by the subtle orange faction whose orientation was mainly materialistic.

The really wise ones left Atlantis for two reasons. First, the separation from materialistic Atlantis was necessary for reasons of matching resonant vibrational frequencies; and on the other hand, they aimed to really help the population of *E-N-K* beings to develop, progress and evolve faster because they foresaw the virtual end of the *E-N-L* branch due to the limitation of its resources for procreation and the potential for progress. At the same time, they knew that the end of Atlantis could not be avoided and wanted to preserve the immense knowledge they possessed, passing it on to the *E-N-K* population that would remain as the only one on Earth.

Due to the fact that the difference in evolution between the *E-N-L* branch and most of the *E-N-K* beings was immense, the Atlantean scholars realized that, if they were not to serve as an active and efficient educational and orientation arm for the *E-N-K* branch, humanity would simply remain at a primitive level of development because its only members would be *E-N-K*.

THE DRAMATIC CLIMAX OF ATLANTIS

The last sequence of images presented to me on the holographic screen included the last seconds of Atlantis, and it involved a great deal of drama. The last exceptional achievement of that extraordinary civilization, which we saw as it sank in the waters, was the huge shining pyramid that towered in the center of the Atlantean continent, near the spaceport. It was much larger than the current pyramids in Egypt, featuring perfectly smooth sides, like translucent metal. I was only shown those moments in which the top of the pyramid plunged into huge waves. At the top of the pyramid, I saw a lighthouse which was actually a huge ruby-colored crystal which flashed intermittently, like a laser, until it was dislocated and destroyed by the huge waves created by the terrible cataclysm. At the same time, the image of the Atlantic Ocean somehow seemed to superimpose itself upon me from above and over that drastic moment in which the huge pyramid sank in the surrounding waters which by that time had become only a vast expanse of water without any large dry surface. In this way, I was shown the complete end of Atlantis which, beyond the very sad visual moment, brought with it a feeling of great suffering and breaking in the soul which I perceived acutely, like a hopeless cry of the submerged continent itself. It was the last cry of a great civilization which belonged to the *E-N-L* branch.

THE GREAT MEETING AND PLAN FOR SAVING MEN

As I mentioned earlier, knowing early on the imminence of the coming cataclysm, the sages who ruled Atlantis wanted to preserve much of their civilization's knowledge but at the same time sought to support the evolution of the *E-N-K* branch of beings that remained after Atlantis. They knew that the branch that led to the formation of the Atlantean civilization and its peaks, that is the *E-N-L* branch, would decline and even disappear, so they set out to support the evolution of the other branch (*E-N-K*) by using the high knowledge they had acquired by then.

Immediately after the images with the total immersion of the continent, I was shown a very large gathering of human beings and aliens under a huge dome in a mountainous area, but I could not identify the exact place on Earth where it happened. From a certain point of view, that meeting resembled the Great Planetary Council 28,000 years ago, but the assembly after the disappearance of Atlantis was more hectic, and the proportion of human beings within it was higher. Even so, I was able to see an amazing variety of races, both human and alien.

I estimated the number of beings present at that meeting as more than 250 souls. My understanding telepathically was that it was a menagerie of life forms and races which had responded to the call for help from the wise E-N-L beings, a call that was made even before Atlantis completely disappeared. Due to the great tension that had been generated by the planetary cataclysm that had just taken place, I could see obvious signs of concern in some of the participants of the meeting. This amounted to unresolved fear that persisted and even a certain nervousness that manifested in such cases.

There, during that special meeting, very important decisions were made regarding the future evolution of our planet and of the E-N-K beings. Practically speaking, the main coordination points of the planet were established. From a certain point of view, these were even more concrete and effective decisions than those established at the Great Planetary Council of 26,000 B.C. because the situation was dramatic as even the initial project for training the intelligent and spiritually evolved human being was in danger of failure. Humanity was at risk of either "anonymously" disappearing or self-destructing.

Following the images, I could not help but notice that the council conducted a kind of "negotiation" of the areas of the Earth which were distributed to every extraterrestrial civilization to be "redone". Initially, I thought that their representatives were interested in the resources of the underground or surface areas where they would have influence. I soon realized, however, that this was not the "negotiation" criterion. It was rather a requirement that there be a large E-N-K population in the assigned area.

The participants at that meeting requested this in order to be able to make genetic changes in the DNA structure of the respective population which would follow the characteristics of the extraterrestrial race that was watching their evolution. It was therefore about a redistribution of the "zones of influence" that had been fixed about 14,000 years ago at the Great Planetary Council in Teotihuacan, only that now, after Atlantis's sinking, the global situation was much more critical.

THE "BREAKING" OF THE VIBRATIONAL FREQUENCY OF CONSCIOUSNESS

The cataclysm influenced not only the physical structure of the planet's crust, it also caused changes in its frequency of vibration, affecting the energetic condition of the subtle planes attached to the Earth. It was a general "fall" in all respects, and humanity took a very big step back.

Many of the results obtained from the evolution of the human race up to that point were almost annihilated by that huge cataclysm which had negative repercussions on a global level. Among others, an entire E-N-L civilization — from what I had seen, the Atlantean civilization was the last of its kind on Earth — that was exceptional by reason of its technological and spiritual advancement had disappeared underwater, along with a large number of evolved beings and the amazing achievements of its progress. Knowledge, experience and advancement in all of the sciences of the time had been annihilated in a relatively short period. The evolutionary resources of Mankind had suddenly become very limited because almost all of the remaining beings that populated the planet at that time were still poorly evolved E-N-K beings.

I could feel all of this telepathically as well as a kind of "impregnation" of the specific state at that time after the great cataclysm. Under other circumstances, I would have described that situation as somewhat desperate for Mankind, but the immediate mobilization of the wise Atlantean survivors and some of the advanced extraterrestrial civilizations has diminished the terrible energy and consciousness collapse that would be felt for thousands of years as a result of the disappearance of the great civilization of Atlantis.

SUPPORT AND RECOVERY PLAN FOR HUMANITY

One of the first measures of that mobilization was the urgent reunion of the extraterrestrial civilizations interested in helping to reconstruct the chain of accelerated evolution of the human being. That is what was meant by the distribution of the extraterrestrial "zones of influence" in regards to the reconstruction of human civilization as it applies to the material plane as well as science, spirituality and knowledge in general. At the same time, the "nursery" of the genetic dowry of human DNA was to be enriched and improved by hybridizations and genetic modifications of the DNA of E-N-K beings. This needed to happen because the "inheritance" of E-N-L beings had been largely lost, due both to the cataclysm as well as their progressive withdrawal into the etheric plane. The new distribution of extraterrestrial "zones of influence" on Earth was going to bring a fresh breath into the DNA structure of E-N-K beings, allowing them to understand and rebuild at least some of the knowledge of evolved E-N-L beings.

The human beings in such an extraterrestrial "zone of influence" have accordingly, over time, manifested some characteristics of the civilization with which they were hybridized because their DNA had been combined to a significant extent with the DNA of that extraterrestrial civilization. They were like the "sons" of that civilization which thus contributed to the structural complexity of human DNA. For example, the aliens wanted to find out how many combinations were able to support the DNA of the E-N-K beings, what was the nature and particularities of those combinations, what were the limits of development for genome structure, and how many "extensions" could it resist. Naturally, the representatives of each alien civilization had a certain margin in which they could control the DNA of E-N-K beings, and this only involved the domain that was related to the specificity of their DNA.

Beyond the altruistic desire to participate in the genetic experiment of forming a very complex being, however, I did not quite understand why the extraterrestrial civilizations wanted to experience this. They probably wanted to reinvigorate and improve their own DNA or plan a "relocation" of E-N-K beings to other planets. This was not too clear to me, but I did not insist on knowing that. I realized, however, that this was a unique opportunity at a galactic level which could not be ignored for many advanced civilizations because its potential was very high. I suppose that was a good reason why many extraterrestrial civilizations answered the call, in addition to those of the Alliance, the latter coming from a sector of the galaxy that was closer.

SOME PERSONAL CONSIDERATIONS

The description of how things went with Atlantis at that time does not coincide with all of those who have spoken or written about it. Most often, in the expositions that are made by different authors, there is a combination of true and imaginary elements in which, unfortunately, the imagination predominates. Also, the lack of details or accurate descriptions of important issues makes science about the distant periods of Mankind remain somewhat blurred or poorly understood, especially since many do not know the parallel existence that E-N-L beings were capable of by reason of their access to the etheric plane where, on the other hand, the lesser developed E-N-K beings did not have access.

It could, of course, be argued that my presentation on the true history of Mankind could be false or that it might be just a product of my imagination. Ultimately, why should the reader believe in me more than other authors who have exposed their own version of events from the very distant past of humanity? The situation is sensitive because undoubtedly clear evidence of a physical nature cannot presently be brought to public notice even if this is currently possible. This is how the system works, and these are its "obligatory requirements". We cannot do everything we want because we are integrated into a society that is still strongly antagonistic. For various reasons, interests that are more or less occult often deprive the human being of true knowledge, and that is the reason many of the elements that have been discovered cannot yet be presented to the world. Given the level of culture and understanding of humanity today, some of these reasons are justified and meaningful. The question remains, however, whether these reasons are enough to prevent the truth from being revealed in the areas that are kept in the top secret and ultra top secret categories.

For example, with regard to the elements related to the true history of Mankind, I was allowed to present only some of its flagged instances, not all of which I managed to see. Even so, there remains the question of the credibility of the facts and aspects presented, but this is already an individual matter. It is the individual reader's decision, discernment, and his knowledge and intuition regarding the aspects I present that are most significant.

The reader is faced with difficult choices because he can hear the information coming from other authors which does not coincide with that which is written here by me. In some cases, this can lead to confusion or even a kind of rejection because he might feel misled in his expectations or manipulated by the nature of the disclosures on one subject or another, disclosures that differ from one author to another.

In such cases, nothing can be done. The only element that I can invoke in addition to that would be that, as far as I am concerned, I have actually seen these fragments of human history, almost everything in the manner as movies are viewed on a screen, but at an incomparably higher level of technology and synthesis. The viewing procedure was doubled by telepathic transmission processes and intuitive understandings, all determined by the interaction with that advanced technology at the cortex level. My descriptions can be taken as such or not, and it is up to everyone to decide for themselves. With the information I present here, however, correlations can be made and things that have never been explained before can be understood, all of which is an important starting point for an individual's analysis.

INTER-DIMENSIONAL PORTALS

During the distant period of Atlantis, better known as the period of the Hyperborean civilization, E-N-L beings had evolved so much that they began to be recognized by highly evolved extraterrestrial civilizations.

The possibilities of our planet in those times were more extensive because the Earth offered not only the variant of the physical plane but also that of the etheric plane into which some of the beings on its surface could reach. At that time, the frequencies of the physical and etheric planes were quite close, even though many of the areas and points of confluence between them had disappeared as a result of the terrible Tarsus War.

Even during Atlantis, there were no great differences between the two planes (physical and the ethereal) as there are today. The initiates knew how to consciously move from one plane to the next and especially knew how to make a difference between them. For *E-N-L* beings, that was an ordinary and very natural practice, but the passage into the etheric plane through the many portals that existed at that time was perfectly possible and easy to do, even for some of the more developed *E-N-K* beings.

These interactions between the physical and the etheric plane were many, and the physical blended with the etheric in a very natural way. In many places on the Earth's surface, especially in the northern hemisphere, there were such "gates" of passage or even vast territories of manifestation of the etheric plane which is, of course, higher than the physical one in terms of vibrational frequency. In fact, many of the unknowns, mysteries, and the so-called mythological events of history of ancient times are precisely explained by that characteristic of the times of several tens of thousands of years ago, when the physical dimension was paired with the subtle etheric one.

It is true, however, that access through those "gates" between the planes was intended primarily for the evolved *E-N-L* beings or the "demigods" and less so or not at all for the primitive *E-N-K* beings, the latter primarily fearing such manifestations, attributing them to supernatural dimensions. The penetration into the etheric plane through those portals was valid only for a certain initiated segment of the population. This fact is important because it made it possible to save part of the wise beings in Atlantis at the time of the deluge and to establish those beings in different parts of the planet. But the most important aspect is that the existence of inter-dimensional portals on the surface of the planet, even if less than in ancient times, has allowed and maintained the links and communication with the evolved extraterrestrial beings and with the higher etheric plane.

THE "REVOLUTION" AND THE FALL OF ATLANTIS

In Atlantis, all human beings belonged to the *E-N-L* branches. After a while, and due to some subtle influences, some of those beings began to turn toward less orthodox actions, pursuing personal interests; and in particular, seizing the power of leadership and control of very advanced technologies. Thus, they began to engage in strange cross-breeding between species, using *E-N-K* beings for this purpose as they were considered to be underdeveloped and, in their mind, could serve as guinea pigs for those strange hybridizations. The main mistake of the *E-N-L* beings who rebelled in this way during the Atlantean period was that they ignored one obvious fact: they, like the *E-N-K*, evolved from the same initial DNA structure. The *E-N-K* beings were therefore their genetic brothers.

By performing the very strange cross-breeding and genetic experiments, the rebels actually broke and altered certain beneficial resonances in their DNA because it was directly related to that of the *E-N-K* beings that they considered to be inferior. As I was shown, those were bad and even evil actions that violated the laws of universal justice, both by intention and by the goals they wanted to achieve.

Thus, even though the E-N-L branch was quite evolved, there was still segregation within it because only a portion of them evolved, remaining connected with the "E-N-L elite group" while another portion remained unevolved because they persisted in those experiments and in the fulfillment of selfish plans, descending to an individual level.

Due to the fact that the rebels were beings who already possessed great powers and advanced knowledge, their negative actions and intentions had very strong reverberations throughout the world. By accumulation, a terrible shock came to human civilization as the frequency of energies dropped sharply.

Uninspired by the E-N-L beings, the game deviated from the beings of the K branch (E-N-K), to which were added the selfish intentions to grab power for personal use, thus undermining the balance of energies on the continent and finally caused the full destruction of it. Thus, instead of evolving, part of the L branch created that very acute problem on the planet which was a real undermining of its own energy level.

AFTER THE CATACLYSM

In the face of the imminent danger of the destruction of Atlantis, some of the benevolent E-N-L beings migrated and sought the help of evolved beings from the "elite groups" of E-N-L from other areas as well as highly advanced extraterrestrial civilizations. It was a decisive moment; and then, at a galactic and planetary level, it was decided that this aspect would be repaired or at least diminished in its gravity.

As a result, Sirian beings began to incarnate into the genetic lines of the evolved and beneficial E-N-L beings that existed on Earth to fully support this process of recovery and to once again support the cradle of human civilization. This was possible because, as I mentioned, a large part of the E-N-L beings had reached an advanced degree of evolution which allowed for the incarnation of wise extraterrestrial beings into E-N-L physical bodies. After the fall of Atlantis, it was necessary that the evolution of the E-N-K human beings, which we know as homo sapiens, be accelerated. Until then, and generally speaking, E-N-K beings had been allowed to evolve freely, without precise targeting. Occasionally, they received an "impulse" through various types of extraterrestrial hybridization which proved to be more or less positive. The DNA complexity of the E-N-K beings was high, and the K branch evolved without any ordering or qualitative targeting, taking an even more difficult path that was only through one's own experience.

When the destruction of the Atlantean continent became imminent and nothing could be done, the sages and a small part of the class of learned nobles left the area, either by turning to other star systems with which Atlantis had close trade and diplomatic ties or by withdrawing to Shambhala to help humanity. Migration from that level of society spread to certain areas of the planet, especially to Egypt, South America or the eastern and northern areas of Europe. During the sinking of Atlantis, a large part of the population retreated inside the Earth, especially due to the decision to give the E-N-K branch the freedom to evolve freely. At first, there were only E-N-L beings; but then, over the following thousands of years, the inner "cavity" of the planet was populated with E-N-K beings. The first to retire there were the "demigods"; and then, gradually, came the sufficiently evolved E-N-K beings.

What I noticed and found interesting was the fact that the Atlanteans that remained on Earth did not travel to other areas using expected transportation. They neither traveled by water nor sailed with their high-performance equipment. What happened in those last weeks and days before the final destruction was actually a passage through the etheric plane, on the ground. For example, they arrived in Egypt by land after first moving into the etheric plane, and then returning to the physical plane when they reached what was called Khem, the Black Earth Country in northern Africa that we call Egypt.

CENTERS OF INITIATORY LINEAGE

With the sinking of Atlantis, the overall vibrational frequency of our planet dropped dramatically. This is precisely why it was necessary to implement spiritual lineages and higher education among the populations of E-N-K beings, the majority of which remained on the surface of the Earth. This way, the evolution of humanity would not be blocked.

Therefore, each civilization or group of civilizations, together with the Atlanteans, have assumed something in this direction. Until then, many of the Alliance civilizations that took part in the process of the formation of the human race have implemented their own DNA or genetic influence into the basic DNA, as designed by the most advanced of them. For a while, they followed the development of those characteristics in human beings; and then, when they considered that they had completed their mission, they withdrew from the area of influence that was distributed to them on Earth, especially after the Great Planetary Council of 26,000 B.C.

After the destruction of Atlantis, however, it was the first time that the cities in charge of the Galactic Alliance, with Shambhala as their central forum, asked for help to start collaborations with other civilizations in the galaxy and to act on Earth in order to restore at least some of what had been lost in the planetary and Atlantean cataclysm. We are talking about knowledge, spirituality, science and technology.

From what I saw on the holographic screen, I realized that their action was fast and efficient. I noticed that the implementation of the spiritual lineages and teachings in that period had to be done directly. The method used before the destruction of Atlantis, when the king or the wise man transmitted certain notions and initiations, was no longer valid because, after the almost complete withdrawal of *E-N-L* beings, the population consisted of *E-N-K* beings, and they had already begun to be divided into different categories of thinking and action.

People not only needed royal lineages but also lineages of wisdom and spiritual paths separate from royalty. As a result, those teachings had to be offered after the destruction of Atlantis, especially at the beginning, by the wise Atlantean and extraterrestrial beings who came among the people and initiated them into different fields of science and spirituality. I saw in those images how they brought that knowledge, first into the middle of small groups, then into the initiation schools formed, and finally, into more complex systems of teaching which involved elements of higher technology. Thus, some peak periods were formed among the *E-N-K* beings which then propagated more and more of that knowledge among the larger populations of people, giving rise to higher lineages and systems of thought.

THE IMPORTANCE OF THE E-N-K BRANCH

Gradually, following those images, I began to realize with astonishment that the *K* branch, in fact, was of major interest to all of those extraterrestrial civilizations. It was astonishing and even inexplicable to me to find out that the most developed branch of human DNA could give rise to such great interest from the point of view of genetic development. As I said, since the beginning, *E-N-K* beings have been allowed to evolve somewhat alone, through their own experience. That is to say, there has not been a massive intervention in their case such as happened in the case of *E-N-L* beings who have been constantly refined, enriched with new frequencies, and chiseled at the DNA level.

The main reason was in a certain kind of "rigidity" of the genetic manipulation of this branch. The *K* branch was very mobile in different types of crossing-breedings, but it was not very evolved. In contrast to the genetic "malleability" of the *E-N-L* branch, the *E-N-K* branch did not have the ability to withstand high frequencies in the DNA macromolecule, and this resulted in a slow evolution for the species, especially as it was not helped by exterior "impulses." In the face of my justified astonishment, the man from Apellos explained to me that a very interesting argument was the basis of such a decision regarding *E-N-K* beings. The alien civilizations in the Alliance became very interested in the *E-N-K* gene because of the special vitality that is manifested by the specific structure of the DNA of this branch. The *E-N-K* gene had preserved and even developed a vital energy intrinsic to the being which made it highly productive, resilient and stable. It is not by accident that the majority of human beings on the surface of the Earth were *E-N-K* beings at that time, and this is still true today. They were well integrated into the Earth's biosphere and resonated effectively with it.

At a certain point in evolution, even if the refinement and level of consciousness is not too high, this vital side matters enormously because it provides the "fuel" needed for gene continuity without it rapidly decaying. Vitality is a "regenerator"; and, at the same time, a "capacitor" of energy for the evolving being. In the case of the *K* branch, it gave the DNA the possibility to make numerous interatomic combinations inside the macromolecule. This made it a fertile field for possible combinations with other types of DNA but also with high vital energy.

Even so, not all *E-N-K* beings were at a primitive level along the lines of evolution. Some of them had been hybridized with higher DNA, most often with that of *E-N-L* beings but also with extraterrestrial beings. Even if the results were not "spectacular" from the start, however, genetic changes were transmitted over time; and at least on certain lines of influence and in certain areas, *E-N-K* beings became very powerful, radiant, charismatic and gifted, even possessing paranormal powers.

As I have said, legends and myths, which actually tell us about extraordinary events that actually happened, refer to such beings as "demigods"; that is, human beings endowed with special abilities, far superior to ordinary *E-N-K* beings. There were also intermediate levels of development, but most *E-N-K* beings were at an early stage of evolution.

Because *E-N-K* beings were spread all over the globe, their level of consciousness also differed greatly. We have seen, for example, small communities of higher *E-N-K* beings living very close to communities of primitive *E-N-K* beings, just as in our cities we meet various categories of beings, ranging from academics to beggars, or cities developed near primitive tribes, all living in the same area of the Earth.

THE REFORMATION OF HUMAN CIVILIZATION

As I said, after the cataclysm of Atlantis, knowledge began to be shared with people in different parts of the globe. Medicine, astrological knowledge, and alchemy then began to appear, as well as other remarkable sciences which had not been known before among the *E-N-K* beings. In a summarized and exemplary series of images, I saw the way in which they were implemented slowly so as to enable the more rigid consciousness of *E-N-K* beings to as-similate everything correctly and to use those gifts more effectively. Much knowledge has been passed on through myths and legends with many celestial events having been expressed through stories of "gods" and "goddesses".

Until then, knowledge was a unitary whole because, as far as I could tell, everything was part of the essential spiritual knowledge of the times. After the disappearance of Atlantis, however, it was necessary for different fields of knowledge to be segmented and explained within the meaning of the *E-N-K* branch in order to be closer to their relevant specificity. For example, some tended to study, others dedicated themselves to art, and a few of them ap-proached the sciences and esoteric. This is why the wise Atlanteans, together with those who represented part of the Alliance's alien civilizations, assumed a domain into which to implement their own specific vibrational frequency into the knowledge of humans; that is, the *E-N-K*.

All the great "gods" who followed in the ancient tradition of Egypt (Thoth, Ra, etc.) represented guardians supporting this reformation of the spiritual branch of human civilization. In fact, the first ancient civilization that really mattered in the evolution of the *E-N-K* was the Egyptian civiliza-tion. The few higher *E-N-L* beings who remained after the fall of Atlantis and who sought help from advanced extraterrestrial beings had to maintain contact with them in order to build the huge pyramids that remain today. The reason for this is that the three great pyramids in Egypt are in fact just that: subtle communication centers which are by no means the version supported by some historians, Egyptologists and contemporary scientists who refer to them as "megalomaniac constructions" that served one purpose: the funeral of the pharaoh. Few of them have the courage to say that "refugee" Atlanteans in Egypt and other places on Earth — such as Central and South America, eastern Europe and even China — have been helped by some advanced alien civilizations in designing and making these pyramids, as I will describe later.

At that time, large spherical Sirian ships were no longer in the sky. As I was shown fleetingly, the presence of ships in the sky continued up to 350,000 B.C., then occasionally up to 330,000 B.C., and very rarely up to a period I estimated to be around 130,000 B.C. By then, in southern Africa, there was already a developed civilization comprising a very large number of *E-N-L* beings. Afterwards, during the flowering of the Lemurian civilization in the Pacific, another huge Sirian ship appeared in the sky, but I did not see details about it. On the celestial vault, however, I saw that it was accompanied by several other types of alien ships of great proportions but smaller than the Sirian ship. Much later, it was shown to me that some of the alien ships would play an important role in the history of Egyptian civilization, helping to build the pyramids and other great temples after the sinking of Atlantis.

CHAPTER THIRTEEN

Building the Egyptian Pyramids

Controversies over the age of the pyramids on the Giza plateau near Cairo are almost meaningless. Any man with some good sense and intelligence, as well as a minimum knowledge, can realize that the "classic" rant that attributes the great pyramids in Egypt to be approximately 4,500 years old, supported by contemporary archeologists and Egyptologists, is hilarious. To this is added the stupid idea that those colossal buildings were built to hold the grave for the pharaoh who lived during the period in which they were erected.

THE TRUE AGE OF THE GREAT PYRAMIDS IN EGYPT

Regarding this, one fact is certain. The way the three pyramids were built has absolutely nothing to do with the present "academic vision". No person with a certain culture and intelligence could possibly swallow the version agreed upon by some Egyptologists and contemporary archeologists about the origin of the pyramids and even less about that of the Sphinx, all of which is completely hidden from modern science. There are so many question marks, unresolved issues, and mysterious elements in connection with these grand constructions that they do not even deserve to be mentioned here.

This "drama" of hidden truth, often ridiculous in the daring way it is supported by today's science, has its roots in the inability of historians, archeologists and Egyptologists to believe that the history of Mankind might be different from the way it is generally presented to the whole world. For example, huge portions of this history, such as the existence of Atlantis and its demise, are excluded on the grounds that they can only be "legends". The "Episode of Atlantis" in the history of Mankind, however, was one of the most important because the disappearance of the great island has radically influenced the situation of humanity and even of the entire planet. To this was added the withdrawal of the land of Shambhala into the etheric plane about 27,500 years ago. The disappearance of these two essential poles of knowledge and evolution of life on Earth has dramatically influenced the course of humanity's development.

We can talk about a lot of counter arguments and elements that demonstrate the falsity of the "orthodox" ideas about the antiquity of the Egyptian pyramids and how they were built, but I do not think it is necessary to present them here. The interested reader can, with a minimum of research, discover such for himself and then be amused by the naivety and superficiality of the opinions expressed by a certain "arena" of scientists.

Interestingly, many people with certain qualities of extra-sensory perception and special endowments have mentioned something other than the tacitly accepted scientific version about these extraordinary constructions. Some of the elements that have been described by these authors correspond to the reality of the akashic records to which I had access, but others are presented incorrectly or are omitted.

There is even a consensus among those who admit that the pyramids are something other than what is commonly stated. This is the idea that the pyramids were built by an alien civilization, and this is not far from the truth. Rather than explanations or accounts of who built them or how they were built, there are, generally speaking, many more mysteries that have been observed in relation to the great pyramids built in different regions of the Earth. The explanations of this nature are often a mixture of truth and imagination, but there is also a special category of them coming from Egyptologists, archeologists and scientists in which they are completely wrong.

If we refer to the architectural complex near Cairo, but especially to the Great Pyramid, the correct dating of the construction is about 13,500 years ago. It was not too difficult to find this "age" from the "interplay" of frequencies, especially since I already had some experience in this direction. I did notice, however, a "movement" of information, a kind of "agitation" for that period, and it was something that initially confused me a little. The announcement of the actual age of the pyramids is not new as many authors and clairvoyants have already mentioned this.

Therefore, for those who are concerned, the opinion of contemporary Egyptologists and archaeologists has nothing to do with reality. Moreover, their entire conception of what the pyramids mean, who built them, and especially how they were erected is completely wrong. Both the images I saw and the calculations resulting from the frequencies I was perceiving showed me as clearly as possible that the three pyramids on the Giza plateau were built immediately after the sinking of Atlantis, approximately 13,500 years ago.

INVASION OF THE REPTILIAN RACE IN OUR SOLAR SYSTEM

The age of the architectural complex near Cairo did not surprise me because I had known for a long time that it could not be "recent". The real surprise, however, came when the pictures showed me that, in fact, the construction of the pyramids on our planet started about 100,000 years ago. That context deserves a brief presentation as it offers a broader and more relevant insight into how the pyramids were erected on Earth and its true builders, as well as the main motivation which determined the accomplishment of those colossal constructions. I came to see and understand these issues because I focused on the construction of the pyramids. Already knowing that the three pyramids on the Giza plateau near Cairo were by no means the first pyramids built on our planet, I wanted to know what it was that determined the construction of these colossal buildings with science and precision that is today unmatched.

At first, it was suggested to me by pictures that the construction of the pyramids on Earth became a necessity at one point. I have thus seen the fragmented initiation of such constructions at different points around the globe and schematic links between them and cosmic space. I was viewing certain directions, symbols and geometric shapes that I could not understand.

Then, in a logical sequence, the images showed the constitution of an extraterrestrial being with reptilian features. It was a quick but complex presentation from many angles with lots of data and adjacent symbols, all of which were highly dynamic within the hologram. The content of the images then changed, showing me brief but precise snapshots of several types of cosmic vessels which were generally elongated. One of the types, however, had the round classic shape of the UFOs presented in literature.

The hologram then "split" in the sense that the image of the reptilian being appeared in the lower left corner of the hologram, and the rest was filled with the image of a huge fleet of ships similar to the ones mentioned above, plus others that were much larger in size. The images were very dynamic, zooming in and out, depending upon the ideas I wanted to be highlighted. The displacement of the fleet was attached to the image of our Solar System which I was able to recognize, especially due to the images of the planet Saturn and the red spot on Jupiter.

It seemed to me that, in this simple way, the reptilians were moving with their cosmic fleet to our Solar System. The feeling and emotion felt at that visual impact was scary because it was not only a simple visualization but also a connection with the state of the moment and the respective context. In the face of the threat, the most important and evolved alien civilizations from the Galactic Alliance who were overseeing the plan for the genetic evolution of the human being on Earth decided to defend our planet and the project on which they had worked thus far. I was amazed to see from the synthesis of the images that, even in this radical action, the advanced extraterrestrial civilizations that had the responsibility for the "laboratory" on our planet acted in such a way that human beings could continue to evolve, even under those conditions. To this end, the original Sirians decided to introduce an advanced technology on Earth that would counteract the reptilian assault.

THE TECHNOLOGY OF THE GREAT RESONATORS

As I witnessed, those events that I followed in synthesis on the holographic screen happened approximately 100,000-108,000 years ago. At that time, E-N-L beings were in full bloom so access to Sirian technology and advanced extraterrestrial civilizations that once lived on Earth was easier due to the fact that the

E-N-L branch already had a refined level of consciousness and understanding.

The technology of the great resonators referred to the construction of enormous buildings at various points around the globe designed to serve as "subtle high energy" headlights which had the capacity to gradually induce important changes in the DNA of human beings through their resonance with those energies. At the moment, I understood and appreciated the idea, but then I asked myself: "Why did the Sirians or even the Alliance they formed with other advanced extraterrestrial civilizations not 'forbid' the reptilians here on Earth or even in the galaxy to do all the evil that they do?" I thought that would not have been too difficult a task for them.

Then, in a very cleverly grouped flashing of images, I realized that, even though the involvement of the evil reptilians was terrible, the role they played in all of those events served a global purpose. I was thus shown that their intervention was, in fact, a necessity because it led, in the end, to a "specialized design" of the DNA of the human being that was so hard wired to the physical plane that it provided the possibility of incarnating a large number of beings from the astral plane into this plane, all of whom otherwise would not have had the necessary facilities to be born into higher level physical bodies.

I therefore understood that the plan of creating a human being with a very complex DNA embraced the consideration of creating, among other things, greater possibilities for certain souls in the astral plane to evolve through incarnation because of their need to understand the meaning of experiences and to bring them to fruition according to individual karma. This could only be done by incarnation into physical bodies with very "specialized" frequencies that are very "concrete" because those souls could not be born otherwise by reason of their own karmic limitations. They could thus continue their evolution only if they were born into a very "concrete" body which would have given them the opportunity to go through certain situations of existential crisis so that they would understand the need to correct the way they conduct their existence.

The fact that human DNA was very "specialized" and "separated" on many different branches and directions of development and evolution also contributed to the birth of a diversity of souls and entities from the astral plane, all corresponding to a wide range of frequencies of vibration, and that is why humanity began to appear as a "multicolored fan" of such frequencies and tendencies which caused it to be called a "nursery".

On the other hand, the reptilians could not control the entire population of the planet but rather only those beings that resonated with them which had in their DNA, at least to some extent, the specific reptilian influence and energy. Some of these influences were harsher, and the respective beings became their acolytes. Other influences were less harsh but were accompanied by an intense struggle for the total subordination of those beings. In fact, the reptilians wanted to suppress the rest of the population, thus conquering the entire planet. They had a rather advanced technological level and so created a "mental network of lower frequencies" as a kind of cage that could influence, to a certain extent, even the beings that did not resonate with them. This is still true nowadays but with certain modifications. By allowing for the introduction to the technology of the great resonators, i.e. the gigantic constructions on Earth, the Alliance gave a new impulse and concrete help to human beings, both to evolve and to use those buildings for defense purposes. The great resonators are, in their vast majority, the pyramids and ziggurats that we can still admire today in precisely aligned areas of the Earth. The accomplishment of these extraordinary constructions was also an extra boost for the spiritual future of Mankind because, after the withdrawal of Shambhala and the sinking of Atlantis, there had to be centers on the surface of the planet to support, to some extent, the light and spirituality of the past.

Even then, however, the pyramids were built during much older periods of Mankind, primarily because of the need to keep in close contact with the "gods", that is to say, with the extraterrestrial civilizations that played a decisive role in the evolution of DNA of the human race on Earth. In the case of such gigantic constructions, this was possible because, in reality, the pyramids are very powerful telepathic transmitters of subtle energy and information.

Second, their construction became necessary in those times because the pyramids constantly create a refinement of the subtle emotional energies of human beings. This was of great help, especially in that ancient context, in which tensions and wars had reached high levels due to the adverse influence of evil reptilians. Therefore, the aggregate of human beings and their specific mental field had to be sustained and helped to evolve further, and that is why one of the main methods to achieve this was to introduce the technology and knowledge of the extremely elaborate and difficult construction of the pyramids which serve as great resonators of beneficial energies in the Universe.

THE COMPLEX ROLE OF THE PYRAMIDS

Over the course of tens of thousands of years, the purpose of building the pyramids has not changed so that, even in times closer to us, that is, after the fall of Atlantis, they played the same fundamental role. Moreover, I was shown that the high priests and pharaohs of those times knew that the immense energy of the pyramid could be used to facilitate the conscious etheric or astral travel of their subtle bodies across very large distances in the galaxy, to the "gods" they worshiped.

Such megalithic buildings, however, were not just a conglomerate of stones, regardless of how complexly arranged they were. The name of "great resonators" is justified by the fact that inside of them were certain rooms designed with colors in which were arranged various devices of great complexity, based mainly on the technology of crystals. In pictures, I was shown as "eloquently" as possible the interiors of such rooms, which are actually control rooms, sometimes being located at either the top or bottom of the pyramid.

By their characteristic shape, the pyramids are extraordinarily powerful subtle energy amplifiers so that the subtle energies emitted by the sophisticated devices and crystals inside of them were greatly amplified and transmitted into space to a well-defined target. On the other hand, the pyramids also had the role of supporting beneficial frequencies over a large area around them so that human beings would not decline under the influence of hostile external factors.

After strengthening the Alliance of beneficial extraterrestrial civilizations and allowing the Sirians to introduce this technology to Earth, the construction of the great pyramids began. The extraterrestrial civilizations that were part of the Alliance and had a territory on our planet realized a coherent and correlated plan to erect these buildings, respecting the subtle energetic influences of the Earth. This included the significant areas of intersection of its magnetic fluxes as well as correspondence with certain areas of the galaxy. These megalithic constructions were not performed randomly but only at certain precise points on the surface of the planet. Although the general shape of the pyramids is the same, they still have their own characteristics, all dependent upon the area in which they were built, the nature of the DNA of the human beings in that area, and the particularities of the extraterrestrial civilization considered to be the "governor" of that territory. For example, I was shown that the pyramids in Atlantis were very complex because they encompassed the knowledge and style of several alien civilizations.

Later, after the great continent sank, the pyramids that were built in different areas of the globe reflected the style of only one of those extraterrestrial civilizations. For example, the three pyramids on the Giza plateau are specific to the original Sirians in the Sirius A system even though, in reality, they were built on the physical plane through the participation of a Sirian civilization derived from the original one and located in Orion's Belt.

The pyramids in Central America, the stepped ones, also have the direct imprint of the Sirian civilizations in the Orion Belt. Things here, however, are a bit more complicated due to the intervention of the reptilians and their acolytes. I saw that the Aztecs went through successive phases. First, there was an initial phase in which their resonance was "healthy" and pure; and then, a second phase in which they were "altered" by the nefarious influence of the "little grays", a degenerative civilization formerly taken over by the reptilian civilization. This converted the actual purpose of the pyramids to be dedicated towards evil.

On the other hand, temples in India, which are somewhat smaller in size but resemble the pyramids, though they are narrower at the base and more "pursed" at the top, have a Pleiadian descent. As far as I could tell, the many details, inlays and roundings in their construction represent something specific to the Pleiadian civilization. I also recognized this feature in the Pleiadian ships that I saw in the holographic projections.

DESIGN OF THE GREAT PYRAMIDS

Looking at the comparative analysis offered to me on the holographic screen, I was keen to see how a great pyramid was conceived and erected, as well as the exceptional technological solutions employed to achieve such a construction. Obviously, I did not expect to see something like the design on a board with a ruler, compass and pencil, nor even on the screen of a computer using various specialized programs for it.

I was, however, very passionate about the process of thinking up and designing the project, especially from the point of view of the advanced technology of an extraterrestrial civilization because I did not imagine that such a grandiose and incredibly sophisticated project, such as the design of a large pyramid, is something common and easy to do. Proof of this is the fact that, despite the level of knowledge and technological possibilities that scientists and engineers have today, they cannot design and erect such a gigantic construction. The difficulties of design and especially of concrete materialization would appear to be insurmountable for them.

As soon as I expressed that desire, the line of synthetic analysis was interrupted and I was shown a map of southern Egypt. The image then changed suddenly and I saw a group of six beings, four of them extraterrestrial and two earthly, gathered in a large room that was possibly inside a ship. I knew three of the four extraterrestrial beings were Sirians because I recognized them by their high stature of more than two and a half meters, the whitish flesh color of the skin and the slightly extended skull towards the back. The fourth extraterrestrial being belonged to a race unknown to me, having very white skin, silver hair and purple eyes. As I telepathically perceived, the two earthly beings came from Atlantis. Everyone was standing around a huge blue hologram which looked like a pyramid in the middle of that hall. The hologram was covered with "milky" light, and the edges of the pyramid gleamed discreetly in white.

Each being in that room intervened by hand movements inside the hologram, modifying or adding elements. At the same time, I saw a lot of information on the edge of the hologram: symbols, shapes and sequential representations that moved and changed continuously. Everything was dynamic, active and full of meaning and coherence. I felt beyond any doubt that what I saw, as a synthesis of the design of a large pyramid, was a very deep work based on cosmic laws and principles, having only peripherally to do with the calculations of its physical structure. As I would soon understand, these calculations resulted directly from the subtle structure of the pyramid, and that is why they were perfect: because the construction of the edifice was not limited to its physical elements, that is to say, the stone blocks, but was directed by the subtle energetic elements and the correct integration into a much larger cosmic structure.

If we consider them in principle, these conclusions are very important because they show us the erroneous basis that scientists rely on when they want to understand the mysteries of the pyramids. Among other things, it is hard to assume and believe that people from the Neolithic Age, about 4,500 years ago per Egyptologists, designed, drew up plans, coordinated and then completed the construction of such colossal buildings. Engineers and contemporary physicists, however, are not able to do so today, even with the help of advanced computers and modern construction technology.

They have not yet understood the fact that there is a well-defined sensibility of handling things in terms of Creation, a realm or reference point where things always comes from the top down. The calculations, results and measurements in the physical plane, which helped to build the pyramid, naturally derive from its higher design in the subtle etheric plane because what I saw synthesized in the image of that hologram was actually the design of the pyramid starting from the etheric plane. So it was not just a simple hologram; but, by a technology that I do not understand even now, it allowed the vision of the pyramid and its design directly in the etheric plane.

In this phase, the pyramid gains meaning and "inner force", but it is not yet related to the physical plane. All calculations and results from this plane are just a natural consequence of structures designed at the etheric level. Perhaps that is why contemporary architects and engineers have not yet had the knowledge of such an advanced project like the construction of a large pyramid. At this level of complexity, only the calculations of strength and structure are sufficient, but it is necessary for there to be a correlation with a deep energy base which gives the project stability and durability. Solutions of a subtle etheric nature are therefore needed as a starting point. They can then generate the concrete solution in the physical plane.

MAJOR CONCEPTUAL DIFFERENCES

From the images presented to me, I realized that such a project starts from a kind of "star astrology"; that is to say, from a certain star configuration serving as a point of reference for the place where the pyramid is to be built.

At the high level of consciousness and understanding of the cosmic laws that advanced extraterrestrial civilizations have, the problem of constructing grandiose buildings implies a different approach which is much deeper and more complex than the ones we are accustomed to on Earth, no matter how amazing these constructions might look.

The big problem with such earthly constructions, whether we are talking about large and sophisticated skyscrapers or other types of buildings, is their durability over time, which is small. A resistance of several hundred years would be a record for the constructions of the modern era, assuming that they will not be subjected to weather or major destructive phenomena of nature. And yet, even with such inclement weather, which at times was harsh, the pyramids in Egypt have been around for over ten thousand years, and others are even much older, near the beginning of the time when the technology of the great resonators was introduced. What buildings do we have on Earth which we can say will last for at least a thousand years? By the very nature of the building materials that are used, they are subject to perishability. Even though, when they are new, they look imposing and beautiful, and the technologies used for interior design seem sophisticated. In reality, however, all of them are very superficial and have a short life. The materials have no resistance in time, and 99% of the technology of it is based upon electricity, the source of which may disappear or be suspended at any time.

However amazing today's technologies might seem, they are at an early stage of development because they have not passed an elementary stage in conception and thought. Most of them depend upon each other, and this weakens the cohesive force of the idea that underlies them. A major leap of conception in contemporary science has not yet been realized; rather, it has not yet been officially accepted on the "mass consumption table" of the population.

It is quite easy to raise skeletons from steel bars to make large buildings and to insulate them with different materials. But, if the largest construction company in the world were committed to designing and erecting a large pyramid only from stone blocks, such as the one in Egypt, it would most likely quit the job in just a few days. It would be great to have the technology necessary to assemble such a construction in a consistent manner, down to the millimeter or even fractions of a millimeter fractions that is similar or identical to the Great Pyramid of Egypt, without having to talk about the design or the work involved.

But, how can contemporary architects and engineers design and build a similar colossus when they do not at present know or understand the construction of the Great Pyramid and its interior structure? Further, the pyramid in Egypt is relatively small in size and complexity compared to what was once the Great Pyramid of Atlantis.

The inability of the science of architecture and engineering in contemporary constructions comes from the fact that there is no superior understanding of what form, energy resonance and support in the subtle dimensions of Creation mean. A magnificent construction, such as a large pyramid, implies an accumulation of interdisciplinary knowledge, and by this, I do not mean architecture, resistance of materials, installations, interior design, and so on. What I want to point out is that true science has a universal nature and also implies, in addition to the laws, equations and norms that define it, a different kind of knowledge, such as the subtle energy relationships between celestial bodies, their mutual impact, the hidden significance of the resonances that develop in this way, the way they can be used over time, the deep science of cosmic cycles, and other aspects that I have seen and understood from the fragments presented to me on the holographic screen.

Moreover, when designing such a construction, both the general macro-cosmic elements, which ensure its stability and durability over time, as well as the microcosmic elements, highlighted by the resonance, are taken into account, specific to the space in which the construction takes place, the general resonance of the DNA of the race of beings that comes into contact with it, but also other specific elements, such as the purpose of that construction. Therefore, the physical pyramid is conceived in relation to all the main aspects of the being and the reality that surrounds it, but especially with those of a subtle nature: the specific resonance of the DNA, the psycho-mental states, the geographical location, the influences of the planetary and stellar energies, the purpose assigned to that construction, and so on.

SPECIFIC STAR CONFIGURATION

I saw how the design of the pyramid by those beings began with the analysis of the star map of the area of the galaxy where the Earth was. Various links were then made between several stars in order to find certain combinations that provided results of both a spatial nature (through the structure of the respective configuration) and a temporal nature (synchronized time periods and their precise duration).

At every move in the huge hologram or in the search for a star, a wealth of information appeared, attached on the edges. From what I saw, I realized that the pyramids are of different types, having different shapes, different angles, being blunt or sharp, including four or more faces, stepped or smooth, and of course, serving different purposes. All of these characteristics were not accidental but correlated with the cosmic energetic influences of a certain star configuration under the "patronage" to which a pyramid was to be built.

As I said, the pyramid is not just a simple material construction but encompasses a whole series of subtle correlated aspects, each of them having a certain vibrational frequency in affinity with a particular geographical area and with a particular psycho-mental state that is specific to it, etc.

After the extraterrestrial beings chose the stellar configuration, I saw how an energetic "cloud" gradually began to form in the central area of that configuration, becoming more and more contoured based upon each new element of construction that was created or chosen by those beings. I then saw how lines were beginning to appear in the middle of that cloud, signifying a precise and quite complicated step. I quickly realized that this was the inside of the pyramid.

The technology that made it possible to achieve that design, which correlated very precisely with other elements, such as stellar energy influx, was amazing. Choosing the stellar configuration resulted in a complicated shape in the middle which represented the interior of the pyramid. The schematic structure was born simply from the agreement with the energetic resonances that were manifested within the stellar configuration. Even more amazing than this was to observe that any stone block, any angle used, any space created and any size that was chosen, were all absolutely in direct connection with something in the respective star configuration. Nothing was accidental or unconscious. Absolutely everything was justified by an extraordinary mutual affinity, manifested between the pyramid and the group of stars that was chosen at the beginning of the construction of that pyramid and which had a precise configuration.

It was a very complicated design, totally executed in the etheric plane. As I said, it started from the level of the inner structure of the pyramid which had gradually appeared in the center of the hologram. It overlapped in a certain way over the star configuration that was chosen, indicating all the areas of correspondence through much data and many symbols. In about the middle of it, at the most important point of energetic influence of the star arrangement, was the space or main room of the pyramid. For example, in the case of the Great Pyramid in Egypt, that space corresponds to the King's Chamber. It was then passed to the secondary rooms, galleries and corridors until the last niche was thus completed.

ETHERIC PLAN DESIGN AND SPECIFIC STAR RESONANCES

In the holographic images I saw, any structural element of the pyramid appeared as a result of the energy resonance created by the configuration of a specific star which had been established for that pyramid. For example, in the case of the three pyramids on the Giza plateau in Egypt, their dimensions — even if they are in harmony with many specific elements and characteristics of our planet — are designed so as to respect the reports corresponding to the geometrical structure of the stellar configuration at the moment of beginning the actual construction and those corresponding to the dimensions of the three main stars of Orion's Belt.* (footnote on next page)

Even this simple fact would be enough to block any attempt of "scientific" explanation of the researchers regarding the construction of the three pyramids because: how could the ancient Egyptians know the diameters of the three main stars of the Belt? This is impossible if you limit yourself to observing the three stars freely which, according to the assumptions of scientists, apparently was the only possibility that the Egyptians had at that time.[**] In such a case, it is obvious that no difference can be made between them. And yet, the three pyramids faithfully and proportionately respect both the dimensions of the three stars of Orion's Belt[***] and their relative position within the belt.[****] In this way, each line and each area of the pyramid was holographically designed in detail on a scale and directly from within the etheric plane. I then telepathically received the information that, practically speaking, designing a large pyramid only in the physical plane is impossible or would be irreparably doomed to failure because it could not effectively solve and correlate the immensity of data necessary for that construction to be viable and resistant.

The calculations and engineering methods from the physical plane do not allow the pyramid to be designed according to the usual methods. With present formulas, calculation techniques and knowledge, it can only be constructed up to a certain stage beyond which problems cannot be solved. This is because the parameters included in the construction of a pyramid are much more numerous and often unknown to contemporary engineers and scientists. This is why, even if they would like to start designing and carrying out such a huge construction, they would reach technical and even conceptual impossibilities quickly enough, making it impossible to build further.

For example, it would be difficult for many scientists and contemporary engineers to understand that pyramids are actually very important communication centers connected to the specific energy of the stars or human spacecraft that have been chosen to form a certain configuration in order to fulfill a certain purpose, usually of a galactic nature.

---

[*] This information coincides with the studies of contemporary researchers, such as Robert Bauval who, in his book *The Mystery of Orion*, undoubtedly shows that the three pyramids near Cairo are a faithful replica of the star configuration in Orion's Belt. Bauval writes: "There is a connection between the texts about the pyramid and the pyramid itself, that is, what the texts tell us is confirmed by architecture, and I have demonstrated this fact beyond any doubt."

[**] This corresponds to 2.500 B.C., the period advanced by Egyptologists and modern science for the construction of the Giza pyramid. At that time, the alignment of the three pyramids with the main stars of Orion's Belt was no longer valid, but it does correspond to 11,500 B.C.

[***] The three stars in Orion's Belt are: Alnitak (Zeta), Alnilam (Epsilon) and Mintaka (Delta).

[****] In his book, Robert Bauval points out that the three pyramids on the Giza plateau in Egypt respect the positioning of the stars in Orion's Belt, but he does not say that they faithfully render, proportionately speaking, the diameter of the three stars.

This is important because the gigantic mother ships of highly techno-logically advanced civilizations often have planetary dimensions, and their missions are sometimes very long lasting, from a few years to several tens of thousands or even hundreds of thousands of years. Therefore, the pyramids were used exactly as we currently use communication centers, and this involves the transmission and reception of information. As they are cosmic interstellar transmitters designed to perform over very large distances, they also had to be very large and powerful, and that is why the pyramids were used as subtle telepathic transmitters.

TWENTY-FOUR YEARS

At that time, in the area where today the three great pyramids stand, there was no desert of sand. Basically, the Sahara did not exist at that time. On the contrary, in the place of today's desert, I saw lush vegetation with large rivers which flowed into the Nile.

In combination with the "play" of the frequencies, it was telepathically transmitted to me quite clearly that the entire operation of building the archi-tectural complex near Cairo, including the preparation of the plateau, lasted about twenty-four years. At first, I was a little surprised because I imagined that, given the advanced technology of the Sirians in Orion, the construction of the three pyramids should take much less; but that was undoubtedly a simplistic evaluation of mine, made in ignorance of the cause. Additionally, the work did not take place continuously because I saw periods when the site was devoid of the presence of aliens and their ships. Later, in amazement over the way the three pyramids were built, I realized that the work was actually moving at a pretty fast pace during the 24 years; and that, under other conditions, their construction could have lasted hundreds of years if not longer.

As the plateau was uneven and covered with earth, the work began with the proper preparation of the place for construction. The images showed me a massive deforestation in that area and a leveling of the surface in order to create the solid rock plateau. There were many ships of different types in the area which stood still in the air at a certain height, all arranged in "layers" or levels. Some of them prepared the plateau using a technology based upon some type of "beams" that leveled the area. As I saw that operation, the air seemed to ripple beneath the ship passing over a certain area, and after it did so, everything became "flattened", and not by violent destruction but rather by a kind of rock liquefaction and proper absorption.

OVERSEAS INVOLVEMENT IN PYRAMID CONSTRUCTION

An interesting aspect I noticed when looking at those extraordinary images was the relation between the origin of the ships and the extraterrestrial beings. In that context of humanity's very distant past, talking about their "extraterrestrial" membership was somewhat improper. The ships and their beings were indeed from other planets, but they had been interrelated on our planet for thousands of years and were living with human beings.

They had therefore not come to Earth just for the construction of the three great pyramids in Egypt, but their presence was old, from the times when Atlantis had a great economic and spiritual power and was influential over all of the other continents, and even long before that.

In Egypt, the three pyramids were built mainly by extraterrestrial civilizations descending from the main Sirian civilization in the Sirius A system. In addition to their representatives, I was shown other ships belonging to different civilizations which also contributed to the construction of the pyramids or had attended the operation during certain stages of it. In total, I saw the participation of four different extraterrestrial civilizations to which was added the important presence of wise Atlantean beings.

The erection of the pyramids was a "team effort" in the sense that the Atlanteans, with their specific ships, worked with extraterrestrial beings from several civilizations, but the major influence of the Sirian civilizations followed, and as I said, the Great pyramid, as well as the other two smaller pyramids, were built in the Sirian style.

On the site and around it, I saw a swarm of air ships which were extremely well organized and precise. Each ship "knew" exactly what to do and everything seemed to be perfectly calculated and managed. There were, however, very few Atlantean and extraterrestrial beings on the ground. At quite a large distance around the area of construction, I could see some locals, quite primitive human beings of the *E-N-K* branch, who were just looking at the activity on the site. In some of the images that followed, however, I was able to see some of those natives performing simple activities within the site.

I was very curious to see the real way in which the pyramids were constructed, without going any further between the hypotheses and assumptions that are made. From the beginning, I understood that this was the exclusive work of the ships and of the Atlanteans and extraterrestrial technology based particularly on the energy of crystals. It was not even a question of whether the locals could do something about building the pyramids or having any initiative to do so. In terms of distance, the metaphorical possibility of such was similar to that between our Sun and the star Sirius. From what I saw, the locals were *E-N-K* beings from one of the lower branches with a primitive level of living. Due to their rudimentary level of living and knowledge, such a work would have been absolutely impossible for them to have accomplished in any phase of its realization.

I then fleetingly remembered the vision of contemporary engineers, archeologists and Egyptologists who seem to have great confidence in the "technical" acumen of the ancient Egyptians, namely: the chisel, the hammer the rope, pulleys, logs and some pieces of copper. In their view, these were the main tools with which the huge and complex pyramids on the Giza plateau were built.

I did not see even one of these tools in the pictures presented to me, but even if the locals had countless such objects, they would have served no purpose. I doubt that those *E-N-K* beings could have cut and carved at least one stone block out of the millions that make up the three pyramids, nor could I see how they could have transported them over such great distances and then assemble them down to millimeters in an extremely complex unit. This is not to mention the construction design, the amazing engineering solutions, nor the dimensions and weight of the stone blocks or many other aspects as well.

It is true, however, that I saw a few pictures at one point of some natives right inside the site, moving and performing simple operations on some stone blocks in the storage area, having a few tools and manipulating some thin metal bars or drawing colored signs with straw bundles. I then received the information that these natives were telepathically guided by some of the tall beings on the plateau who were dressed in silver-white and walking slowly between different points of the construction site

THE CONSTRUCTION OF THE THREE
GREAT PYRAMIDS ON THE GIZA PLATEAU

Beyond all of these general elements, I firstly focused on the design of the pyramids. This aspect, which could not be fully understood until today, is attributed to near primitive beings effectively lifting giant stone columns. Seeing the extraordinary complexity of such works in the holographic images presented to me, I was stunned by the lack of discernment and even the logic with which contemporary researchers and renowned Egyptologists argue the "modern version" of how the pyramid complex near Cairo was erected.

I repeat these things over and over again precisely because of my desire to draw attention to the illogics that are perpetuated in the form of "competent" opinions, but what is really sad is that the population considers all of these "academic solutions" as being true. However, they represent only the manifestation of immense scientific pride and the inability to understand and accept something higher than the current level of technological development. To these is added a lamentable indoctrination of the population

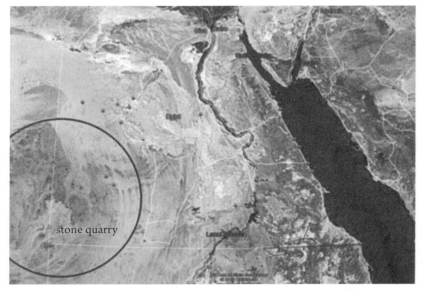

THE APPROXIMATE POSITIONING OF THE STONE QUARRY

so that they do not know the truth and thus give unseen wings to the desire for progress and freedom.

As for the actual construction of the three pyramids, the first thing that was shown to me was the way in which the stone blocks were cut. In other words, we saw the stone quarry that provided the building material of the three great pyramids. Unexpectedly to me, it was not in the territory of today's Egypt, but further south, in the territory of what is today Libya, not too far from its border.

The image then focused on cylindrical devices which were stuck in the ground at different points in the construction area. They were similar to the ones we saw in the pictures of the Persian Gulf 400,000 years ago that were being used by the Sirians for "drilling". It was not clear to me what role they played in that stone quarry, but I still saw the correlation between the rays of laser-like lights coming out of those cylinders and the "lasers" of the "construction ship" floating noiselessly above the mountain. It was a large ship, impressive by its somewhat irregular appearance which, in fact, gave me the impression of it as a "construction ship" because it had many attachments on its sides. I saw that it was responsible for the vertical sectioning of the stone blocks in the quarry because the stone was extracted vertically from the top of the mountain. The ship was always positioned above another place in the mountain, being guided by its own "lasers"; then vertically sectioning the mountain stone along the four sides of the upper surface through thicker rays of light which were bright white. Thus, the shape of the stone block was generated, after which the mother ship went to the section of another stone block in another area of the quarry.

After the stone block was thus delimited in the mountain, a transport ship came above it which correlated its movement with that of a sphere-like device resembling an automatic drone. It came through the air near the respective block cut in the mountain, and with the help of "laser" beams that it emitted, sectioned the block both at the top and at its lower part, allowing it to be "caught" and raised to the transport ship through a special force field. Before this, however, I saw that the drone "inscribed" the stone block, always in the bottom right corner. The code was not carved or painted, but I understood that the area in which it was inscribed was energetically activated in such a way that the composition of the stone was modified in that region. It was becoming more structured there, as if it were a neat and luminous crystal. The "code" as such was a rectangle in which several lines and squares were printed, as is the electronic signature nowadays. It would illuminate when a certain ray of light was directed at it, as a kind of specialized "reader".

The transport vessels were rectangular, and each of them had two symmetrically arranged hemispheres which most likely generated an attraction field that supported the stone blocks below. As I said, when a ship reached over a block of cut stone from the mountain, it was sectioned below, and it was then "trapped" in a specific energy field emanating from the ship. I clearly saw the way this one was done because a diffused beam of white light came out of the two hemispheres which "covered" the stone block. It began to levitate almost immediately, rising up to the bottom of the ship to a short distance from those hemispheres. The ship then sped on an aerial "highway", transporting the stone block to the site.

If the stone blocks were relatively small in size, a ship would carry two such blocks on one road; but if they were larger, the ships carried only one block. For very large blocks or with special shapes, I saw that, after being cut raw from the mountain, they were transported to an adjacent area where they were finished in a meticulous manner, being brought to the required dimensions by several mobile devices that seemed to be guided automatically.

At a considerable height in the air above the quarry was a much larger ship whose diameter I estimated to be at least 120 meters. Then I received a telepathic knowing that her role was to oversee and direct the work project. I could see perfect rows of small transport ships which were coming to the quarry and departing with medium-sized stone blocks. The precision and dynamics of the movements of those ships and "drones" was irreproachable. It seemed like a gigantic computer was ordering every operation, both for the flight and steering of the ships as well as for the cutting and lifting of the stone blocks. I also telepathically understood that this was always happening with precise science. When the stone blocks were cut, it was already known exactly where

THE STORAGE AREA OF THE STONE BLOCKS
AND THE CONSTRUCTION SITE OF THE PYRAMID

each of them would be placed in the construction of the Great Pyramid. The cut blocks were always those blocks that were waiting to be put in the order that had been established, but as I was to notice, the complete "finishing" took place at the construction site.

I saw two main areas: the storage of the stone blocks and the actual construction. The blocks were taken in a certain order, never by chance. I could say that not one stone block was the same as any of the others, each having its specific integration in the construction of the pyramid. I did not see, for example, stocks of stone blocks forming a pile. There were, of course, blocks on the ground but not in piles, and the existing ones were immediately taken and integrated into the extremely laborious construction of the pyramid.

COLLABORATION BETWEEN ATLANTIS
AND THE EXTRATERRESTRIALS

On the ground, I saw a tall Atlantean man, dressed in white and resembling a priest, who oversaw the general construction. I could not say how I knew that tall man was an Atlantean, but the information was nonetheless accurate in my mind. I saw two extraterrestrial Sirian beings in the warehouse area whom I recognized because of their white skin, their elongated head towards the back, and their beautiful blue suits with golden signs.

These three seemed to coordinate the general work, but I saw other beings on the perimeter of the site, about ten, carrying out different tasks. Two of them were also Atlantean.

My attention was drawn to three of those beings who were taller than the others — I estimated that they were more than 2.5 meters high — and wore some kind of whitish-silver slightly translucent color combinations that flowed into a cape-like flair in the back. And on the plateau was a mixture of races, some beings having hair on the head and others not, while the skin of some was darker, even brown, but most of them were white.

The Atlantean priest and the two Sirian beings who were leading the general work had a monitor in their hands that resembled a large tablet, correlating the various actions that were needed. Absolutely everything under construction was made by the ships in levitation. I could only hear a fine noise, like a hum, but this was probably due to the movement of ships through the air because the sky was filled with their presence.

I realized that those beings, especially the tall ones dressed in white and silver suits, were permanently in telepathic connection either with the general command center, which I could not see, or with the central "brain" coordinating the movement of the ships. At his right temple, the Atlantean priest had a device that appeared as if it were stuck on his long blueish white hair. It was comparable to a bluetooth of today except that it was larger and more elongated.

Every being and ship out there knew exactly what to do and everything was running with extraordinary precision and perfection. The timing and correlation of all operations was truly impressive. Moreover, in the magnitude and complexity of such construction, I do not know how the activity could have been otherwise so efficient. Even so, as I said, the construction of the entire architectural complex lasted more than two decades.

An important fact to mention is that I did not notice the existence of pilots in small transport vessels. These were fairly simple ships, rectangular in shape but without crew, something similar to today's drones. I concluded that everything was correlated and guided from a general command center.

ADVANCED TECHNOLOGIES

I was then shown very clearly how the respective stone blocks "came in" to be assembled perfectly in the intended place. The process was entirely technologically based. I saw cylindrical devices on the ground that were like smoky-dark pillars. They were similar to those in the quarry but greater in height, each measuring about five feet high. Each had a hemisphere on the top which made them resemble tall mushrooms to some extent. As far as I was aware, those cylindrical devices were arranged on a certain path and at certain points, somehow in pairs, forming a kind of "corridor".

When a stone block was to be moved and recessed into the body of the pyramid, two beings from those present on the plateau moved in front of such a cylinder. With only a hand gesture, probably triggering an internal command, the sphere from the top of the cylinder in question began to vibrate imperceptibly, at the same time emitting a specific and non-disturbing high-frequency sound. A ray of light like a laser appeared from the hemisphere, intersecting with the radius emitted by another cylinder. The two "lasers" then scanned the multitude of stone blocks, exactly identifying the block with the code needed to be placed in the pyramid assembly in the exact order established for the construction.

I do not know what that technology was based on, but I could see that the stone blocks actually rose in the air, levitating, and then passing through the rows of cylinders heading towards the pyramid. There they were driven exactly into a certain area of it, rotating in the air until they reached the position where they could be perfectly integrated. I also saw how some of the beings on the ground checked each time how these operations were performed, the pace being precisely sustained. They never spoke, but I felt that there was always an exchange of telepathic messages between them which correlated the different phases of the work.

It started with the Great Pyramid, and I noticed that the development of the construction was not just one-sided but that it was being approached in several regions. As I said, the stone blocks were brought and placed precisely in a predetermined order, creating the feeling of a "living organism" in the construction process. Even though it is a difficult concept to assimilate, this is how I felt when the images were presented to me because, as I said, the holographic technology of Apellos not only facilitated the perception of those times visually but also, to a certain extent, psychically and mentally.

I thus understood that everything had a well-defined meaning in that construction, that each stone having a direct meaning and correlation with a certain cosmic influence, and that nothing was left to chance. If it were not so, how could those magnificent buildings remain "standing" even after more than thirteen millennia? Following the way the pyramids were made, from conception to their practical construction, I realized once again the immense gap that exists between humanity's current understanding of the laws that govern life and the universe and the ancient advanced civilizations of Earth or the extraterrestrial civilizations that guard us.

For example, I felt a kind of "symbiosis" between each piece that was added to the pyramid and its general assembly. Absolutely every detail of the stone blocks was in correlation with a certain cosmic element which facilitated the continuity of important energy flows towards the pyramid, always in relation to the respective star configuration.

I saw, for example, the exact moment when they cut a certain side of a stone block along a certain precise line with the image then focusing exactly on the embedding of that stone block on one of the edges of the pyramid which, for this purpose, we will call the direction of the line cut at an angle aimed at a star in the Orion Constellation. The image then immediately presented to me, in a separate quadrant in the upper right corner, the sector of the cosmos to which that star belonged to. The same construction principle involved complex geometrical arrangements of the stone blocks and the angles between them were correlated with astral movements and important cosmic configurations, all corresponding in detail to all the stones in the pyramidal ensemble. In their final form, the pyramids were perfectly polished, like very valuable pieces of art.

For contemporary science, such aspects that go beyond the strictly material framework mean nothing because the scientists do not understand their significance. In fact, this is the main reason why it has not yet come out of the "mechanical era" with the same somewhat primitive ideas of propulsion and energy being perpetuated. It is true, however, that there is also a very high-level world elite that has had and continues to have access to much extraterrestrial knowledge as well as complementary contacts. This elite has amazing technologies which it uses for its personal interest, even on an impressive scale, but I will not develop this topic here.

All of the three main pyramids on the Giza plateau near Cairo were erected at the same time, but the first works were those that targeted the Great Pyramid. Immediately after that, construction began for the other two pyramids. It was a monumental and far-reaching work which, as I said, lasted about twenty-four years. Further south and a little after the construction of three large pyramids, smaller ones were erected as well as some temples, but they were all part of the same general project. I was shown that they faithfully respected the correspondence with the stellar arrangement in the cosmos which was chosen to energetically influence this subtle architectural ensemble.

From what I was shown, I saw the construction phase of the Great Pyramid where the base and its corners had already been slightly raised. In the middle of the inside, I noticed a much larger activity. It was a special movement, an activity of another kind because it represented, in a way, the "beginning" of the pyramid; that is to say, its essential structure that was to give it "life" and make it effective.

If the stone blocks from the outside were simpler and somewhat similar, things were different inside, requiring a great deal of attention and a great refinement to make the construction extremely complicated. Those blocks were much different from the ones on the outside, although after they were assembled, they seemed to be simply rectangular. In fact, they had different shapes and very precise angles so that they fit into each other perfectly. Each stone block there was practically unique.

I then saw that, in some areas inside of the Great Pyramid, another kind of material was used, different from the stone taken from that great quarry. The consistency of those blocks was different. Some of them were black and glossy while others with red inserts were very polished, all of them cut at many different angles and with complex shapes. As a unique element, I noticed that beneath the King's Chamber was placed a structure with a round shape with a circumferences of "rays" looking similar to a gear wheel. The piece was a very complex assembly. I felt that this mysterious form, like a star with many rays, whose presence is completely unknown to contemporary researchers, plays a very important role but one which I did not understand. No one imagines that there would be nothing more than massive blocks of stone a little below and between the King's Chamber and the Queen's Chamber in the Great Pyramid, but I was clearly shown that this is false and that both that area and many others in the Great Pyramid are actually full of tunnels, small rooms or even larger rooms.

THE FINAL ASPECT OF THE THREE GREAT PYRAMIDS

In their final phase of construction, the pyramids had perfectly smooth faces on the outside, being completely different from what we see today. They were dazzlingly shining in the sunlight, but as I immediately realized, that glow was favored not only by the shining of the white stone that covered the faces of the pyramids but also by a special substance that was applied over them.

The grandeur of the three pyramids could also be admired at night, being a perfect spectacle, as from another world. At first, only the Great Pyramid was illuminated, but in the images that followed, I saw all three pyramids spreading a fairy light, accompanied by the less intense light emanating from the other secondary constructions around the whole complex. The splendid images showed me the whole architectural complex from a certain height, the three pyramids being just like real "cosmic headlights". At the top of each pyramid, I saw a crystal, but the one on the Great Pyramid was huge, like an obelisk with the brightest light. Thus, contrary to scientific assumptions and "calculations", there was never an object of any other form except that huge crystal at the top of the Great Pyramid, and it fulfilled the function of a formidable cosmic relay, both for receiving and transmitting information.

I was then shown an image close to a face of the Great Pyramid and saw that its brightness was mainly due to a somewhat transparent and somewhat phosphorescent film which covered the entire pyramid. If I were to make a comparison, I would say that the substance resembled a kind of transparent "gel" which was shining brightly. It was not a diffused brightness, but it was something that reflected the light so when you looked at the pyramids, the general impression was that they were made of that substance. Even more so, its structure became somewhat translucent, leaving it to be seen what is inside. The stone blocks were not observed at all, but everything was perfectly polished and covered with that special substance. After several thousand years, however, as I could see in the pictures presented to me, the substance has lost its qualities and even started to disappear from certain areas of the pyramid. For example, around 5,200-4,800 B.C., as far as I could see, only the area at the top of the Great Pyramid kept traces of that amazing substance. The crystal, however, was still at the top of the building. Otherwise, the pyramid had become matte and, to my great surprise, it was buried about half in the sand. The other two smaller pyramids were even more covered with sand. We could also see that the faces of the pyramids were beginning to be "eaten" away by the passage of time and the weather as the stone blocks were being reinforced in many places on the outside. It had, however, been almost 6,000 years since its construction.

SECRET STRUCTURES AND RITUALS
INSIDE THE GREAT PYRAMID

Intrigued by the fact that the pyramid was half buried in the sand, I wanted to see other elements related to that upsetting transformation. The images changed, showing me a view from a larger angle, and then, instead of the abundant vegetation and water that existed in the area at the time of the construction of that architectural complex, I saw the sandy desert that was everywhere. Climate change must have been terrible and quite rapid, but I understood telepathically that it was largely determined by a brief but rather intense war between certain extraterrestrial factions.

I was then shown "more recent" images of pharaonic palaces and temples built around the pyramidal complex with an obvious growth and evolution of the Egyptian population that abounded in that area. I was shown again the Great Pyramid buried in the sand, but the image somehow penetrated inside the pyramid, through its walls, so that I could simultaneously see both inside and outside. In its interior space, through the galleries and rooms that have not yet been discovered in the physical structure of the pyramid, I saw more human beings doing different jobs and even gaining access, in a way that I did not immediately understand, by moving some blocks of stone in the interior when entering certain hidden areas of the pyramid. Not surprisingly, as I insisted, the image changed, showing me three Egyptians who, after dressing and appearing in their attire, seemed to be of high rank, most likely priests.

They were in a rather large gallery but not in the Great Pyramid Gallery. I was not shown how they got there, but I saw how the older priest stopped at a certain time near a stone block. He was holding a support in his left palm upon which was a small sphere that shined with a bright yellow light. I saw how the priest then uttered a string of sounds with a special intonation of his voice, modulated and quite strong. I noticed that the sounds produced were "swallowed" by the structure of the pyramid rather than reverberating from the walls. As the priest issued those incantations, I realized that it was necessary to reach a certain frequency in order to trigger a certain process. After a few seconds and while he was still making those sounds, the other two lower-ranking priests lightly pushed a stone block from the floor level with their hands and then another one that was above the priest. Both stones then rotated easily at an angle of about forty-five degrees. The three priests then entered a rather large room.

The image then showed a dynamic and overall view of the pyramids in which we saw much of its structure which is not currently known. There are many other hidden rooms and corridors that are not even suspected by researchers; however, some of these have been identified recently by the improvement of a certain technology, but it is not enough as the data is still too elusive.*

From what was presented to me, however, I can say that things do not appear as scientists think. For example, all of these numerous rooms, galleries and spaces that are in the pyramid did not have the main purpose of storing things; although, in some of them, as we saw in that extraordinary overview of the internal structure of the Great Pyramid, there are objects, some of them even amazing, but other spaces are empty.

Certain priests and initiates therefore had access to some "keys" to enter the secret spaces of the Great Pyramid. This also happened when we saw many beings inside the pyramid who were mostly workers. By telepathic transmission, I understood that these people were engaged in actions to repair and maintain the pyramid, probably due to the damage recorded after the war. In parallel, I could see vast work outside to release the pyramid from the burden of the sand that surrounded it. Indeed — this work was done by the native

---

* The author probably refers to the discovery made in 2015 by the ScanPyramids team made up of an international group of researchers. The team identified a large empty space in the Great Pyramid by the x-ray method, but behind that empty space, one does not know for sure what it might be (a room, several rooms or a gallery) and what is inside it. Even this discovery, however, is called into question by some Egyptologists such as Dr. David Lightbody.

Egyptians, probably at the order of the pharaoh of that period who knew very well that the pyramids represented the legacy of the "gods" and that they had to be treated with the utmost respect.

From the images, however, as a subtle transmission, I felt that these magnificent constructions no longer transmitted the same kind of information and energy as they did in the first phases after their construction; that is, at a time when they had a colossal and profoundly transformative effect. It was as if a kind of "wave of forgetfulness" had seized the minds of people who saw the pyramids only as physical objects, extraordinary in their grandeur, but appreciating them only at this limited level of understanding. Somehow, they had lost over time the ability to understand what the pyramids truly represented and were no longer feeling their subtle extraordinary energetic influence. There had been a "hardening" of their energetic structure and level of consciousness which no longer allowed them to understand the occult elements and higher learning so as to achieve a "resonance bridge" with the energy of the pyramids on the plateau. Therefore, only the priests and the initiated retained some of the true knowledge, but even among them, the terrible seals of oblivion had begun to manifest.

CHAPTER FOURTEEN

The Sphinx — The Eternal Enigma

The famous Egyptian edifice is a sensitive topic because, for contemporary archeologists, Egyptologists and scientists, its mystery seems to be even deeper than that of the great pyramids. Generally speaking, the sphinx in Egypt is believed to be older than the pyramids, and this is true. Even the fact that it was not always as we see it today is true. What is not known, however, is its history, and as I was convinced by following the synthetic images on the holographic screen, this lack of information is due to its very old age which make even the oldest references that can have once existed to be eroded by the patina of time. If, as far as the three great pyramids in Egypt are concerned, a few mentions of it or various stories have been lost, nothing is known about the Sphinx except what was intended to be invented.

From the beginning, I must specify an important fact: the place where the Sphinx is currently located, that is on the same plateau in Giza near Cairo where the three great pyramids were built, does not, in fact, represent its "native place". This fact was revealed to me as soon as I formulated the wish to know the elements related to the origin of the Sphinx in Egypt. I expected to see, as in the case of the three pyramids, a chronological progression of the stages of its construction on the same plateau. Instead, the images suddenly changed, showing the northern part of the country in the area of the Nile's delta.

THE OLD METROPOLIS OF HELANAS

I saw that, at that time, the northern territory of Egypt was constituted of an "alliance zone" of the different races of E-N-L and extraterrestrial beings and soon became one of the first and most powerful outbreaks of culture and spirituality for the population of those very distant times. That area had its center in a port city built around the mouth of the Nile on the Mediterranean Sea. The images showed me two huge lions on the banks of the river where it entered into the sea. Carved in stone, the lions were in a position identical to that of the Sphinx that still stands next to the Great Pyramid. I looked closely at those images and noticed that the two huge sculptures were identical in body with the current Sphinx on the Giza plateau, but their heads were that of lions. By telepathic transmission, I already knew that those big statues were going to be related to the area of the later pyramids.

As for the city in the north of Egypt, where the two immense lions were, this was already during its full creative bloom through 23,000 B.C. It was most likely much older, but I did not go any deeper. It is possible, however, that its origins can be traced back to 32,000-30,000 B.C. The name of the city appeared in my mind as Helanas, Halanas, or Helios. Practically speaking, it was more than just a city. It was a real metropolis, a city as a state, comprising both crowded and rarer areas on the outskirts.

Its distinguishing sign was the two gigantic lions from the entrance of the Nile to the Mediterranean Sea. At that time, the Nile Delta was practically nothing and in an incipient form of what we know today. Also, the Mediterranean Sea was smaller than it is now; and there was no connection between it and the Black Sea through the Bosphorus and Dardanelles straits. The configuration of the Earth was a little different then because the soil was higher in altitude.

I immediately realized that Helios (or Helanas) was a city built and populated largely by E-N-L beings because its inhabitants were tall, three to four meters high, and some even more. I also noticed some higher E-N-K beings, but they were much smaller, about two meters high or even less, as well as humanoid extraterrestrial beings, some of them wearing some kind of special costume. I admired the nature of the activity and movement of the beings in that city, the magnificent constructions, and a kind of surrealistic brilliance coming from the multitude of surfaces plated with gold or even objects of massive gold which could be seen everywhere in the city. Especially conspicuous were statues, roofs, columns or fountains, all of pure gold and which shined very brightly in the light of the sun's rays. It was all fascinating.

In the middle of that city was a large and artistically carved stone market. I saw, in fact, several such markets at different points of the huge city and also on its outskirts which stretched far to the south, to what is today the Sahara Desert. The entire settlement, immense indeed, resembled a confederation because, in the images presented to me, I could identify several smaller cities or states linked together by numerous paths and roads, admirably constructed. Those cities were separated by areas with rich and even lush vegetation. There was therefore a lively and complex communication between all of those regions which, as a whole, formed a kind of state, even larger than a metropolis of today.

In the middle of the central market in Helanas was a very tall obelisk, measuring probably 70-80 meters. At its peak, I saw a sphere of the same gold, the diameter of which I estimated as about five meters. The obelisk had a round circumference and was perfectly smooth. As I have seen telepathically, the sphere at the top was a product of extraterrestrial technology and uninterrupted light, like a true sun, even at night. It was amazing, and I could even say magnificent. The entire building resembled an ocean lighthouse, but the light was several hundred times stronger. Paradoxically, however, it did not hurt one's eyes; being warm and penetrating the darkness of the night up to tens of miles away. Its intensity was formidable, and if I were to make a comparison, I do not find anything today in the entire world that is similar or that even comes close to the power and qualities of that light. I also understood that it had healing properties, helping beings to regenerate better during the night.

I also saw that when Atlantis sank, Helanas was almost in ruin because, in the last thousands of years and before the final cataclysm of the Atlantean continent, almost all *E-N-L* beings were no longer reincarnated when they died but continued pure and simple existences in the etheric plane without any discontinuity of consciousness. It was a gradual sunset of that flourishing civilization, also accompanied by the rigors of nature, for the area was deserted and the sand had begun to invade even the great central city of Helanas. The vegetation, however, was still quite rich at that time.

The *E-N-L* gene information had reached the end point of its existence in the physical plane, and according to the law of evolution, that branch was beginning to resorb into the higher dimension of the etheric plane. So, as we have seen in the pictures, after the destruction of Atlantis, the metropolis that was Helanas was already largely submerged in the sand, and another part was under the waters of the Mediterranean which had invaded it because the sea level had risen.

Being intrigued by these aspects, I was shown in a brief visual synthesis that there are several areas on the globe where real metropolises and megalithic cities are currently under water due to the configuration of the land having changed a lot. An example is Japan. In the extension of its coasts, there are amazing cities, and what is left on the bottom of the ocean is also covered with sand. In addition, Japan was not always the island we know today, but before Atlantis sank, it was linked to the continent and extended far offshore as a part of the continent.

The same happened with the great metropolis of Helanas in northern Egypt which was covered by the vegetation of those times, and to a certain extent by sand, but especially by the waters of the Mediterranean which had swallowed up much of it. At the time of the construction of the architectural complex on the Giza plateau, the fate of that region was already sealed. In a few pictures, I was at one point shown a delegation of three Sirian beings who were inspecting with a ship, flying low but hardly visible below by reason of the splendor of that extraordinary metropolis. The ruins were covered almost entirely with vegetation and vines, much like some pyramids or temples recently discovered in the Amazon jungle. One of the two gigantic lions, the one on the left bank of the Nile, had disappeared under sand and water, and the other was on an incline with water rising to a level above the chest.

RELOCATION OF ONE OF THE STATUES TO THE GIZA PLATEAU

I was then suddenly shown pictures with the Sphinx on the Giza plateau which had been placed in the position we know today. It was actually one of the two large statues of Helanas, the other one having not yet been discovered beneath water and sand. I concluded that it was simply taken from Helanas and transported by air to the plateau where it is now. Probably, however, they decided not to let the last trace of the big city that was Helanas disappear, and that is why they decided to complete the architectural ensemble at Giza, thus giving a precise connotation to the place. For, if we interpret things from another angle, the specificity of the plateau with pyramid-shaped constructions, it has no meaningful connection with the presence of the Sphinx. It was, however, an important symbolic justification which I will discuss below. There are two notable aspects of the Egyptian Sphinx, both disturbing to the reader. The first refers to the fact that when the Sphinx was brought to the Giza plateau near the pyramids, it was, in fact, a huge lion with the carved head of a lion with a specific mane. What we see today in place of the lion's head was a change made much later because the stone sculpture was severely damaged at this level, following the fierce war I mentioned.

The fact that only one of the two lions sculpted in Helanas was brought there signified the emergence of a new spiritual center that was born in Egypt. When the two immense lions were placed on both sides of the Nile, in the old Helanas, they were there to express the adoration of the Sun, the light, the leadership and sovereignty. A single lion brought in to the architectural ensemble from Giza, however, represented the idea of a center. In any case, it was clear to me that neither the Atlanteans nor the other beings from the extraterrestrial civilizations that helped to build the pyramids in Egypt did not set out to restore Helanas but only to establish a new center of culture, science and spirituality on the Giza plateau area that was adapted to the E-N-K beings and to the new global situation after the great cataclysm of Atlantis.

The second aspect also shakes up the current ideas about the Sphinx. It is known that it is actually older than the three pyramids, thus corresponding to the truth because it was built in Helanas, and its age would rise to at least 25,000 years. Bringing it to the Giza plateau after the pyramids were built, however, makes it "younger" than they are.

Beyond the special "destiny" of the Sphinx in Egypt, however, remains its metaphysical spirit, its unfathomable mystery and its ancestral beauty which has unambiguously crossed the millennia in a sovereign silence.

EGYPT, AFTER ATLANTIS

The ruins of the great metropolis Helanas are very well preserved and now under sand. Egypt could now, once and for all, cut the so-called "unknowns" about the true history of the pyramids and the Sphinx or those about the identity of the "gods" of Antiquity, thus revealing these vast and exceptional ruins. This, however, requires political will and not only that. I understand these aspects very well as they are especially valid for the Bucegi complex.

On the other hand, the E-N-K beings were not capable of sustaining the greatness of that city, either physically — because its dimensions corresponded to the E-N-L beings which were noticeably higher — nor spiritually because their level of consciousness was not very high. The memory of a special spiritual place, however, remained in that part of Egypt so that, after the Atlantean sinking, some of the Atlantean sages retreated to Egypt, and helped by several extraterrestrial civilizations, built the pyramids on the Giza plateau but also others, further south. Some smaller ones are also hidden under the desert sand along with other suburbs of the Helanas metropolis.

As I said at the beginning, the presence of Atlanteans and extraterrestrial beings among the almost primitive E-N-K beings who "inherited" the territories of today's Egypt was physical and constant for a period of time. This was necessary in order for the science shared with those beings to take a solid foundation and create firm roots to form certain stronger and more evolved individuals in the E-N-K population. The idea was that they would then spread those teachings to as many as possible. Thus, the E-N-K beings helped their genetic branch to grow and refine more and more.

Over time, however, extraterrestrial beings began to withdraw. As a result, direct contacts with the E-N-K population became rarer as the E-N-K gene was strengthened and full respect for its free will was an absolute necessity for these beings to manage their own existence and destiny. Later, the withdrawal of extraterrestrial and E-N-L beings from the lives of the inhabitants of Egypt at that time continued until they finally no longer appeared physically or directly among the people.

Instead, communication with them was maintained through pyramids which played the role of intermediaries between the world of humans and the world of "gods", that is, highly advanced technologically and spiritually extraterrestrial beings who laid the foundations of their ancient culture. For example, the initiated Egyptians used some pyramid chambers to easily perform the "conscious astral projection" which allowed them to move to the planets where their "gods" lived. The guidance came from the specific vibrational frequency of the pyramid, as designed by the "gods".

HIDDEN INITIATIONS INSIDE THE PYRAMIDS

I saw in a few pictures how initiations were carried out in the King's Chamber of the Great Pyramid. The sarcophagus was filled about three quarters with a semitransparent and viscous light blue liquid in which usually the High Priest would be immersed while naked, save for only a scarf around the hips. The sarcophagus, however, was also used for the same purpose by all who received the initiation for the journey to the "gods" and not just by the High Priest.

The body did not sink into the liquid but remained floating on the surface of it. Although I did not quite understand it, I think that the liquid was meant to facilitate "astralization" of the being or perhaps it was meant to cause certain biochemical transformations in the body that were necessary for the conscious detachment of the astral body from the physical one. It is certain that the human being in the sarcophagus was entering a trance state quite quickly. Other priests were standing around the sarcophagus reciting certain incantations. These "incantations" were not common liturgies, but they often played a decisive role, as far as I could tell, in the process of initiation for the initiate and their travel in the subtle planes.

The images also showed me the etheric reality, and I could see that, after the body was immersed in liquid and the ritual began, tall silhouettes of extra-terrestrial beings appeared through the stone blocks that made up the walls of the room. They were translucent and imposing with some carrying a scepter. They were situated behind the priests who officiated during the incantations, and in my opinion, they were supervising and helping to properly conduct the ritual, providing the necessary subtle protection.

THE SHORT-TERM WAR AND THE
REORGANIZATION OF THE GALACTIC ALLIANCE

The images then jumped pretty quickly to another historical reality which was, from what I calculated, about 4,800 B.C. I saw that among some of the civilizations that had supported that process of transmitting the legacy of ancient scientific and spiritual knowledge, all of which had helped to form strong centers of spirituality on Earth, certain dissensions began to emerge. These turned into a powerful war, but that did not last long. People were also involved, and the end result led to a reorganization of the Alliance so that many of the initiative centers on the planet came under the tutelage of civilizations other than those from the beginning. It also involved changing customs, the names of deities and even knowledge. There were also some "mutations" in the religions of the people.

In principle, and as far as I could tell, the reason for the conflict, which this time was less intense than the one of 100,000 years ago, had the same root: the negative influence of the evil reptilians. The problem was that some of the extraterrestrial "gods" of antiquity lived in areas of the galaxy that had begun to be "shadowed" by the evil presence and influence of evil reptilians. It was therefore difficult and even dangerous to tolerate such a negative infusion of conception and even genetic modification into the DNA of humans if the pantheon of the Egyptian gods remained unchanged. This aspect was quite delicate as all human civilizations that pervaded over time, especially after 30,000 B.C., were endorsed by those extraterrestrial "gods" who contributed to the formation of spiritual centers on the planet, the construction of the pyramids, and other buildings serving a priestly purpose.

Due to the reptilian influences that slowly propagated even among some of the rather advanced extraterrestrial civilizations, the Galactic Alliance was forced to change its pantheon several thousand years ago, some "gods" being replaced by others from other civilizations of the Alliance. This change, however, was not to the liking of some *E-N-K* beings who wished to remain faithful to the old "gods"; thus, tensions began to emerge between human populations which later expanded between certain alien civilizations in the Alliance.

With these changes in the Egyptian pantheon, certain totemic tendencies were amplified which made the representations of the new "gods" to usually be a combination of the human body with the head of an animal. For example, the pharaohs of ancient Egypt or the important persons in the administrative management were depicted with the mask of a dog (jackal) or ibis on the head, while some female deities had a cow's head. Controversies of interpretation thus arose, suggesting the possibility of the corruption of these civilizations by the malefic reptilians, and therefore, their hybridization with reptilian DNA.

ANUBIS AND OTHER TOTEMIC HEADS

I had to view the images several times to understand why they wanted to "explain" all this to me because the subject was quite abstract. Some modern authors have rushed to the conclusion that those masks with animal heads, with which the gods and sometimes even the pharaohs were represented, did not necessarily represent symbolic aspects but were used to hide certain reptilian traits. But, if that were the case, why did not the "gods" of that extraterrestrial civilization appear as having those features before the time of Ancient Egypt? I have seen pictures of them over a period of 400,000 years and have not noticed such "anomalies" even once. If that were true, it means that the Sirian Tenekau himself, who came from the Orion constellation and can, from a certain point of view, be called the "Father of Mankind" should also be regarded as having reptilian features. I noticed, however, that he was a human being with high moral qualities who was noble, wise and good and contributed his own DNA to the first hybridizations of human DNA.

On the other hand, the vast majority of Egyptians at that time were made up of *E-N-K* beings who came from the direct line of large primates and still had a strong animal influence in their DNA. As a result, they needed to show special respect, stemming from their admiration for the animal kingdom. As a personal opinion, I could say that this was the origin of most of the animal sacrifices; that is, this gift was offered to the being who "shaped them" because each pharaoh associated the origin of the domestic animals with his image. In a way, this assumption can be true because the domestication of many animals took place concurrently with the period when the pharaohs came to power and supported that phenomenon.

Later, when human DNA (*E-N-K*) evolved, it was necessary for man to gradually reject these totemic associations because he had became too dependent on the animal kingdom without being able to detach from the energies of the Earth. An eloquent example is that of Moses with the Jewish people who, during the Exodus, rejected the association with the animal kingdom that was characterized by praying to idols and went on to a more abstract understanding of Yahweh, meaning, he wanted to make a particular qualitative leap. Here, however, things are more complicated, but I will not insist in this direction.

After the great cataclysm and disappearance of Atlantis, each "god" or extraterrestrial being who sustained spirituality in Ancient Egypt represented a constellation. They were Sirius beings who came from both the Sirius system, meaning from the Big Dog constellation, and also from the systems associated with some stars from the Orion constellation. The teachings they offered were in agreement with the specific energy of that period that was necessary to give the human gene a certain ability to resonate with those subtle forces. Therefore, each "god" was associated with a form that represented the symbol of the area from which he or she came, or in other words, that specific "sign".

Due to the totemic and animistic character of the belief that "folk people" had at that time, these representations were meant to provoke a certain emotion in those who saw those animal heads, those associations being necessary for the human being to understand what that "god" signified. With the passage of time, however, they no longer tried to make the association between the symbol and the deity, but they united the symbol with the respective "god" or "goddess" itself, thus resulting in the rendering of the human body with the head of cow, a lion, or a dog, etc.

Generally speaking, the human being is accustomed to associate various symbols directly with certain human beings, and in the case of Ancient Egypt, this was done with the "gods" and pharaohs of those times. From here, it was only a step until the representations of this nature were put on frescoes, cartouches or pictograms. When, for example, a pharaoh was known after his reign or even during his reign to have been "like a lion" because of his strong personality, the best representation of this idea was for that pharaoh to have a lion's head. The examples are numerous and continue.

The problem that arose with the passage of time was that these associations began to become entangled with the connotation of symbols being altered or simply "borrowed" for occult purposes. An example of this is the symbol of the "Eye of Horus" currently used by the Illuminati in the most diverse situations but having a corrupt meaning.

This is how the ancient Egyptians gradually forgot the true meanings of the symbols associated with their "gods" or, better yet, surrounding them with so many multiple meanings and characteristics and transferring them from one to the other so that they reached the point where they no longer knew what the truth was. Faith, lacking a viable support, began to crumble, and Egyptian spirituality declined in a short time.

This is exactly what is happening nowadays with a society that is almost completely distanced from deep moral and ethical principles and values but rather only mimics fairness and decency which, in reality, is only a screen for the manipulations behind it by very powerful and dangerous occult groups and organizations. Their main purpose is the total destruction of any spiritual support within the being because, so disheveled and inconsistent, it tends to dismantle without having any force of reaction or opposition. Unfortunately, this plan has given worrisome results so far as humanity seems to have "lost its compass". As will be seen, however, the spiritual revival is close, but in order for it to happen faster, it is necessary to become truly aware of the current situation.

CHAPTER FIFTEEN

Troy and the Retreat of the Mayans

Closer to our times and to contemporary history, there are some landmark historical moments that need to be considered, especially due to the mystery surrounding them and the lack of authentic sources of information. I focused on Troy, an enigmatic painting in the memory of Mankind of which there are no other references than those in Homer's *Iliad*. After viewing the images on the holographic screen, I developed the topic in a very interesting discussion I had with Cezar a few weeks later.

THE CITY OF TROY

The first images I saw about the existence of the great city of Troy was when I was shown the "descent" of the Hyperborean civilization. A branch of it had descended to the south and reached the northwestern coast of today's Turkey. The spread to that area, however, was not dictated by geographical needs but rather by the existence of a large inter-dimensional portal, one of the few that remained at that time on Earth. As I was shown, the city — which later became known as "the fortress" — was built around that space-time discontinuity which allowed for the connection with the elevated areas of the etheric plane and especially with Shambhala.

I was very impressed by that presentation and that is why, in one of the conversations I later had with Cezar, I brought up this topic which I confess that I had not yet fully understood. There were indeed several strangers.

The descendants of the Hyperboreans who founded Troy, even if they were only pale reflections of what once was the Hyperborean civilization, still possessed enough secrets and even occult methods to resist enduring attacks from other peoples.

Even so, it would have been no problem for the two malefic alien civilizations who had some control in today's southern Europe to immediately shave off any trace of the city, including its inhabitants, from the surface of the Earth by using the advanced weapons of mass destruction that they had. Such an "intervention", however, could not be done so easily thanks to the supervision by the Alliance, and this was confirmed by Cezar. What I did not understand, in fact, was what was at stake with the fortress In other words, why did the ancient world focus so much on that area?

Cezar explained to me that, even if evil was allowed to manifest and be spread amongst Mankind, that action still had its own "economy", a sensitivity related to the formation of humanity passing certain tests to allow for the manifesting of free will. Troy was sought out in antiquity because it was located at one of the "edges" between the physical and the etheric plane; that is, in the area of a large and powerful "energetic vein", an important place that allowed easy passage from the physical plane into the etheric plane.

THE TRUE STORY OF THE TROJAN WAR

When Cezar went on to the next point, his explanations became more nuanced:

"Troy was practically the last city in Europe to maintain a strong bond with the subtle etheric plane," he told me. "It was the last city where one could enter the subtle ethereal plane naturally and widely. With the defeat suffered during the war with the Greeks, the city suddenly 'broke' from the physical plane, and then the reality on the surface of the Earth was 'mortified' somehow because it had eliminated even the last redoubt of what was still superior, pure, and good. At that point, the last clear trace of the Hyperborean civilization probably then disappeared."

I asked if the war had anything to do with that delicate aspect.

"The 'crossing area' in the etheric plane that was inside the fortress was the main aim of the Trojan war. It was, in fact, occult forces that suggested and directed it, using human beings as vehicles to achieve that massive 'energy break'. This fall threw humanity into a darkness even deeper than it was before as result of what had been generated by the destruction of Atlantis."

"And what happened to the city afterwards?"

"It resurfaced in the etheric plane, and the city as such cannot be found in the physical plane. What Schliemann* discovered, however, is only a small area of his own, one that had a resonance closer to the physical plane. However, it does not represent the "City of Troy" such as archeologists have been quick to announce."

I now understood the mystery that surrounded that mythical fortress, as well as the long war that was waged for its conquest.

"From Troy, it was very easy to go into the etheric plane in the subtle dimension," Cezar told me. "I do want you to understand, however, that this passage was not admissible to all. The city was perfectly circular and surrounded the central point where the distortion was, the source through which one could penetrate into the etheric plane corresponding to that area of the city of Troy, with only a few having access to the higher dimension.

---

* Cezar refers here to Heinrich Schliemann, credited for the so-called discovery of the city of Troy in 1870 in the area of Hisarlik village in northwestern Turkey today.

NUCLEUS OF THE MAYAN CIVILIZATION

"It seems that those closer to us in antiquity knew that not everyone could enter these subtle worlds nor could they do it in any manner they chose," I said.

"Obviously, and Troy is not the only example. The Mayans are even more representative in this regard because almost no trace of human activity or cities could be found behind them. They simply 'disappeared' without being identified in any area. I refer to the core of the original Mayan civilization from the past, from which the Aztec and Inca lines extended, but the 'seeds' of that very special civilization which were Mayans remained in the form of a small number of priests and sages, as well as their descendants that settled in an area of the Yucatan, near the ocean coast. Some of the families, however, wandered throughout various areas of the former Incan empire. The collapse of that nucleus, which did not exceed one hundred thousand members, favored the almost unaltered preservation of the ancient and original knowledge and tradition of the Mayan civilization, strengthening their determination to evolve. For the most part, they did not even interact with the Incas who were still there. Even though they also had a considerable degree of knowledge and development, they still lost the power of the original gene. As an example, the 'mythical' city of El Dorado or the Golden City of the Incas was foreign to them. The Incas knew the tradition, but they had forgotten how to get to that settlement that their heritage told them about. The less the Spaniards found, the more desperately they looked for it. Such cities were never discovered by conquerors, and the reason is the same as for the city of Troy: they were cities that were not necessarily part of the physical world but more of the subtle world of etheric frequencies. At one point, they completely resurfaced in that dimension of existence and simply disappeared from the physical world. Some of the Incan priests and initiates, however, knew about the reality of the 'Golden City' and a very small part even had access to it by passing through an inter-dimensional portal. The Mayan sages from the remnant nucleus of the ancient civilization had unrestricted access because they possessed that special knowledge and had the necessary vibrational level, manifested in a few specific genes and most likely inherited from the E-N-L."

Cezar's explanations were very clear and succinct, and even though I had not explored that part of the world or the civilizations that had inhabited it until then, what I had learned here was not entirely unknown to me. My recent experience in Utklaha*, the city within the Earth, had been uplifting and many of the inhabitants of that city in the subtle etheric plane were actually forerunners of the ancient Mayans. I took the opportunity to find out more, and that is why I asked Cezar to clarify the mystery of the Mayan civilization, a culture which I knew could not be deciphered by today's archeologists or scientists.

---

* Utklaha is a city within the Inner Earth mentioned in *Inside the Earth — The Second Tunnel.*

"VIBRATIONAL JUMP" IN THE ETHERIC PLANE

"The great problem of the Mayans was symbolized by the Spanish conquerors," said Cezar. "Their invasion meant the disaster of the Mayan civilization from the physical plane, but at the same time, in a certain way, this 'forced' its passage to a higher plane."

Seeing that I was looking at him questioningly, he went on to explain.

"The Mayans were a people with an old culture with exceptional knowledge. To them, the 'break' between the physical plane and the subtle planes, at least conceptually speaking, almost did not exist. After the Spanish invasion, their priests quickly realized that the only viable alternative to the threat of extermination was a massive exodus of the Mayan population from the physical to the etheric. In other words, to make a vibrational leap in their existence. Such actions are quite rare in history and only occur in exceptional cases, when the situation cannot be resolved otherwise."

I asked how it was possible for an entire people to move from one plane to another. Cezar said that really was a thorny problem, but for the most part, they succeeded.

"Mayan priests knew very well the area of passage into the etheric plane that was in one of their jungle towns. The Mayans understood the importance of the communion between man and Nature, and that is why their cities coexisted extensively with the surrounding vegetation. The only problem was that other authentic Mayan groups had migrated and had to be gathered from other areas of the Inca empire in order to achieve that transition between planes. In this way, they could escape the madness of the Spaniards and their desire to kill them."

I realized then that the drama of that period in which a somewhat primitive civilization, through knowledge and attitudes but strong at the military level — and here I refer to the Spaniards — threatened to exterminate another civilization that was noble and elevated: the Mayans. Neither the Aztecs nor the Incas were able to cope with the ferocity, disease and firearms of the Spaniards. They were conquered, as is well known, but as far as the core of the ancient Mayans was concerned, that could not be achieved.

Cezar told me that there was a "general call" so that the Mayan population who were scattered throughout the Incan empire began to "run" to the special crossing place where there was a large portal, that is, a space-time discontinuity known to Mayan priests and sages. That area was defended for about two months by a large number of Mayan soldiers who created a corridor of protection for the civilian population coming from different areas of the empire to avoid possible attacks by the Spaniards.

"On the other hand, the robbery of the conquerors was not a war or a continuous battle, and it did not take place in one place," Cezar continued to explain. "There was no real fight but rather a messy robbery. Attacks by the Spaniards were mostly spontaneous when they simply seized a village or a city in the jungle. On the other hand, the Mayan soldiers had a precise mission to counter such attacks in order to ensure the escape route of the civilian population to the area between the planes."

"Have you personally seen all this?" I asked.

Cezar nodded his head affirmatively, assuring me that this was one of the most amazing moments in history, both through its drama and the mystery surrounding it.

"It was more like the war with the Americans in Vietnam. It was not at all clear to the Spaniards how much they had conquered, and not just from the Incan empire, but also in the area of the Yucatan peninsula where the core of the Mayan sages remained. This is because, near the great passageway, the physical plane often blends into the etheric plane so that the phenomenon of 'psychological blindness' is in full force. The wise men of the ancient Mayans had the power to manipulate the surrounding reality through their specific invocations and occult methods. You could meet a group of twenty conquerors, and a little further on there would be a Mayan village where normal activity went on without the Spaniards having any idea of its existence, even if they passed it by. They simply did not see that village because, as far as they could see, there was only the jungle in that area. Such strange phenomena, which was often repeated, seemed quite confusing to the conquerors; but in the end, their increasing number would have led to the extermination of the Mayans had they not taken the radical decision to leave the physical plane and move to the etheric plane where they could safely continue their existence. In fact, this moment had been predicted many hundreds of years before by the Mayan priests."

THE GREAT "TRANSITION" OF THE MAYANS

Cezar said, however, that the transition to the etheric plane could not be done under just any conditions. There were only certain areas and only certain periods when the transition from the physical to the etheric plane could take place. I then asked him why, if this secret data were still known, did not all of the population pass? It seems that a certain part of the Mayan population, about one fifth of the total "pure gene" group, did not want to go into the etheric plane, preferring to remain in the physical dimension. For the most part, it was based on the law of affinity, that is, vibrational frequency, that did not allow a certain category of people to go through that passage.

"The first ones who passed into the etheric plane were those who met the resonant conditions of the frequencies because some of the Mayans were not prepared from this point of view, even if they wanted to cross the portal. I saw, however, that many of them were helped by the shaman priests who stood near the "gateway" and supported them in this process through the powers they held by temporarily raising their individual vibrational frequency so that they could cross into the etheric plane. Once they reached beyond, those beings were able to maintain that vibrational frequency, thus managing to remain in the new plane of existence.

I became very curious to know what that big "portal" looked like from the perspective of the physical plane. In the images that had been shown to me on the holographic screen of the Apellos, the "contact" points between the physical and the etheric dimensions usually appeared as a surface that is slightly blurred, slightly foggy, or completely invisible in most cases. Then, it was indicated in the hologram by certain symbols and a bright red point where the discontinuity between the planes was. I wanted to know, however, based upon what Cezar told me, about that Mayan passage in the etheric plane that seemed to cover a larger area.

"I was watching closely what was going on there and seeing the events," he told me. "I clearly realized exactly where the crossing was made; but nevertheless, I could not see any distortion in that boundary area. There was apparently no discontinuity of space. I could not see anything that could have hinted that there could be an ethereal plane. Instead, I noticed that as the Mayans approached that area to cross it, something seemed to happen in their being because each one of them was shaking with a fine tremor. I was interested in the phenomenon, so I focused on the beings that crossed the area of spatial discontinuity."

I knew all too well that all of the high-tech extraterrestrial devices that facilitate the investigation of space and time have the particularity of offering the ability to feel everything that is being researched in the context of time and space, if desired. In other words, you live what you see, as if you were right there in the space-time zone you are researching. I could say that feeling is more refined and nuanced than even one's normal feeling, offering an extra sensation, intuition and perception. It is as if all the senses are sharpened and the field of perceptions widens. So, I understood Cezar's story too well because I myself had the same experience many times. In some cases, it can be traumatic; but fortunately, I learned that I had the opportunity to "adjust" it by manifesting my will or even suppressing it altogether, in which case only visual information remained. I was thinking though about whether that was a similar experience or not to the ones I myself had lived through in the Second Tunnel or on the way to the "inland" in Argentina. Accordingly, I asked Cezar if it was different from our experience inside the Earth.

"No. Basically it was an identical phenomenon, but I wanted to convince myself that the portal connected the physical plane with the etheric plane. You can't get it wrong in this regard, once you feel that vibration. I felt that, before passing, those whose level of consciousness was high enough perceived the city and the jungle from which they came, but at one moment, they saw how a much larger and more developed city was beginning to spread in front of them in which the jungle vegetation no longer existed. Those who did not have the ability to move into the etheric plane were still observing their old city in the jungle, but they were confident because they knew that there was something else beyond in the subtle dimension. When they reached the priests who were guarding the invisible gate of passage into the etheric plane, the priests helped them, raising the vibrational frequency of their consciousness for a short time but as much as was necessary for them to see the city from the etheric plane and pass through and beyond.

"But the priests — what were they doing?"

"They stood from place to place, on a certain path towards the gateway, creating a kind of 'subtle tunnel' of initiation. Those who had the native ability to cross entered a certain specific state of consciousness as they approached the gate. Others were hesitant, and some even tended to turn back."

So it is that the "great Mayan passage" into the etheric plane was not a great "migration" nor travel by cart or ship to another area of South America, as scientists suppose, but it simply signified a retreat to another part of their city but one that was ethereal. Cezar told me that, after the access through the gateway was closed, the etheric plane into which the Mayans had passed through the portal was strictly delimited by the physical plane. They continued their life there but at higher energy parameters because the vibrational frequency of the etheric plane is higher than that which is specific to the physical plane.

CHAPTER SIXTEEN

The Anunnaki: A Delicate Problem

In universities, the existence of extraterrestrial beings and of highly advanced civilizations has always been a kind of "Pepelea's nail"* for today's humanity. Due to poor education and manipulation through the media, most people are doubtful and skeptical when it comes to this topic. For many of them, the benevolent presentation of the aliens "sounds too good and too beautiful" to be true. It is thus considered that they should also have some shortcomings, including a desire for hybridization due to their desire to be perceived as being closer to the present human condition. In some cases, they are even viewed as a source of threat to our civilization.

A STRANGE INVESTMENT OF VALUES

Such a vision may in fact reflect the distrust of human beings in their own enormous potential. Watching closely everything that was presented to me in the holographic images of humanity's past, I can say with all conviction that the Earth was and is blessed by great protection and great care from advanced extraterrestrial civilizations in our galaxy. Most people consider that the fraternal state and attitude of our wonderful friends in the cosmos is a subject for science fiction and that the holographic network of extraterrestrial connections in the galaxy which have been shown to me are, in fact, the product of a mind full of overflowing imagination.

There is, however, a category of human beings who are genuinely interested in these subjects and who want to know the truth. Unfortunately and sometimes unintentionally, such subjects are either hidden or misrepresented. A good example of this are people's perception of the race of extraterrestrial beings known as the Anunnaki.

This name has triggered many bizarre ideas but especially erroneous beliefs which are based both on false or incomplete information as well as a certain superficiality in dealing with the subject. Many books have already been written in which the Anunnaki are blamed for all of the evils of the Earth, but most often, they are associated with extraterrestrial beings with reptilian traits. The fundamental error, which is based upon incorrect information and conclusions, is the correlation of the evil reptilian beings with the Sirian beings

---

* Pepelea's (pronounced *Peh-Peh-leah*) nail is a Romanian folk tale of a poor man who had inherited a beautiful house. When a rich man wanted to buy it, Pepelea sold it upon only one condition: that Pepelea would retain ownership of a nail on the wall of the living room upon which he could hang whatever he wanted. When the rich man was having guests or otherwise enjoying the house, Pepelea would drop by and hang a dirty old garment. Eventually, the rich man got so exasperated and disgusted that he returned the house to Pepelea for free.

known as the Anunnaki. This is even more strange, given that the Sirians are the ones who initiated and supported, in direct collaboration with the plans of the subtle celestial entities who serves as governors of the galaxy, the process of birth and evolution of human beings on Earth.

Such a reversal of values has also been encountered in other times and circumstances, but in this case, it is amazing that the enthusiasm of some authors, who only imagine that they know the truth, in reality, are in grievous error. The pressure on this subject is very high because it has been "targeted" repeatedly in very negative parameters which makes it more challenging to return to the true knowledge and the real values, both of which have been lost. I will, however, on the one hand, specify some of these elements based upon what images I could see from prehistoric times to those of modern history; and on the other hand, based upon the heartfelt explanations I got from the man from Apellos in response to some confusion I expressed. As I said, the Sirians are at the root of the birth and formation of the human civilization, and they are also at the root of human DNA, supporting its evolution for ages and helping humanity in the key points of its development, both from the spiritual point of view as well as the material. I myself have seen many aspects of the history of Earth and of humanity, and some of the more important ones I have described in this book. In some cases, when it was needed, the Sirians even influenced the course of history so that the evolution of the human being could take place in the best conditions. At one point, the man from Apellos told me that from their original basic branch, which is in the Sirius A system, secondary branches have appeared over time in different areas of the galaxy, but the Sirians in the Sirius A system are called Anunnaki which means "those who came from the Divine Light".

SEGREGATION OF POPULATIONS
AND MIGRATION TO OTHER PLANETS

At one point during my investigation, the confusion of what I knew about the Anunnaki and what I saw in the holographic images had become so great that I had to interrupt the flow a little to seek some explanation from the man from Apellos who had been silent and motionless, a little behind me. I asked him, if possible, to give me some details about the Anunnaki in order to clarify the dilemma that is still valid for most people today.

"The origin of this civilization is in the planetary system of the star Sirius A," he told me. "They are the original Sirian race, the oldest and basic branch from which other branches broke off before migrating to other areas of the galaxy.

He then told me that, in the Sirian language, when someone is given a name, the root is put first. In other words, the basic name is complemented by adding a certain defining trait or characteristic of that being to that root, often representing a group of beings. Thus, if some of the original Anunnaki migrated at one time to a planet from another part of the galaxy, they are then also called Anunnaki as a whole, but they also have another name that differentiates them from the original Sirians. This is one of the aspects that many authors have missed, giving rise to controversial views. From the basic Sirian civilization, many other secondary civilizations have developed which have "relocated" over time to other planets and other star systems of the galaxy. Most of them, however, have settled near the constellation Canis Major, especially in the constellation Orion and in the star systems of Orion's Belt. The mistake, which was perpetuated among contemporary authors, was to consider one or more of these secondary civilizations that spread throughout the galaxy as the original Sirian civilization of Sirius A.

From time immemorial, Earth has also received other civilizations that either came from other areas of the cosmos or evolved on its surface. Man, as a being who has already undergone many transformations before reaching the present condition of homo sapiens, can be considered to be "young" (almost 400,000 years old) compared to other extraterrestrial beings.

In the discussion I had with the man from Apellos, he synthesized these aspects very well in a natural, calm and profound way.

"When one is born, a being begins the cycle of continuous evolution. A planet can only support the evolution of that being or civilization for a certain time, but there comes a time when a civilization must mature. This happened with the E-N-L branch which, at its maximum level of development, withdrew into the subtle etheric plane. This will be the case with the current human civilization as soon as it reaches its peak; but for now, contrary to what most people believe, homo sapiens' civilization is still far from the beginning of its maturity. To make a parallel, you are about somewhere between fourteen and sixteen, an age when all teenagers think they are extraordinary; but, in reality, this is far from the truth. They have much more to learn."

This was a harsh remark, but in my opinion, perfectly true. In any case, he emphasized the need for scientists of today to re-evaluate their possibilities and concepts and to give up at least some of the immense pride that characterizes them.

A common strategy, which is used by the vast majority of advanced alien civilizations, is to send certain members of a particular civilization which have not evolved as quickly as the rest of the population to a more suitable planet. In other words, they are "relocated" to another planet which better corresponds to their vibrational frequency where they will evolve at their own pace. Those who remain on the home planet can thus accelerate their evolution without being hindered by those who have been relocated.

An example is that of the Anunnaki because they proceeded in this way in successive phases, relocating entire segments of the population of their planet, originating from the Sirius system A, to other stellar systems. Such "migrations" to other planets follows the cosmic law of vibrational affinity because no being can remain in an existential reality unless it corresponds to that local frequency. An "adjustment" of the situation is then sought out with the most natural solution being this kind of "redistribution" of the vibrational frequencies which corresponds approximately to the wise old saying: "The right man for the right place."

THE SPECIAL DESTINATION OF HUMANITY

The course of the discussion with the man from Apellos brought me close to a very sensitive aspect. What was the reason why the Anunnaki Sirians chose our planet to shape, develop and protect the human species?

"Indeed. To many of the other civilizations who have come to observe us, this choice of the Sirians is almost incomprehensible," he said. "There are 'observers' in space around our planet who simply attend events on the surface without intervening. It is a moment, even for them, to understand and experience how the destiny of a civilization 'flows'. And one of the most difficult things to understand for those who do not have access to a thorough knowledge of the true history of man and his origin, is why Sirians, along with the other extraterrestrial civilizations in the Alliance, assist humanity with great care and attach extreme importance to Mankind in the context of the fundamental transformations that are taking place today."

I replied that we are not the only ones enjoying such attention.

"I have seen that as the Anunnaki assist this planet and transformations taking place at this level, so have they supported many other civilizations in the last hundreds of thousands of years, having laid the foundations of humanity. But now, in this very special convergence of space and time in the galaxy, they support us, not others."

This was a good question and that is why some extraterrestrial civilizations are curious to attend events on Earth in order to observe what is happening in our Solar System. For them, the situation is a great mystery: people remain at the level of industrial production, they are technologically and ideologically backward, they are violent, and many have a very low intellectual level and even exhibit animal behavior. Under these circumstances, why do the Anunnaki from the Sirius A system, known to be true spiritual masters in the galaxy, consider us to have such great importance? As far as I could tell, even if our civilization is in such a condition, we are important to the Anunnaki. It is therefore obvious that this area of cosmic space in which the Earth resides is a special focus for the future.

"All this happens because they are the ones who, in fact, guide the galaxy and are the ones who support humanity," said the man from Apellos. "From many points of view, humanity is a quite backward civilization; not primitive but backward in terms of understanding, principles, and behavior. In contrast, the resources within human beings are immense; and it is precisely because the Sirians saw this extraordinary potential in humans that they give their endorsement through the very undeniable authority that they have among other civilizations at the galactic level. In fact, many alliances were formed precisely because they gave their endorsement and insisted upon our integration.

Due to the agreement given by the Anunnaki and the alliances formed by them, humanity has become a kind of "attraction point" at this moment in the galaxy. From a certain point of view, it may be that the Earth, by the example it offers and the situation it is in, is now a kind of "stone border" for the future of this galactic sector and perhaps even for a larger area of the galaxy.

A GALACTIC "WEDDING"

At this point, the man from Apellos pointed to a deeper and even extraordinary aspect of this entire scenario.

"All the transformations that take place now and that will take place in the future, in addition to their local and immediate effects, are actually related to the preparation for the union of our galaxy with that of the Andromeda galaxy. Although this will take place over several billion years, preparations and collaboration for it have been made in both galaxies. It is like a 'galactic program' useful for aligning life to the new vibrational frequency of the galaxy that will result from the union of the two current ones. We could say that, at the cosmic level, it is as if they are preparing for an important 'wedding' of galactic proportions. The spiritual levels must be aligned, the subtle energies must also be correlated, and the frequencies must be arranged in such a way that, at the time of fusion, the civilizations and life of the two galaxies do not suffer extinction but rather evolve in an amazing way."

I expressed my astonishment sincerely.

"But why worry about the extinction of the worlds that might come? Ultimately, the chances of the stars or planets of the two galaxies colliding, even if the galaxies are intertwined, are very small."

"Their extinction would not come from brutal phenomena but rather from a major and subtle vibrational leap. Such an extraordinary cosmic event causes the vibrational frequency to rise, and this will cause chaos in most of the new galaxy. This is precisely why the present preparations and the ones that will follow, even if the galaxy's unification will take place over several billion years, envisage that the civilizations that will be born will appear on the basis of ideas already assimilated and embedded into the consciousness of intelligent beings. In this way, the differences of the energetic and conceptual nature between the life of our galaxy and that of the Andromeda galaxy are minimized. It is a galactic and even universal evolutionary program and is the very idea of evolution at the macrocosmic level."

The man from Apellos also told me that this very complicated and long "cosmic action" is coordinated by celestial entities far superior to most extraterrestrial civilizations which govern the galaxy from subtle planes. For example, they are the ones that give approval or not for certain specific actions that have to be carried out in different areas of the galaxy by advanced civilizations.

These celestial entities, organized in a strict hierarchy, are the ones that coordinate and correlate all the colossal transformations that will take place here. Any specific action or influence is thought out and oriented towards a higher purpose. It is a huge plan which, in relation to our lifespan, cannot be understood or integrated mentally. It is so distant in time and at the same time gigantic that it goes far beyond the usual capacities of perception or thought. The comparison with the "wheel that fits in a huge gear and has its own important mission, contributing to the smooth functioning of the mechanism" is very true for humanity and for life on Earth with regard to this idea of integration into the great future of the galaxy, all of which will take place over a huge period of time.

For most people, the aspects and motivations presented may seem irrelevant due to the huge temporal dimension that is involved in this vast divine plan. However, at a high level of perception and action such as the causal plane, time becomes insignificant, and events are perceived simultaneously and equally. The man from Apellos told me that the causal entities that govern this cosmic process and its proper development have noticed that, in the current cosmic context, the evolution of our planet is important, representing a "boundary" of reference.

Even if most people do not realize this, however, crucial events take place at the galactic level. Every being, every action, and every attitude is important in its own way because it integrates into this whole unity in the pursuit of a particular goal. Society changes from "having" to "feeling". In other words, the sense of possession, selfishness, competition and violence tends to be gradually replaced with pure positive emotions and feelings, among which love, altruism and compassion are fundamental. Practically speaking, every human being is invited to take part in the great spiritual transformation of our humanity and our planet, to humbly demand with dignity that his life be a germ of light, of spirituality, and of hope for the bright future to which we can have access. All these seem to be just beautiful words; but in reality, they are the basic bricks for the transformation and evolution of the contemporary human being.

From this perspective, the information I provide here is an integral part of this "game" and has a certain significance, as both Méntia and the man from Apellos have brought me to understand. By properly assimilating this information, many people will probably understand things more deeply and will awaken to a higher reality which allows for a much broader view of life in the Universe. In particular and in relation to the subject I am discussing here, they might acquire a different view of the Anunnaki civilization and thus might reconsider the nature of these highly advanced extraterrestrial beings in a new way, both technologically and spiritually.

Sirians know how to pour out their wonderful love, but at the same time, when needed, they know how to react very strongly in fights or other terrible cosmic conflicts. They do so, however, at a different level of understanding than is perceived by most human beings. The Anunnaki are considered to be true spiritual masters in the galaxy; and that is why, if they support us, this is implicitly a kind of "recommendation" to other advanced extraterrestrial civilizations who will understand that this is important.

The presence of spirituality and an implicit sense of a high morality are strongly felt, and that is why they are still known by many civilizations in the galaxy as "those who came from the Spirit". Wherever they go, they emanate purity, the force of righteous action, and high knowledge in different forms. Metaphorically speaking, we can think of some highly evolved monks who are spiritually worthy, but at the same time, humble and wise. They do not attack, but if attacked, they defend with great efficiency and always defeat their adversary.

EPILOGUE

As Radu clearly alludes to in the last chapter, what he has offered us is in stark contrast to the preponderance of literature about aliens. Two major influences in my own life, that being L. Ron Hubbard and Preston Nichols, certainly portrayed extraterrestrials in a most negative light. While Preston did also convey a positive connotation, particularly in regard to the Pleiadians who educated him, Hubbard portrayed aliens as being rather dedicated with implanting human beings so as to make them docile and controllable.

I think everyone would agree that there is a huge chasm between the state of mind of the average human being and that which could be considered a highly superior entity who has advanced technology as well as skill in navigating the etheric dimensions. If we are to heed Radu's comment about humanity's evolutionary status being at the equivalency of a young teenager, there is a long way to go, and what is offered in these books is part of the process of humanity's evolution.

Radu has at least five more books to present to us, and I have received a hint that the next one will be forthcoming soon, but I cannot say specifically. As soon as I receive a computer file, I will begin the translation and editing process immediately.

I will also continue my own personal adventures to Romania; and in particular, to Cioclovina Cave. This is a cave which time control scientist, Dr. David Anderson, has stated is the most significant with regard to containing scientifically documented traces of a powerful discharge of space-time motive force, i.e. the name of for energy that is released in conjunction with a Time Reactor™ (time machine).

For those of you who want to keep up-to-date, you are invited to subscribe to my quarterly newsletter, the *Montauk Pulse.* This is where I will report on any new developments with regard to Radu or the other characters that he writes about.

Peter Moon
Long Island
November 11, 2019

THE TRANSYLVANIAN SERIES

TRANSYLVANIAN SUNRISE is the story of an unprecedented archeological discovery beneath the Romanian Sphinx in the Bucegi Mountains. Radu Cinamar visits this secret site where he witnessed a holographic Hall of Records left by an advanced civilization and three mysterious tunnels leading deep into the bowels of the Inner Earth. *Transylvanian Sunrise* chronicles the political intrigue surrounding the discovery of these artifacts which represents the dawn of a new era for Mankind.
288 pages, ISBN 978-0-9678162-5-8.............................$22.00

TRANSYLVANIAN MOONRISE corroborates Radu's story with newspaper articles as he is sought out by a mysterious Tibetan Lama who takes Radu on a mystical journey to Tibet where he receives a secret initiation and a sacred manuscript from the blue goddess Machandi. This is an initiation of the highest order that will take you far beyond your ordinary imagination in order to describe events that have molded the past and will influence the future in the decades ahead.
288 pages, ISBN 978-0-9678162-8-9......................................$22.00

MYSTERY OF EGYPT features an expedition to explore the First Tunnel in the holographic chamber: the one to Egypt. Ancient artifacts are discovered which tell the history of the Earth in holographic form, the most controversial of which include remarkable adventure that includes explorations in time to the First Century A.D. This book also includes updates from Cezar since their last meeting.
240 pages, ISBN 978-1-937859-08-4.....................................$22.00

THE SECRET PARCHMENT — FIVE TIBETAN INITIATION TECHNIQUES presents invaluable techniques for spiritual advancement that came to Radu Cinamar in the form of an ancient manuscript whose presence in the world ignited a series of quantum events, extending from Jupiter's moon Europa and reaching all the way to Antarctica, Mount McKinley and Transylvania. An ancient Romanian legend comes alive as a passage way of solid gold tunnels, extending miles in the Transylvanian underground is revealed to facilitate super-consciousness as well as lead to the nexus of Inner Earth where "All the Worlds Unite."
288 pages, ISBN 978-0-9678162-5-8......................................$22.00

THE WHITE BAT — THE ALCHEMY OF WRITING
Told in a personal narrative, Peter Moon relates how he was being drawn to Transylvania via the dream of a white bat, long before he became involved with Montauk, only discover that there are actual white bats in Transylvania that are unknown to science. This book synthesizes the dream process with the creative process and teaches you to do the same.
288 pages, ISBN 978-1-937859-15-2.....................................$22.00

INSIDE THE EARTH
THE SECOND TUNNEL

Stories of the Inner Earth have both fascinated and perplexed mankind since the dawn of time. Now, for the first time, hard scientific data is provided that the Earth's core is not what conventional science has always assumed.

More amazing than the science, however, are the personal adventures of Radu Cinamar whose position in Department Zero, Romania's secretive intelligence division, allows him to penetrate ancient subterranean passage ways and meet citizens of civilizations in the Inner Earth.

Familiar characters from the **Transylvania Series** also reappear, including the enigmatic Tibetan lama, Repa Sundhi, also known as Dr. Xien, who states:

> "If someone had a device or machine that could start up and go everywhere they want, especially towards the center of the Earth, the machine would be blocked and stop at a certain point because of the frequency of vibration to be found there. Just how far you can go with such a machine can be limited by reason of your own consciousness which can in and of itself restrict the dimensional range of such a device or the extent to which it can penetrate other realms. This applies to both human beings as well as material objects. Your ability to access such a region is determined by what your own individual consciousness can or will allow you to experience."

In this exhilarating description of mysteries inside the Earth, Radu Cinamar presents a unique way to penetrate the Inner Earth through the process of feeling and the effects that will develop from such an experience. To enhance the reader's understanding of this very guarded subject, **Inside the Earth — The Second Tunnel** includes multiple illustrations that include depictions of Inner Earth geography.

Within the core of the Earth is intelligence reaching far beyond the scope of ordinary human consciousness. Inside the Earth is an opportunity for initiation as you explore the frequencies of your own inner nature.

240 pages, ISBN 978-1-937859-20-6.....................................**$22.00**

THE STORY BEHIND THE STORY

(How Radu Cinamar's Works Came to be Published)

Radu Cinamar's books include some of the most uplifting tales imaginable, more often than not leaving the reader with a desire to experience what the author has put forth. His most recent book, *Inside the Earth — The Second Tunnel*, teaches us that a significant ascendancy in consciousness is required to even begin to penetrate these fantastic realms. The potential that his work represents makes his books some of the most positive in the entire history of literature.

It is important to note, however, that it was only after the *The Montauk Project: Experiments in Time* was published in the Romanian language that Radu Cinamar sought to have his original manuscript (*Transylvanian Sunrise* in English) published.

The way this came to pass was when Sorin Hurmuz was working as an editor at a major Romanian publishing house and his boss asked him to review *The Montauk Project* in order to see if it was suitable for publishing in Romanian. Although Sorin advised him to do so, the publisher declined and Sorin responded by opening his own publishing house, Daksha, in order to publish *The Montauk Project*. It was only as a result of this that Radu saw the Romanian version and approached the publisher via the internet. A deal to publish the original manuscript was soon arranged.

It should not be too much of a surprise that the publication of *The Montauk Project* would be the catalyst for these remarkably positive books, the reason being that the Montauk Project itself represents the antithesis of what is presented in Radu's work. It is therefore only natural that a book exposing it would be the key to bringing the incredible stories of his experiences out of the woodwork

The Montauk Project has been a very powerful instrument in waking up the world with regard to its heritage as well as the potential for the future. In celebration of the 25th anniversary of its original publication, we have released a Silver Anniversary Edition. In addition to this, there is a major media series in the works that we hope will debut in the next few years. We are also sad to comment that the release of the new edition coincides with the death of the primary author of *The Montauk Project*, Preston Nichols, who passed away on October 5, 2018. A tribute to the memory of Preston has been put up youTube. In the meantime, research into the nature of time will continue.

The Montauk Project
EXPERIMENTS IN TIME

SILVER ANNIVERSARY EDITION

A BRAND NEW VERSION

The Montauk Project was originally released in 1992, causing an uproar and shocking the scientific, academic, and journalistic communities, all of whom were very slow to catch on to the secret world that lurks beyond the superficial veneer of American civilization.

A colloquial name for secret experiments that took place at Montauk Point's Camp Hero, the Montauk Project represented the apex of extensive research carried on after World War II; and, in particular, as a result of the phenomena encountered during the Philadelphia Experiment of 1943 when the United States Navy attempted to achieve radar invisibility.

ISBN 978-1-937859-21-3 $22.00

The Montauk Project attempted to study why and how human beings, when exposed to high powered electromagnetic waves, suffered mental disorientation, physical dissolution or even death. A further ramification of this phenomena is that such electromagnetic waves rescrambled components of the material universe itself. According to reports, this research not only included successful attempts to manipulate matter and energy but also time itself.

It has now been over twenty-five years since *The Montauk Project* originally appeared in print. In this *Silver Anniversary Edition*, you will not only read the original text, accompanied by commentary which includes details that could not be published at the original time of publication, but also an extensive summary of a twenty-five year investigation of the Montauk Project which culminated in actual scientific proof of time travel capabilities.

ORDER TODAY FROM SKY BOOKS

THE SEQUELS

The stir and controversy produced by *The Montauk Project* was overwhelming to the society it was released into in 1992. The powers that be behind the military industrial complex had a lot to explain. A whole new genre of television shows were spawned in an attempt to absorb the fallout of questions and to do damage control on the trail of information thus exposed. In the meantime, Peter Moon set about trying to verify the Montauk Project and the result was of the first sequel to this amazing series:

Montauk Revisited: Adventures in Synchronicity
by Preston Nichols and Peter Moon

This sequel pursues the mysteries of time brought to light in *The Montauk Project* and unmasks the occult forces behind the science and technology used in the Montauk Project. An ornate tapestry is revealed which interweaves the mysterious associations of the Cameron clan with the genesis of American rocketry and the magick of Aleister Crowley and Jack Parsons. *Montauk Revisited* continues the Montauk investigation and unleashes incredible new characters and information.
ISBN 0-9631889-1-7, 249 pages, illustrations, and photos...................**$19.95**

After *Montauk Revisited* was completed, and much to his surprise, Peter Moon discovered that the mysterious trail of synchronicities led to the revelation that the site of "The Montauk Project" experiments was sacred Native American ground that was once accompanied by ancient pyramids which could be clearly seen in old photographs of Montauk. The result of this brand new investigation was:

Pyramids of Montauk: Explorations in Consciousness
by Preston Nichols and Peter Moon
This astonishing second sequel to *The Montauk Project* and *Montauk Revisited* awakens the consciousness of humanity to its ancient history and origins through the discovery of pyramids at Montauk. A full examination of the mysteries of the pyramids at Montauk Point reveals that the Montauk Tribe were the royal family of Long Island and that they used the name Pharaoh as a designation that connected their heritage to ancient Egypt and beyond. The discovery that these pyramids were placed on sacred native American ground opens the door to an unprecedented investigation of the mystery schools of earth and their connection to Egypt, Atlantis, Mars and the star Sirius. This book explains why Montauk was chosen as a select location for pyramids and time travel experimentation. *The Pyramids of Montauk* stirs the quest for the end of time as we know it.
ISBN 0-9631889-2-5, 256 pages, illustrations, photos........................**$19.95**

In 1995 Preston Nichols revealed his mysterious UFO experiences as a young child. This resulted in a new book blending the history of physics and UFOs:

Encounter in the Pleiades: An Inside Look at UFOs
by Preston Nichols and Peter Moon
This book is the incredible story of a man who found himself taken to the Pleiades where he was examined and instructed by intelligent life forms who appeared human. The Pleiadians proceeded to give him an expereience that enable him to regain his health and attain an unparalleled understanding of electromagnetic science and its role in UFO technology. A new look at Einstein gives insights into the history of physics and how the speed of light can be surpassed through the principles of reality engineering. New concepts in science are offered with technical but simple descriptions even the layman can understand. These include the creation of alternate realities; mind control aspects of the Star Wars defense system; implants; alien abductions and much more. Never before has the complex subject of UFOs been put together in such a simple language. Peter Moon adds further intrigue to the mix.
ISBN 0-9631889-3-3, 256 pages..**$19.95**

After *Encounter in the Pleiades* was published, Peter Moon had accumulated information connecting Montauk to Tibet. Peter's research culminated with a visit from world-renown German author, Jan van Helsing, who shared his photos of the mysterious German flying craft as discussed in:

The Black Sun: Montauk's Nazi- Tibetan Connection
by Peter Moon
After World War II, Allied military commanders were stunned to learn the depth of the Nazi regime's state secrets which included the world's best intelligence organization with meticulous research files on secret societies, eugenics and other scientific pursuits that boggled the imagination of the Allied command. Even more spectacular was an entire web of underground rocket and flying saucer factories with accompanying technology that still defies ordinary beliefs. A missing U-boat fleet possessing the most advanced submarine technology in the world left many wondering if the Nazis had escaped with yet more secrets or even with Hitler himself. Behind these mysteries was an even deeper element: a secret order known to initiates as the Order of the Black Sun, an organization so feared that it became illegal to even print their symbols and insignia in modern Germany. *The Black Sun* probes deep into these strange associations and their connection to Montauk Point where an American military facility was used by the Nazis to further their own strange experiments and continue the hidden agenda of the Third Reich.
ISBN 0-9631889-4-1, 304 pages, with photos, illustrations.................**$24.95**

SYNCHRONICITY & THE SEVENTH SEAL

Peter Moon's consummate-work on Synchronicity begins with a layman's scientific description of the quantum mechanics of the universe and how the observer or spirit experiences the principle of synchronicity as a divine expression of the infinite mind.

Besides exploring parallel universes, numerous personal experiences of the author are included which not only forges a pathway of how to experience and appreciate synchronicity, but it goes very deep into the magical exploits of intriguing characters who sought to tap the ultimate powers of creation. This not only includes the most in depth analysis and accurate depiction of the Babalon Working in print but also various antics and breakthroughs of the various players and that which influenced them. These characters include the legacies and personas of Jack Parsons, Marjorie Cameron, L. Ron Hubbard and Aleister Crowley.

Peter Moon adds exponential intrigue to the mix by telling us of his personal experiences with these people and their wake which leads to even deeper encounters which penetrates the mysterious legacy of John Dee. This pursuit of synchronicities leads Peter Moon to an captivating encounter with Joseph Matheny who had similar experiences to Peter but has his own version of a space-time project known as Ong's Hat. Matheny's incredible synchronicities led him to create one of the highest forms of artificial intelligence known to man, a computer known as the Metamachine designed to precipitate and generate synchronicities. These synchronicities lead to the book's climax, a revelation of the true Seventh Seal. The proof is delivered with no counter claims ever having been made. You can make up your own mind.

455 pages, ISBN 0-9678162-7-0...........................$29.95

SPANDAU MYSTERY · BY PETER MOON

The end of World War II precipitated more intrigue and struggle for power than the war itself. Much of this centered around the secret projects sponsored by Rudolph Hess which included not only the Antarctic project but the construction of Vril flying saucers. These tasks eventually crossed the path of one of the most colorful characters of the Second World War: General George S. Patton. Patton's job, as the war came to a close, was to recover the secret technology of the Germans and safeguard it for American use. After accomplishing his mission and compiling a German history of the war, General Patton was killed in a dubious accident, the mystery of which has never been solved and has been magnified by government refusal to declassify the file on the investigation of his death. Far more conspicuous and powerful than Patton was Rudolph Hess, the Deputy Fuhrer of Germany, who flew to England in 1941 as an envoy of peace and was imprisoned for life and suspiciously killed just before his imminent release. The current of intrigue and power which permeated these two individuals and led to their downfall was the same current which led to a repatriation of the U.S. Government and an undermining of a constitutional government that is run by and for the people. It was thus that Patton and Hess wore different uniforms but shared common interests and held within their grasp a force so powerful that it resulted in murder for both.

350+pages,ISBN978-0-9678162-4-1...................................$22.00

SkyBooks

There is an order form on the back of this book if you would like to purchase the above book, and if you would like more information on these or additional titles, you can visit the websites below.

WEBSITES

book store: www.skybooksusa.com

www.digitalmontauk.com

www.timetraveleducationcenter.com

THE MONTAUK PULSE

The *Montauk Pulse* originally went into print in the winter of 1993 to chronicle the events and discoveries regarding the ongoing investigation of the Montauk Project by Preston Nichols and Peter Moon. It has remained in print and been issued quarterly ever since. With a minimum of six pages and a distinct identity of its own, the *Pulse* has expanded to not only chronicle the developments concerning the Montauk investigation, but has expanded to include all the adventures that have surrounded Peter Moon since that time. This includes his adventures with David Anderson and the ground-breaking events that are occurring in Romania. For regular updates, subscribe to the *Montauk Pulse* newsletter. Subscribing to the *Pulse* directly contributes to the efforts of the author in writing more books and chronicling the effort to understand time and all of its components. Past support has been crucial to what has developed thus far. We appreciate your support in helping to unravel various mysteries of Earth-based and non-Earth-based consciousness. It makes a difference. You can subscribe for $20.00 annually if you are in the U.S.A. or $30.00 if you are overseas. See the order form on the back of this page.

The Time Travel Education Center

The **Time Travel Education Center** was created in 2015 in order to educate the public on the simple math and science behind the concept of time travel (with free videos) and also to keep people informed on related aspects to this very avant-garde and rarified subject. The science and math, based upon the genius of Dr. David Anderson, are introduced at an eighth grade level of mathematics yet the concepts are astonishingly profound.

Peter Moon has also prepared an on-going video series on the **Psychology of Space-Time** in order to help people understand the issues surrounding this phenomenal technology and why it is not readily available for everyone. There will be further videos as time allows.

You can become a free member of **The Time Travel Education Center** by going to the website below, and you can also become a paid subscriber which will give you access to further information including books in progress by Peter Moon. Your support is important.

VISIT THE TIME TRAVEL RESEARCH CENTER:

www.timetraveleducationcenter.com

SkyBooks   ORDER FORM

We wait for ALL checks to clear before shipping. This includes Priority Mail orders. If you want to speed delivery time, please send a U.S. Money Order or use MasterCard or Visa. Those orders will be shipped right away. Complete this order form and send with payment or credit card information to:
Sky Books, Box 769, Westbury, New York 11590-0104

Name	
Address	
City	
State / Country	*Zip*
Daytime Phone (In case we have a question) ( )	

☐ This is my first order ☐ I have ordered before ☐ This is a new address

Method of Payment: ☐ Visa ☐ MasterCard ☐ Money Order ☐ Check

____ — ____ — ____ — ____

Expiration Date   *Signature*

TITLE	QTY	PRICE
The Montauk Pulse (1 year - free shipping US orders)...$20.00		
The Montauk Pulse (international - free shipping)...$30.00		
Montauk Project SILVER ANNIVERSARY EDITION...$22.00		
Note: There is no additonal shipping for the Montauk Pulse. **International subscription is $30.00.** *Subtotal*		
For delivery in NY add 8.625% tax		
U.S. Shipping: $5.00 for 1st book plus $1.00 for 2nd, etc.		
Foreign shipping: $20 for 3 books		
Total		

Thank you for your order. We appreciate your business.